# POLICY SIMULATIONS WITH AN ECONOMETRIC MODEL

# POLICY SIMULATIONS WITH AN ECONOMETRIC MODEL

GARY FROMM
PAUL TAUBMAN

THE BROOKINGS INSTITUTION · WASHINGTON, D.C.

1775 Massachusetts Avenue, N.W.
Washington, D.C. 20036

*Distributed outside the United States and Canada by*
NORTH-HOLLAND PUBLISHING COMPANY – AMSTERDAM

*Library of Congress Catalog Card Number 67-30593*

THE BROOKINGS INSTITUTION is an independent organization devoted to nonpartisan research, education, and publication in economics, government, foreign policy, and the social sciences generally. Its principal purposes are to aid in the development of sound public policies and to promote public understanding of issues of national importance.

The Institution was founded on December 8, 1927, to merge the activities of the Institute for Government Research, founded in 1916, the Institute of Economics, founded in 1922, and the Robert Brookings Graduate School of Economics and Government, founded in 1924.

The general administration of the Institution is the responsibility of a self-perpetuating Board of Trustees. The trustees are likewise charged with maintaining the independence of the staff and fostering the most favorable conditions for creative research and education. The immediate direction of the policies, program, and staff of the Institution is vested in the President, assisted by an advisory council chosen from the staff of the Institution.

In publishing a study, the Institution presents it as a competent treatment of a subject worthy of public consideration. The interpretations and conclusions in such publications are those of the author or authors and do not purport to represent the views of the other staff members, officers, or trustees of the Brookings Institution.

# FOREWORD

As our knowledge and understanding of the complex world in which we live increases, so must our tools become more refined and our descriptions more detailed. This is as true in economics as in physics, where in the span of a few decades the relatively simple Bohr proton, neutron, electron model has given way to the current version with its multitude of particles and anti-particles. But today's nuclear diagram could not have been found without the earlier pioneering work. And so it is in the realm of models of the economy. The large-scale Brookings model is an outgrowth of continuing work in the field and owes much to the spirit, if not the detail, of the post-Keynesian models of Tinbergen, Klein-Goldberger, and Duesenberry, Eckstein and Fromm, and others.

This monograph is the second in a series of volumes describing the structure, solutions, and simulations of the Brookings model. The first volume, *The Brookings Quarterly Econometric Model of the United States*, J. S. Duesenberry, G. Fromm, L. R. Klein, and E. Kuh (eds.), was published by Rand McNally – North-Holland in 1965. It contains detailed descriptions and goodness-of-fit statistics for most of the equations utilized here. Another compendium of papers, *The Brookings Model: Some Further Results*, will be issued by the same publishers in the near future. An earlier version of parts of chapters 2, 3 and 4 of the present monograph was presented by the authors at the First World Congress of the Econometric Society held in Rome, Italy in September 1965. At present, Gary Fromm is a member of the senior staff of the Institution and Paul Taubman a member of the faculty of the University of Pennsylvania.

As is usual with any project involving a large number of individuals, the authors owe much to their colleagues. Without doubt, the greatest debt is to the original participants who formulated many of the specifications in the model. Special thanks for research assistance go to John Ahlstrom, L. C. Chugh, James A. Craig, Vijaya Duggal, Mark Eisner, and Michael D. McCarthy; Ross Preston wrote the initial version of the complete system solution computer program. Alix Ryckoff and Nancy Vensel typed and Deborah A. Holmes edited the manuscript. Florence Robinson prepared the index.

The comments and suggestions of James S. Duesenberry, Robert A. Gordon, Lawrence R. Klein, Edwin Kuh, Marc Nerlove, and Roger Bolton were also most helpful. They, of course, are not to be held responsible for any errors. The econometric model project is part of Brookings' Economic Studies Program, which is under the direction of Joseph A. Pechman. The research on this project was supported by a grant from the National Science Foundation. The International Business Machines Corporation also generously provided computer time at various installations.

The views expressed in this book are those of the authors and are not presented as the views of organizations with which the authors are affiliated or the staff members, officers or trustees of the Brookings Institution or the National Science Foundation.

Kermit Gordon
*President*

The Brookings Institution
September 1967

# AUTHORS' PREFACE

For a system as complex as the modern economy, there are very few issues that can be examined in the simple, single-relationship ceteris paribus framework which has formed the basis for so much economic analysis in the past. What is needed is a quantitative specification of the relations among economic variables which models the economy as a system rather than as a set of unrelated random processes.

In the summer of 1961, an interuniversity, interagency group began building such a model. This model, although similar in form to earlier models, has several distinctive features. With over 300 equations, it is much larger in scale – on an order of seven to eight times – than any other econometric model and also has a more detailed sector breakdown. Furthermore, it explicitly introduces government policy parameters and variables. Size is not a virtue in itself, but it does appear that only a large-scale, disaggregated system can be used to examine structural questions with any degree of validity. Several sectors are given a more extensive analysis than previously possible. Monetary influences are specifically and extensively taken into account; this sector alone consists of nearly thirty equations. Input-output analysis is integrated into the structure of a short-term cyclical system. New statistical techniques and concepts are developed. A set of notation and data library for more than 2,000 variables (time series) have been constructed and compiled; these should be extremely useful to other investigators.

We believe we have demonstrated that group, interuniversity research can be fruitful. The experts who participated in constructing the model contributed many insights which might have been lost had a small number of scholars attempted the task alone. Finally, we hope that the project will be a continuing venture, thus making model building a cumulative and collective process and also providing a means for testing subsectors within a complete system context.

The continuity which is characteristic of the model should be remembered when reviewing and interpreting the results presented in this volume. The model is still in preliminary form and much remains to be done in the way of respecification of equations, testing of the system in response to exogenous shocks and changes in initial conditions, and, generally, determining the model's reliability and validity.

The present model has been estimated without the benefit of the recent 1947–65 revisions of the national income and product accounts. These revisions, a complete set of which only became available in December 1966, are still being modified, but are being used to re-estimate the complete system in a simultaneous equation framework. The solutions with this revised model should be available early in 1968.

For these reasons, the present results should not be taken too literally; they are offered primarily as an example of how policy actions can be analyzed in the milieu of a large scale econometric model. Also, because the results can be contrasted with a priori notions of the reponse of the economy to policy changes, they provide an additional test of the model's validity. Furthermore, they offer a partial basis for establishing priorities in selecting sectors and equations in need of refinement.

Gary Fromm
Paul Taubman

September 1967

# TABLE OF CONTENTS

FOREWORD . . . . . . . . . . VII
AUTHORS' PREFACE . . . . . . . . . . IX
LIST OF TABLES . . . . . . . . . . XIII
LIST OF FIGURES . . . . . . . . . . XV

## 1. STRUCTURE OF THE MODEL

1.1. Introduction . . . . . . . . . . 1
1.2. Sectoral specifications . . . . . . . . . . 2
1. Consumption 2. Residential construction 3. Inventories 4. Orders 5. Investment realizations 6. Investment intentions 7. Foreign sector 8. Government revenues and expenditures 9. Production functions and factor income payments 10. Wages and prices 11. Agriculture 12. Labor force 13. Monetary sector 14. Automotive industry
1.3. Disaggregation . . . . . . . . . . 14
1.4. Price and output conversion . . . . . . . . . . 15

## 2. COMPLETE SYSTEM SOLUTIONS AND SIMULATIONS

2.1. Description of the system . . . . . . . . . . 17
2.2. Method of solution . . . . . . . . . . 18
2.3. Pseudo-realistic solution results . . . . . . . . . . 19
2.4. Impact multipliers . . . . . . . . . . 23
2.5. System simulations . . . . . . . . . . 24
1. Simulation experiments. 2. Simulation results 3. Dynamic multipliers

## 3. ANALYSIS OF EXCISE TAX CHANGES

3.1. Excise taxes as a policy instrument . . . . . . . . . . 53
3.2. Excise changes and disposable income . . . . . . . . . . 54

3.3. Translation of excise reductions into price changes . . . . . . . 55
1. Markup mechanisms 2. Changes in the price structure 3. Implicit excise tax rate estimates
3.4. Nonlinear considerations . . . . . . . . . . . . . . . . 60

## 4. EXCISE TAX REDUCTIONS: SIMULATION RESULTS

4.1. Input . . . . . . . . . . . . . . . . . . . . . . . 63
4.2. Results . . . . . . . . . . . . . . . . . . . . . . 64
1. Absolute impact on *GNP* 2. Multipliers 3. Economics of scale in excise effects 4. Impact on other variables
4.3. Summary . . . . . . . . . . . . . . . . . . . . . . 80

## 5. EVALUATION OF ALTERNATIVE POLICIES

5.1. Derivation of real input multipliers . . . . . . . . . . . . 82
1. Government expenditures 2. Income taxes 3. Excise taxes 4. Monetary policies
5.2. Real input multipliers for distributive shares . . . . . . . . . 88
5.3. Fiscal multipliers . . . . . . . . . . . . . . . . . . . 91
5.4. Response path considerations . . . . . . . . . . . . . . 92
5.5. Multiplier results . . . . . . . . . . . . . . . . . . . 93
1. Actual or equivalent incremental inputs 2. Dynamic multipliers 3. Discounted multipliers
5.6. Other policy ranking criteria . . . . . . . . . . . . . . . 101
5.7. Utility evaluation of alternative policies . . . . . . . . . . 106
1. Utility functions 2. Ambiguity of quadratic utility functions 3. Adjustments for dynamic response 4. Scaling 5. Summary of utility evaluation procedure 6. Illustrative results
5.8. Conclusion . . . . . . . . . . . . . . . . . . . . . 123

APPENDIX A. BROOKINGS ECONOMETRIC MODEL CONDENSED SYSTEM OF EQUATIONS AND LIST OF VARIABLES AND DEFINITIONS . . . . . . . 125
APPENDIX B. CODING OF BROOKINGS INDUSTRIES . . . . . . . . . . 159
APPENDIX C. PRICE BEHAVIOR AFTER EXCISE TAX CHANGES . . . . . . 161
APPENDIX D. ADJUSTMENT OF MODEL EQUATIONS FOR EXCISE TAX REDUCTIONS . . . . . . . . . . . . . . . . . . . . . . . 171
INDEX . . . . . . . . . . . . . . . . . . . . . . . . . 177

# LIST OF TABLES


2.1 Unconditional forecasting of first differences, actual and predicted complete system solution . . . 20

2.2 Quarterly impact multipliers . . . 26

2.3 Simulation results: impact of government expenditure increases, personal income tax cut, and monetary policy . . . 30

2.4 Ranking of simulation effects after ten quarters . . . 48

2.5 Dynamic multipliers . . . 48

3.1 Markup factors for ad valorem tax rates and value-added prices: 1965–67 . . . 59

4.1 Simulation results: impact of excise tax reductions . . . 66

5.1 Constant and current dollar actual or equivalent incremental inputs . . . 94

5.2 Dynamic multipliers for real gross national product and real consumption . . . 96

5.3 Average quarterly discounted multipliers for gross national product and real consumption . . . 99

5.4 Rank order of policy multipliers for real gross national product and real consumption . . . 100

5.5 Indexes of utility in selected quarters . . . 117

5.6 Quarterly averages of indexes of discounted utility . . . 118

5.7 Rank order of utility indexes—proportional weights . . . 119

5.8 Rank order of utility indexes—equal weights . . . 120

5.9 Comparison of multiplier vs. utility rank ordering . . . 122

B.1 Coding of the thirty-three-sector Brookings industries . . . 159

B.2 Coding of the eight-sector Brookings industries . . . 160

C.1 Retail price movements in regular gasoline in response to a $0.01 increase in tax: July 1, 1956 and October 1, 1959 . . . 163

C.2 Distribution of changes in retail price of regular gasoline in response to changes in excise taxes, for individual stations . . . 164

C.3 Distribution of retail price changes for regular size cigarettes in response to a tax change of $0.01 price from individual stores, various cities . . . 165

C.4 Comparison of old and new prices for face powder and face cream, March–June 1954, for tax reduction from 20 to 10 per cent, April 1, 1954 . . . 166

C.5 Frequency distribution of percentage changes in suggested retail prices, April 1 through August 31, 1954 by appliance group . . . . . . . . . . . . . . . 167
C.6 Refrigerator, standard model retail prices by city; tax decrease from 10 to 5 per cent . . . . . . . . . . . . . . . . . . . . . . . . . . . . . 168
C.7 Ratio of retail prices March/June 1954—1.00; tax decrease from 10 to 5 per cent for toasters, 15 to 10 per cent for light bulbs . . . . . . . . . . . . . . . 168

D.1 Ad valorem tax rate markup factors for consumption sectors: 1965–67 . . . 172
D.2 Expected shifts in levels of $(TX+V_{BUS})_i/TX+V_{BUS})$ . . . . . . . . . . . 174

# LIST OF FIGURES

1.1 Condensed flow diagram of Brookings econometric model . . . . . . . . . 4

4.1 Consumption and employment effects of excise tax reductions . . . . . . . 76

5.1 Derivation of equivalent real input multipliers for monetary policies . . . . . 86
5.2 Policy response paths . . . . . . . . . . . . . . . . . . . . . . . . . 92
5.3 Static Phillips price curve . . . . . . . . . . . . . . . . . . . . . . 101
5.4 Static Phillips price curve envelopes . . . . . . . . . . . . . . . . . . 102
5.5 Phillips price curve sets and fiscal action . . . . . . . . . . . . . . . . 103
5.6 Fiscal action Phillips curve envelope . . . . . . . . . . . . . . . . . . 104
5.7 Choice of optimum size fiscal action . . . . . . . . . . . . . . . . . . 105
5.8 Utility functions . . . . . . . . . . . . . . . . . . . . . . . . . . 108
5.9 Quadratic utility function ambiguity . . . . . . . . . . . . . . . . . . 109

# 1

# STRUCTURE OF THE MODEL

## *1.1. Introduction*

Few would deny that the structure of the economy is complex. Most would also agree that a model that is to be used for studying this structure and for examining policy alternatives must mirror this complexity. As can be seen from the condensed flow diagram of the system, figure 1.1, the Brookings model portrays the economy in considerable detail.

In the model, as in the economy (for any time period), certain variables [1] in the following diagram are largely determined by past values of other variables. Other sets of variables, [2] and [3], are for the most part simultaneously determined within the current period, while a final group [4], depends on the values of variables previously determined within the period. In all four instances, exogenous forces from outside the system (for example, long-term factors such as population and short-term influences such as government policy actions) may also affect the solutions. This framework (which has become known as a block recursive structure) may be displayed as follows [1]):

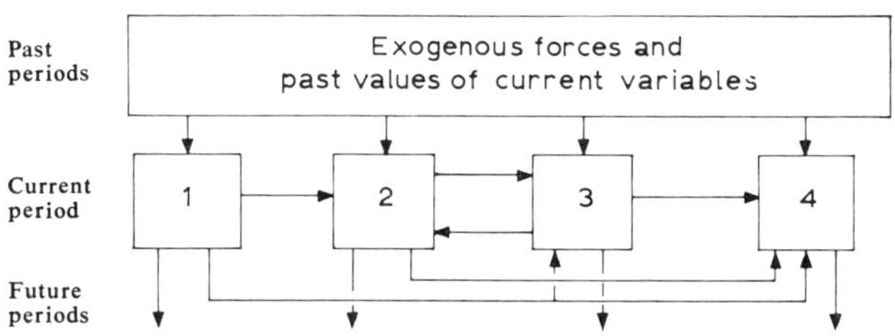


[1]) Mathematically, where $Z$ stands for exogenous variables and $X_t$ for current endogenous variables, the system might be represented by:

$$X_{1_t} = f(X_{t-j}, Z)$$
$$X_{2_t} = f(X_{t-j}, Z, X_{1_t}, X_{3_t})$$
$$X_{3_t} = f(X_{t-j}, Z, X_{1_t}, X_{2_t})$$
$$X_{4_t} = f(X_{t-j}, Z, Z_{1_t}, X_{2_t}, X_{3_t}).$$

In matrix notation, for a linear system, this can be written as $\boldsymbol{A}+\boldsymbol{B}\boldsymbol{X}_t+\Sigma_j\,\boldsymbol{C}_j\boldsymbol{X}_{t-j}+\boldsymbol{D}\boldsymbol{Z}=\boldsymbol{0}$, where $\boldsymbol{A}$ is a vector of constant terms, and $\boldsymbol{B}$, $\boldsymbol{C}_j$ and $\boldsymbol{D}$ are matrices of time invariant coefficients.

Each block contains equations which relate so-called current endogenous dependent variables to other variables. For example, in the first block, business plant and equipment investment in the durable manufacturing sector is a function of lagged values of the industry's output originating and capital stocks, and long-term interest rates. The specification of the various sectors of the model is discussed in a previous volume [2]), and need not be repeated here. (The equations of a slightly modified condensed model are listed in appendix A.)

However, as the U.S. economy evolves, econometric models must also be changed in order to depict its structure faithfully. Furthermore, as economic theory advances and empirical investigations are conducted, we learn more about the economy's historical path and behavioral characteristics. Also, internal and external review of previous results gives rise to ideas for further improvement. Thus, notwithstanding the considerable efforts which have already been expended on the analysis of individual sectors, continuing research is required to keep the model current and to increase its accuracy and validity. This research might be divided into three areas: (1) further analysis of the present sectors; (2) disaggregation of production sectors; and (3) the conversion of *GNP* component demands into industry outputs and industry prices into prices of *GNP* components. These areas are discussed here to anticipate the reactions of some readers to particular equation specifications, to indicate how specific functions might be modified to increase their structural validity and predictive ability, and to assist in the interpretation of the simulation results.

## *1.2. Sectoral specifications*

### *1.2.1. Consumption*

The consumption functions employed in the simulations of this volume are of a classical type, making expenditures (by category) dependent on income, relative prices, capital stock or lagged consumption, and a few additional variables. It seems likely, however, that outlays for durable goods are responsive to changes in credit terms and the availability of installment financing. This would have the effect of increasing the sensitivity of the

---

[2]) *The Brookings Quarterly Econometric Model of the United States Economy*, J. S. Duesenberry, G. Fromm, L. R. Klein, E. Kuh (eds.), (Rand McNally and North-Holland, 1965).

model's "real" sector to alterations in monetary policy and shifts in financial market conditions [3]).

It is also desirable to develop improved measures of consumers' capital stocks of durable goods and to determine the impact of these holdings on consumption. Moreover, it may be desirable to examine whether a "portfolio" approach with asset substitution and complementarities is relevant. That is, it might be helpful to postulate that consumers behave in such a way as to maximize utility, subject to income, financial assets, durables and housing assets, and inertial constraints. Also, the utility independence assumption could be relaxed to permit the consumption of each item to have an effect on the utility derived from consuming other items. This would lead to an "optimal mix" formulation of the consumption function. Other questions in the consumption area which concern us are the independent impact of buying plans and expectations on expenditures and the degree to which the propensity to consume varies with different kinds (wages, salaries, transfers) and time paths of income.

### *1.2.2. Residential construction*

In its present formulation, the equation for total new construction starts depends on the gap between household formation and removals plus vacancies, a relative price rental-construction cost index, the Treasury bill or bond rate of interest, and a distributed lag of past starts. The constant dollar value per start is a function of real income per household and the same rate of interest (which, for reasons of uniformity, should also be put in real terms). This dichotomy of the value per start being dependent on household income while the number of starts is independent of it, should be examined. One should likewise investigate whether there is some relationship between credit conditions and housing *demand* or whether the influence of monetary factors impinges mainly on housing *supply* in the form of the willingness of builders to increase their inventories under construction.

It would also be appropriate to integrate the analysis of the housing and financial sectors since the two are functionally related. In particular, account should be taken of financial institutions' forward commitments of mortgage loans and the availability of funds from the Federal National Mortgage Association (FNMA). Furthermore, while U.S. Treasury interest rates

[3]) An analysis of consumer credit is being conducted for the project by Michael Evans and Avram Kisselgoff. Their preliminary results reveal that durables demand is significantly affected by credit terms.

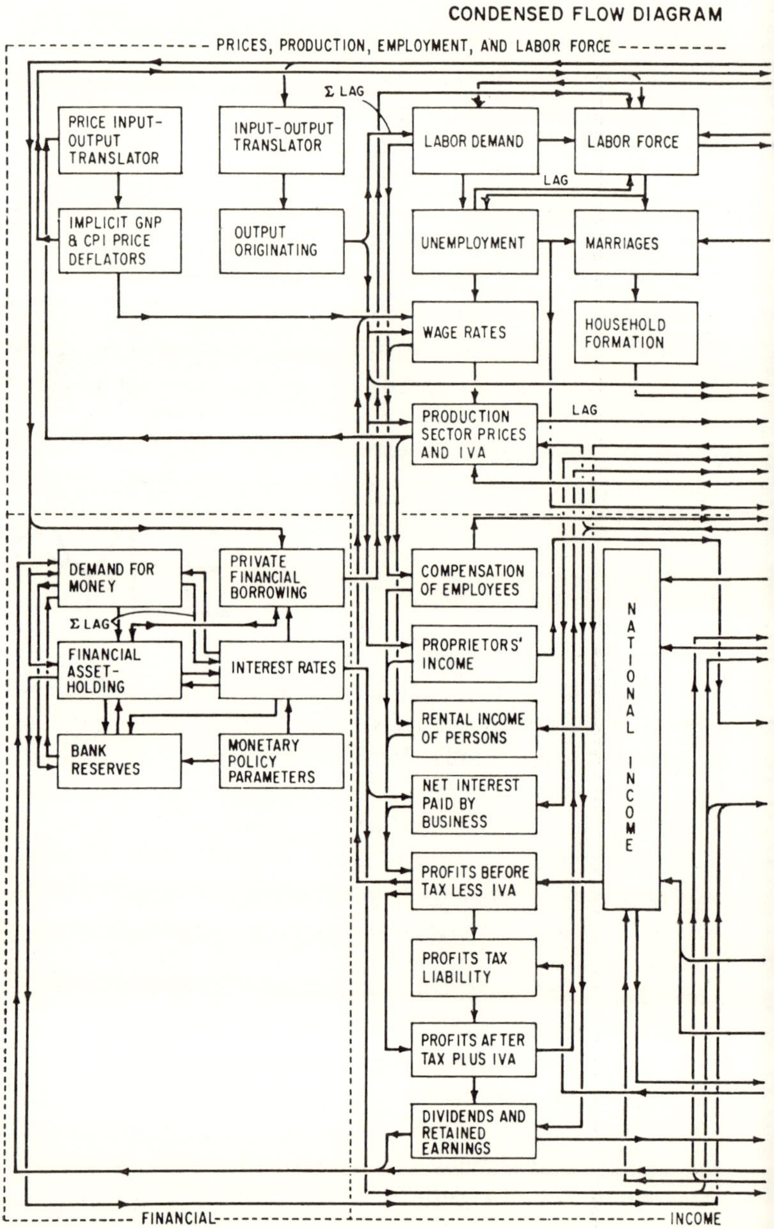


*Figure 1.1. Condensed flow diagram*

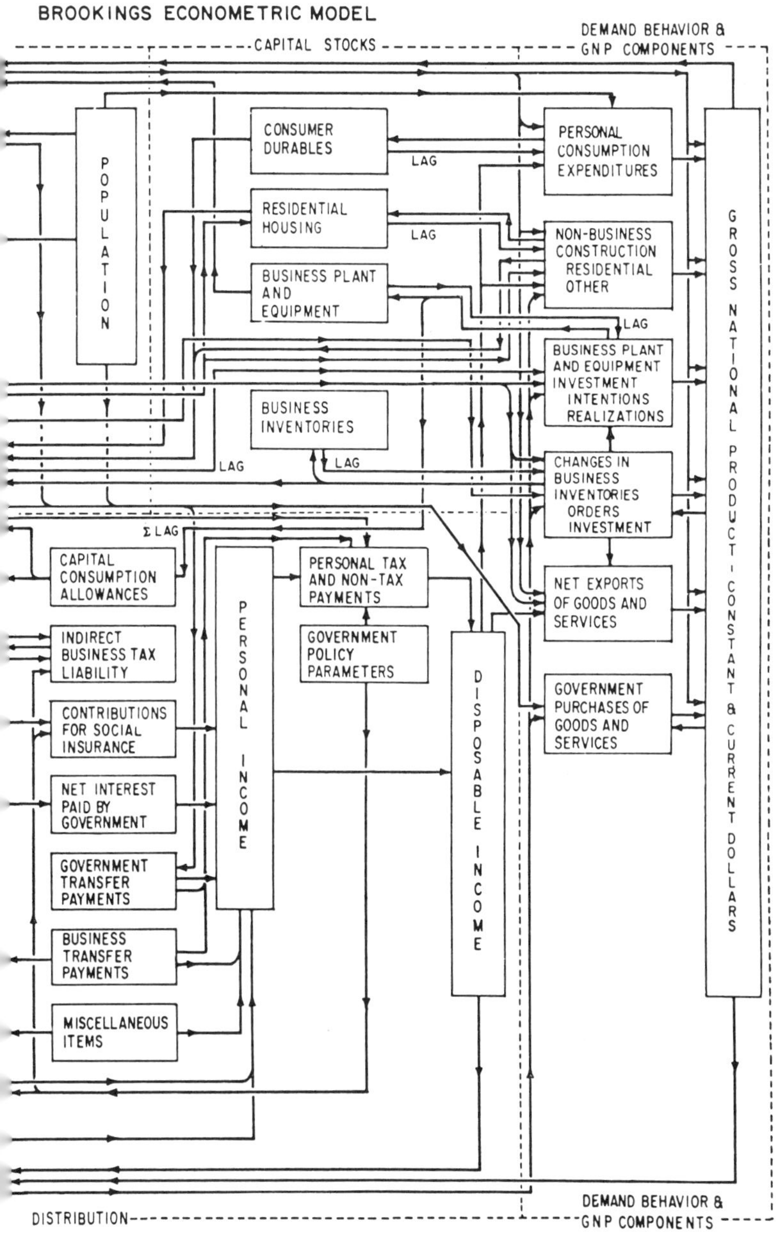


*f Brookings econometric model.*

serve as an indicator of the cost and availability of funds in the private housing market, they do so very imperfectly. Whenever possible, more direct measures should be used. This probably requires a substantial increase in detail in the housing-financial sectors.

Another aspect of residential construction that probably bears closer scrutiny is the difference between single and multi-family dwelling unit starts. While the former have had a downward trend since 1955, the latter have been rising rapidly. In other words, rental housing is becoming more significant in the total market. This is partially accounted for by the increasing concentration of population in metropolitan areas (although not in the urban core) and, perhaps to some extent, by urban renewal. However, these are not the only forces at work.

### *1.2.3. Inventories*

In the initial work on this sector, the approach taken followed traditional lines by positing an inventory decision process based on a stock adjustment mechanism. Inventories were disaggregated by production sector (durable manufacturing, nondurable manufacturing, trade, and other), and some attention was given to industry capacity and government military orders. Other relevant factors were relative prices and short-term interest rates. While the performance of the final equations taken individually was satisfactory and comparable to the results obtained by other researchers, in the complete system they produced significant errors. Therefore, additional research was indicated and has already been initiated.

This research is twofold. First, the traditional approach might be followed, but with greater disaggregation. Inventories might profitably be split into their stage of fabrication (finished goods, work-in-process, and raw materials) as well as industry components. Also, further breakdowns of some of the independent variables, particularly government demands, should be undertaken. Finally, an examination of retail trade inventory movements reveals that the automotive component behaves differently from the total. Therefore, the trade inventory function might well be split into separate relationships for wholesale trade, retail trade other than automobiles, and automobiles. Second, as noted, with sales given, inventory accumulation can be treated as a residual from a production decision. Instead of minimizing the costs of holding inventories, the objective function provides for minimizing the cost of production to meet fluctuating demands. This approach is now being investigated for the model by David Belsley of Boston College.

### *1.2.4. Orders*

The present model contains four orders functions for durable and non-durable manufacturing: two identities for the change in the level of unfilled orders (that is, new orders minus sales) and two new orders equations. In the latter, new orders are a function of current and lagged final sales, an own rate of change of price variable, and the first difference in government military outlays. As in the case of inventories, these relationships might benefit from further disaggregation, both by sector and by reduction of the time period to a monthly basis. It may be of value to trace the generation of new orders from industry to industry, given expenditures on final demand. This would require a greater degree of industry detail than our present seven sectors, but should be quite feasible on a thirty-three sector basis. The primary sequence for orders arising from an industry's final demand might be determined from the coefficients in the 1958 input-output table and the production lead-time statistics gathered by the National Planning Association's PARM project.

### *1.2.5. Investment realizations*

A significant result of the work on the Brookings model has been the demonstration (by Robert Eisner) that realization functions on investment intentions produce superior predictions of investment expenditures than the use of fixed automatic payout mechanisms on the intentions. Eisner's interpretation of his equations imputes a rate of return rationale for the included profits variable. Alternatively, these terms might be regarded a constraint on the availability of investment funds. In this case, a more appropriate variable would be retained earnings plus depreciation allowances. Additionally, it might be argued that increases in sales arising from an increase in the real value of purchased inputs per unit of output should not give rise to greater investment demands. That is, the sales terms might well be replaced by value-added originating variables. Both these hypotheses require testing. Finally, it would be interesting to compare the predictive power of equations combining the investment intentions-realizations functions with the predictive power of equations which estimate investment directly.

### *1.2.6. Investment intentions*

Dale Jorgenson's treatment of investment intentions is pioneering and powerful. However, it leaves room for further inquiry. As in the investment realizations functions, output originating might be considered the demand variable instead of sales. Also, the depreciation variable in the user cost of capital is in real replacement terms while, for tax purposes, a current, historical cost basis might be more relevant. Furthermore, no funds availability constraints are imposed, which implies that a firm, in any time period, can acquire unlimited capital at a marginal cost equal to the average user capital cost.

Then, too, the underlying production function is a homogeneous of degree one Cobb-Douglas, and technological change is exponential. Therefore, such change appears necessarily embodied, neutral, and time invariant. Also, it is implied that capital services per constant dollar of capital stock are fixed. These assumptions could be modified (discrete innovational shifts might be introduced) as could those relating to the lag structure of the investment decision, especially since the parameter estimates are highly sensitive to shifts in the lag distribution [4]).

Moreover, the treatment of investment lags as being merely a technological phenomenon of the lag between placement of plant and equipment orders and their delivery is far too restrictive, given the uncertainty of future output, revenue, cost, and financing predictions. Furthermore, the use of very complicated forms of lag functions in the presence of serially correlated disturbances is suspect. The use of Durbin-Watson statistics is inappropriate as a serial correlation indicator because of the inclusion of lagged dependent variables in the fitted equations. Simpler types of distributed lags should be tested as alternatives.

It might also be valuable to extend Jorgenson's preliminary examination of the effect of substituting the National Industrial Conference Board's investment appropriations series for the OBE-SEC investment intentions

---

[4]) In most production and investment functions, innovational shifts are treated as a constant, time invariant exponential factor. For example, take the highly simplified Cobb-Douglas case, $Q = e^{\lambda t}L^{\alpha}K^{\beta}$, where $Q$ = output, $\lambda$ is the technological shift parameter denoting increased output per unit of factor input in each time period ($t$), $L$ and $K$ are labor and capital inputs, and $\alpha$ and $\beta$ are elasticities of output with respect to the factors. Then, the marginal productivity of investment at time (t) equals $(\partial Q/\partial K)_t = \beta e^{\lambda t}L^{\alpha}K^{\beta-1}$.

It is unrealistic to assume that in the "real world" $\lambda$, $\beta$ and $\alpha$ are fixed. The rapid introduction of new technology will have marked effects on the coefficients in the short run, even though they may return after a period of time to so-called equilibrium values. (A recent example of this phenomenon is the application of the oxygen blast in the steel industry.) At the model's present high level of aggregation of seven industrial sectors, discrete innovational shifts might not be detected. But, with two-digit industry detail, they might become important.

statistics. As published, the latter are corrected for "bias." Thus, any imperfections in the correction procedures are transmitted to the parameters.

### *1.2.7. Foreign sector*

The present formulation of the foreign sector is highly simplified and limited to U.S. import and export functions for a few classes of commodities. Constant dollar trade flows are related to real income, relative prices, production demands, and past levels of expenditures. However, to be truly useful, analyses in the foreign sector should be disaggregated into principal product groups and key regions. In addition to such a treatment of trade flows (which are only one ingredient in the balance of payments), it is also necessary to study direct foreign investment and capital movements. The responsiveness of the latter—long and short-term—to monetary sector variables (particularly interest rates) is especially vital in the consideration of stabilization and growth policies. Obviously, the construction of a submodel that is suitably descriptive of the foreign sector is an immense task which nearly necessitates a model of the world economy, requiring resources far beyond those available to our project. Fortunately, other economists are undertaking econometric analyses in this area, and it should be possible to integrate their findings into the framework of the Brookings model. Among the principal investigators are Rudolph Rhomberg of the International Monetary Fund and Lawrence B. Krause of the Brookings Institution.

### *1.2.8. Government revenues and expenditures*

The government sector of the model offers one of the most extensive econometric descriptions of government fiscal activities ever prepared. For example, in the complete model, approximately twenty equations are employed to explain U.S. Treasury tax collections and to translate them into national income and product account statistics. Further analysis is needed, however, especially in the areas of federal government purchases of goods and services, state and local expenditures, and state and local tax receipts.

The federal purchases subsector might be improved in two ways. First, several components that are now exogenous can be made endogenous by relating them to other variables already included in the system. For example, government employment of civilians in nondefense areas can be related to such variables as population growth, and transfer payments for social insurance. Nonmilitary construction, a large component of which is office buildings, can be related to population and government employment. Second, for all types of expenditures, and especially those having long lead times and gestation periods, it is desirable to determine payout functions to indicate the time pattern of translating Congressional appropriations into actual expenditures. It would also be beneficial to obtain data on government obligations (by type of program) to have additional observations (conditional constraints) which the distributed lag functions must satisfy. Obligations data would also be vital in the inventory and orders functions and, therefore, essential in terms of the speed of their impact. Unfortunately, at present, only a limited set of such information for Department of Defense obligations is available; efforts are being made to broaden this coverage.

On the state and local level, further research is needed on methods of relating expenditures for government activities to economic and demographic variables. The areas involved include road and sewer building, education, construction, and employee compensation. Many of these areas may depend not only on population and economic factors in the aggregate, but also on shifts within and between states. Concerning revenue, the need for more accurate state and local tax functions is becoming evident because state and local receipts have been rising faster than federal receipts. Furthermore, a careful study of borrowing versus taxing decisions should be undertaken. Much of this work is already under way, but a great deal of additional effort is required before many of the complex questions in this sector are resolved.

### *1.2.9. Production functions and factor income payments*

In what is equivalent to an implicit linear approximation of a production function, the model's employment and hours variables are dependent on the level and rate of increase of real output, beginning of period capital stocks, and their own lagged values. Judged by the usual statistical criteria these equations appear quite satisfactory; however, some restructuring of this framework may prove helpful.

Shifts in factor productivity and utilization might be incorporated in the employment functions; also, the underlying production functions could be explicitly specified. It seems reasonable, too, to assume that an important determinant of the change in hourly workweek would bc the desired change in employment *not* achieved in a given period (at present, changes in sector output alone are used in the hours equations). In the area of income shares, functions must be developed for indirect business taxes and business transfers at the production sector level; currently, the total of these items is distributed by an autoregressive proportional share mechanism. Also, further analysis of rental and interest income should be undertaken.

### *1.2.10. Wages and prices*

An examination of the complete model solutions for 1961–62 reveals that the wages and prices sector is one of the larger contributors of errors in the aggregate results. Even on an individual equation basis, the forecast residuals (actual minus predicted) turn negative in late 1960 and grow increasingly from quarter to quarter. There are two possibilities to explain this phenomenon. The equations may have been misspecified over the entire sample period (there may be missing, incorrectly defined, or superfluous variables); or a structural change (long-run or short-run) has taken place since the advent of the Kennedy administration. Certainly there has been an increased use of governmental moral suasion (witness the Council of Economic Advisers' wage-price guideposts) in recent years. Both possibilities require study, especially for the wage equations where the use of four-quarter rates of change (that is, overlapping first differences) biases the goodness of fit statistics because the effective degrees of freedom are less than seems apparent.

The variables in the wage equations include the four-quarter change in the consumer price index, distributed lags of profits per unit of real output and the reciprocal of the unemployment rate, and past wage changes. Here, aside from alternative specifications, some further disaggregation might be advisable since key wage bargains have been shown to affect other industries' wages. Thus, for example, steel wage increases might be used as an independent variable in a wage equation for manufacturing durables other than steel. Also, account might be taken of fringe benefits which do not impinge on current compensation but do raise future labor costs, for example, certain pension plans which require no sinking funds. Finally, the impact of the structure of unemployment on wage changes should be investigated, e.g., the unemployment rate of married males 25 years and older probably has a greater effect on wage bargains than that of teenagers.

In the area of prices, additional study is needed of the impact of purchased input costs on the market prices of goods and on trade, regulated, and service sector margins (i.e., on the prices of value added). Also, for manufacturing, unfilled orders/output originating ratios may be better indicators of demand conditions than corresponding inventory/output originating ratios. Finally, in every period, wages and prices are closely connected; therefore, functions for these variables should be estimated as a simultaneous subsystem.

### *1.2.11. Agriculture*

The present agricultural sector has been formulated in two alternative versions: a highly disaggregated set of equations (by Karl Fox) and a condensed subsector (by G. Fromm). Much of the former is cast in terms of specific product classes and, consequently, many independent variables were used that are only appropriate at this level of detail. To use the disaggregated version in simulations with the complete model, explanatory equations for these variables must be supplied. Otherwise, the endogeneity of the overall system cannot be maintained without resorting to arbitrary numerical assumptions. While undertaking this task, the specification of several functions might well be reviewed to determine whether their heavy reliance on autoregressive terms is truly appropriate. Comparisons with the extremely large-scale, commodity model of the U.S. Department of Agriculture may also prove useful.

The condensed version of the agricultural sector is in many respects similar in form and specification to the other production sectors: it includes equations for investment, inventories, output originating, and employment. The difference is that sales and production costs are treated explicitly and rental income is divided into several components; more work is needed to refine all the nonstandard equations (the standard equations are highly satisfactory).

### *1.2.12. Labor force*

The solutions presented in the following chapter use a total aggregate labor force equation. This function makes the absolute size of the labor force dependent on current employment, the level and rate of change of unemployment in the previous quarter, and a time trend. The unemployment variables have a positive sign, presumably reflecting, on a net basis, the entrance of wives into the labor force when their husbands lose their jobs and the discouragement of potential or presently unemployed labor force participants. The positive sign on the time trend can be interpreted as a net indicator of increased participation of women in the labor force and a secular decline in the proportion of teenagers seeking employment due to the longer average period of education as well as a proxy for population growth.

The foregoing function, which has an $\bar{R}^2$ (explained variance) of 0.993, was adopted as a temporary measure because earlier results of labor force equations by sex and age group (from 14 to 19 and 20 and over) were somewhat disappointing [5]). Even greater disaggregation than already undertaken may be necessary. Also, further study of the composition of unemployment within the same groups is needed. An investigation of structural change in the labor market in recent years may also furnish some useful insights, especially in relation to teenagers and college-age youths and minority groups.

### *1.2.13. Monetary sector*

The monetary subsector is one of the most interesting aspects of the model. While previous model-building efforts have all but neglected monetary influences, the complete Brookings model has an extensive set of equations (numbering nearly 30) relating the financial and real sectors. Money and near-money demands of households and businesses are treated separately as are the various classes of financial institutions. However, the interactions between the monetary and real sectors are weak, and are reflected only in the form of interest rate terms in the housing, business investment, and factor share distribution functions and income and investment terms in various financial equations. A stronger linkage would probably be found if additional variables were introduced [6]). An analysis should be made of the impact ot personal and business balance sheet positions (together with flow variables) on consumption and business investment behavior patterns. It seems that such an empirical study has never been undertaken; it is likely to provide a stimulus to the resolution of some of the current controversies between the proponents of the Chicago theses and those who believe that, in the postwar years, the money supply has had little influence on the course of economic events. Although not wholly comparable or consistent with the national income account statistics, the balance sheet data contained in the FTC-SEC

---

[5]) By definition, those who are employed are also members of the labor force, and employment over the period of estimation ranges from 93 to 96 per cent of the labor force, so the high $\bar{R}^2$ obtained for the function is not surprising. For a review of recent work on this question, see Jacob Mincer, *Labor Force Participation and Unemployment*, Multilithed Paper (National Bureau of Economic Research) New York, 1966.

[6]) The linkages between the monetary and real sectors are currently the subject of extensive research in a Federal Reserve Board—M.I.T. project directed by Albert Ando, Frank de Leeuw, and Franco Modigliani. The Brookings model project is also doing further studies in this area.

*Quarterly Financial Report for Manufacturing Corporations* and in the Federal Reserve Board's flow of funds tables (and other series) provide a basis for an exploratory analysis.

### *1.2.14. Automotive industry*

An item-by-item examination of the national income and product accounts shows that the automative industry plays an important role in the cyclical path of the economy. Not only does it bulk large in absolute size, but fluctuations in its sales, investment, inventories, labor compensation, and other variables have an important and pervasive influence on the rest of the economy. For example, the extremely high, economy-wide utilization rates which occurred in 1955 can be explained in large measure by the record consumption of new model cars in that year. Nearly all the "noise" in retail inventories comes from the fluctuations in automotive inventories, and it seems vital to treat them separately because of their magnitude and long production lead times. This is also a distinctive industry in that production is tied directly to individual orders from retailers to manufacturers. Also, the high volatility of consumer durables demand can be attributed largely to this sector. Thus, a complete representation of automotive production and retailing might significantly improve the validity of many of the most important parts of the model.

## *1.3. Disaggregation*

With continuing work on the model, the need for greater disaggregation of production sectors has become increasingly apparent, especially when structural characteristics are analyzed and the composition of *GNP* component demands is changing. Differing capital intensities, rates of technical progress, market power, unionization, automation, and product types cause divergent behavioral responses to increases in aggregate demand, unemployment and taxation. Some preliminary analyses of production functions have shown that there are significant differences between durable and nondurable manufacturing aggregates and their components. Also, compositional changes in business construction and private durable goods demands cause acute problems in price and output conversion. Therefore, for both reasons, it is desirable to broaden our present eight-sector coverage; an approximate thirty-three-sector breakdown is planned (see appendix B, table B.1 for a detailed list). Work is underway on productivity and price and wage equations on this basis. Investment, depreciation, inventory and other functions must also be estimated.

Just as greater accuracy of estimated relations should result from greater disaggregation, so an important area for study is the development of criteria for evaluating proper levels of aggregation. The static effects of aggregation error require attention. Two types of dynamic aggregation error also need further exploration: time aggregation and aggregation of dynamic systems, the latter topic having already received interesting theoretical treatment by Ando, Fisher, and Simon [7]). The former topic is especially pertinent to the treatment of the production-decision inventory relations which form a major part of the short-run dynamic response of the present model. Whether the estimated responses of the underlying dynamic structure have been biased by using quarterly instead of monthly data is a problem urgently requiring investigation. At the other end of frequency response, it is possible that more efficient estimates of long-run behavior parameters can be obtained from averaged data which most closely correspond to steady state behavior.

## *1.4. Price and output conversion*

The relationship between *GNP* expenditure components and industry outputs and between industry prices and *GNP* component prices is not a simple one. For example, even with only eight producing sectors, the prices of five of these industries (agriculture, nondurable manufacturing, trade, regulated and services) must be combined to yield the price of consumer food outlays. The following techniques might be used to specify these relationships.

1. F. Fisher, L. R. Klein, and Y. Shinkai proposed the explicit use of an input-output table [8]). Unfortunately, only a 1947 and a 1958 table are available for the United States, and it appears that shifts in the coefficients have taken place and will continue. Thus, if either 1947 or 1958 coefficients, or even interpolations between them, are employed, the conversion results may either be increasingly biased over time or lack consistency (in the statistical sense). Accordingly, correction factors are needed to maintain

---

[7]) A. Ando, F. M. Fisher, and H. A. Simon, *Essays on the Structure of Social Science Models* (Massachusetts Institute of Technology Press, 1963).

[8]) "Price and Output Aggregation in the Brookings Model," in *The Brookings Quarterly Econometric Model of the United States*, op. cit., pp. 653–78.

conversion accuracy (we are using an autoregressive mechanism to obtain such factors at present). An alternative to utilizing continuously updated correction factors would be to restructure the conversion equations, using short-run relationships with lags for translating *GNP* component demands into industry outputs and long-run relationships on the value added composition of final expenditures for translating industry prices into *GNP* component prices. That is, instead of using a single set of conversion matrices, two would be employed.

2. In order to bypass the input-output table, each industry's output originating might be directly related to the set of *GNP* component expenditures. Using an iterative procedure, the coefficients so derived may be updated subject to row and column constraints on the sums of the coefficients. This procedure was derived independently by David Kresge, Michael Bacharach, and Richard Stone. Bacharach has shown that the process iterates to a unique solution [9]).

3. A related, alternative method obtains nonstochastic, linear simultaneous solutions of each row of coefficients (relating industry output originating and *GNP* component demands) for specified time intervals. (The length, in number of quarters, of each interval in the absence of singularity is equal to the number of coefficients in the row.) These are then treated as stochastics in time, and interpolation formulas (limited to monotone transforms) are derived for each element. Given the interpolation formulas, a new set of nonstochastic solutions and interpolators is derived. This iterative procedure is continued until the sum of squared deviations of actual from the predicted *GNP* components (in each row) is minimized. The final set of coefficients may then be extrapolated beyond the sample period by the last interpolation formula.

At present, it is not clear which of the alternatives is best: the first suffers from fixity of the coefficients and possible bias; the second, from multicollinearity in the regressions; and the third, from arbitrary interpolation and possible inconsistency. The relative merits of each of the procedures should be determined.

Some of the difficulty in conversion arises from the high degree of aggregation. With only eight producing sectors, each industry delivers much of its outputs to itself; thus, little account can be taken of compositional changes on either the production or demand side. This problem will be alleviated when we disaggregate to a thirty-three-sector breakdown.

---

[9]) Michael Bacharach, *International Economic Review*, (September 1965).

# 2

# COMPLETE SYSTEM SOLUTIONS AND SIMULATIONS

## *2.1. Description of the system*

The test of any model is not only how well it performs for individual equations but also how it functions as a complete system in predictive and simulation tests. During the past year we have been determining the characteristics of various subsets of the present "full blown" 359-equation version of the model. Eight-quarter solutions (for 1961:1–1962:4 and 1957:1–1958:4) were obtained with a 177-equation version in which the parameter estimates were fitted to 1948:1–1960:4 by ordinary least squares [1]). (Longer runs for as many as thirty-eight quarters—1953:3–1962:4—have also been calculated.)

Given the structural shifts in some parameters after 1953, it would have been desirable to have employed equations fitted to 1953:3–1960:4. However, these equations had not been estimated when the interperiod covariance analyses were undertaken, and special calculations to obtain them would have involved considerable expense and delay in complete system testing. An alternative to reestimation would be to use the parameters fitted to 1953:3–1962:4, but this would produce positively biased indications of accuracy in the 1961-62 period because the observations in these two years would influence the parameter estimates. Conversely, in utilizing the 1948-60 equation estimates, the forecasting results are negatively biased, that is, smaller errors would be obtained if 1953:3–1960:4 equation estimates were the basis for the post-1960 system solutions.

The 1948-60 equation estimates appear in appendix A. With few exceptions, the specifications are the same as those published in the first volume on the model[2]). In the automobile consumption equation, the (exogenous) attitudes index has been replaced by the (endogenous) rate of unemploy-

---

[1]) Consistent estimates have been derived for many equations but not on a wholly compatible set of data. All parameters in the model will be reestimated in a few months when the complete revisions in the national income and product accounts become available.

[2]) *The Brookings Quarterly Econometric Model of the United States*, op. cit.

ment as a cyclical indicator. Also, a dummy variable has been added to reflect the major easing of credit terms in 1955. In the durable manufacturing inventory investment function, the orders terms have been lagged one quarter, and the relative price and index of hours-worked terms have been deleted. For nondurables, inventory investment, lagged sales, and inventory investment have been added, and the change in unfilled orders has been dropped.

Several elaborate sector specifications have not been used for the present solutions. Labor force participation is treated in the aggregate rather than by sex and age group. The direct, alternative business investment functions were employed instead of the two-step intentions-realizations functions. The government receipts sector has been condensed to seven equations, and the financial sector to six. However, with the availability of more data, the function for manhours in the regulated industries has been separated into employment and hours functions, and many equations have been added to explain income shares (entrepreneurial, interest, rental income) by production sector.

Agriculture and government expenditures are treated exogenously. Furthermore, some components are related to totals (for example, durables exports to total exports) on the basis of historical averages. Also, because data are taken from various sources, in certain instances an exogenous difference has been added to reconcile two series. Finally, the use of the fixed coefficient, 1947 input-output table necessitated autoregressive corrections on the conversions from industry prices to *GNP* component prices and *GNP* component demands to industry outputs.

## *2.2. Method of solution*

The solution to the system is iterative and is achieved by making use of the model's block recursive structure. First, a block of twenty variables wholly dependent on lagged endogenous or exogenous variables is solved; this block contains investment, capital stock, and capital consumption allowance variables. Second, an initial simultaneous equation solution is obtained for seventy-eight variables in the "quantity" block (consumption, imports, exports, inventory investment, orders, output, employment, *GNP*, taxes, and various income items) using predetermined variables and prices of the previous period. Third, a simultaneous equation solution is obtained for fifty variables in the "price" block (prices, wage rates, interest rates, and demand and time deposits), using predetermined variables and the initial solution from the "quantity" block. (All nonlinearities in the two simultaneous blocks other than price-quantity interactions were linearized by Taylor's expansions around the previous quarter's values.) Fourth, because prices and quantities are interdependent, the "price" block solution is used as a new input to the "quantity" block, and the second and third steps are iterated until each variable changes (from iteration to iteration) by no more than 0.1 per cent. Fifth, three blocks of seventeen, six and six variables each, respectively, are solved recursively. These blocks contain inventory and housing stocks and certain production sector income shares. The entire procedure is then repeated to derive the following quarter's solution.

## *2.3. Pseudo-realistic solution results*

Taken as a whole, the solutions derived for 1961:1–1962:4 are fairly accurate. The model fails to produce a decline in real *GNP* in the first quarter. The actual rise from that period to the end of 1962 exceeds the predicted only slightly. Actual constant dollar *GNP* increased by \$48.8 billion. With a condensed version of the tax sector, predicted real *GNP* rose by \$48.5 billion. This is an error in the first differences of \$0.3 billion, or approximately 0.6 per cent, over eight quarters. With the condensed tax sector, the predicted rise in real *GNP* is \$46.2 billion. For either version, in the fourth quarter of 1962, the predicted exceeds the actual level of real *GNP* by less than 2.0 per cent. Similarly predicted total real inventory accumulation over the entire period exceeds the actual by only \$4.1 billion, that is, an average of \$0.5 billion per quarter. Errors in the levels of other variables are also, for the most part, small.

While interest attaches to the level figures, small errors in these figures can mask large errors in predicting cyclical movements. Therefore, first differences are more relevant for judging the performance of the model. A set of actual and predicted first differences for a summary set of variables is shown in table 2.1. For each variable, the first line gives the actual first differences, the second line shows the predicted first differences with initial conditions of 1960:2, and the third line gives predicted first differences with initial conditions of 1960:4. As can be seen, most of the major swings in real magnitudes are captured reasonably well after the first quarter, especially with some corrections for timing by averaging of contiguous values. After the first quarter, the model accurately mirrors the slowdowns in the rate of growth that the economy actually experienced. The rate of

TABLE 2.1

*Unconditional forecasting of first differences, actual and predicted complete system solution* [a]).

| | Year and quarter | | | | | | | | | |
|---|---|---|---|---|---|---|---|---|---|---|
| | 1960:3 | 1960:4 | 1961:1 | 1961:2 | 1961:3 | 1961:4 | 1962:1 | 1962:2 | 1962:3 | 1962:4 |
| Current dollar *GNP* | | | | | | | | | | |
| Actual | −0.6 | −1.4 | −0.7 | 12.5 | 8.5 | 14.5 | 8.6 | 7.9 | 5.6 | 7.6 |
| Predicted | 2.0 | 6.6 | 4.3 | 12.9 | 12.9 | 15.8 | 13.0 | 10.2 | 8.5 | 7.8 |
| Predicted | | | 8.8 | 15.9 | 11.9 | 17.9 | 13.4 | 12.5 | 6.4 | 7.6 |
| Constant dollar *GNP* | | | | | | | | | | |
| Actual | −1.9 | −3.1 | −2.9 | 10.2 | 6.2 | 11.9 | 6.6 | 6.0 | 3.2 | 4.7 |
| Predicted | −1.3 | 0.7 | 0.8 | 8.8 | 7.8 | 11.5 | 8.9 | 3.6 | 1.4 | 3.6 |
| Predicted | | | 5.8 | 10.3 | 6.4 | 12.2 | 7.9 | 5.4 | 0.3 | 3.7 |
| Total real investment (excluding inventories) | | | | | | | | | | |
| Actual | −0.8 | −0.5 | −2.6 | 1.0 | 1.4 | 1.7 | 0.9 | 1.6 | 1.5 | −0.2 |
| Predicted | −0.5 | −0.6 | −1.5 | 2.3 | 2.3 | 3.0 | 0.5 | −0.3 | 0.6 | 2.6 |
| Predicted | | | −2.5 | 3.1 | 2.9 | 3.1 | −0.2 | 1.0 | 0.2 | 2.3 |
| Total real consumption | | | | | | | | | | |
| Actual | −0.9 | 0.0 | −0.5 | 3.7 | 3.3 | 4.9 | 4.2 | 2.4 | 3.2 | 3.8 |
| Predicted | −0.0 | 1.4 | 2.7 | 3.3 | 3.9 | 4.1 | 5.0 | 2.1 | 2.3 | 3.0 |
| Predicted | | | 4.1 | 3.7 | 4.1 | 4.8 | 4.8 | 2.5 | 2.9 | 3.2 |
| Real consumption of automobiles | | | | | | | | | | |
| Actual | −0.4 | 0.0 | −2.0 | 0.3 | 0.5 | 0.9 | 1.1 | 0.1 | 0.2 | 0.8 |
| Predicted | −0.5 | 0.1 | 0.1 | 0.2 | 0.4 | 0.4 | 0.5 | 0.1 | 0.1 | 0.1 |
| Predicted | | | −0.6 | 0.5 | 0.7 | 0.7 | 0.5 | 0.1 | −0.1 | 0.0 |
| Real consumption of durables other than automobiles | | | | | | | | | | |
| Actual | −0.2 | −0.5 | −0.2 | 1.1 | 0.5 | 1.0 | 0.0 | 0.0 | 0.5 | 1.2 |
| Predicted | −0.5 | 0.0 | 0.4 | 0.6 | 1.1 | 0.8 | 1.0 | −0.3 | 0.0 | 0.2 |
| Predicted | | | 0.4 | 0.8 | 0.9 | 1.0 | 0.8 | −0.1 | −0.1 | 0.4 |
| Real disposable income | | | | | | | | | | |
| Actual | 1.6 | −0.5 | 1.3 | 5.2 | 4.7 | 5.6 | 3.6 | 3.7 | 1.4 | 2.8 |
| Predicted | 2.2 | 0.1 | 2.8 | 3.7 | 6.0 | 5.3 | 6.9 | 0.5 | 1.4 | 2.1 |

| | | | | | | | | | | |
|---|---|---|---|---|---|---|---|---|---|---|
| Implicit price deflator for *GNP* | | | | | | | | | | |
| Actual | 0.004 | 0.005 | 0.006 | 0.001 | 0.003 | 0.002 | 0.002 | 0.002 | 0.004 | 0.004 |
| Predicted | 0.008 | 0.012 | 0.008 | 0.005 | 0.008 | 0.005 | 0.005 | 0.013 | 0.014 | 0.007 |
| Predicted | | | 0.005 | 0.008 | 0.009 | 0.008 | 0.009 | 0.013 | 0.012 | 0.006 |
| Wholesale price index: durable manufacturing | | | | | | | | | | |
| Actual | −0.007 | −0.001 | −0.001 | 0.000 | 0.001 | −0.001 | 0.000 | 0.001 | −0.002 | −0.001 |
| Predicted | 0.034 | 0.001 | 0.014 | 0.005 | 0.006 | 0.006 | 0.009 | 0.021 | 0.021 | 0.007 |
| Predicted | | | 0.038 | 0.009 | 0.004 | 0.006 | 0.022 | 0.018 | 0.018 | 0.004 |
| Consumer price index | | | | | | | | | | |
| Actual | 0.002 | 0.006 | 0.000 | 0.001 | 0.006 | −0.001 | 0.005 | 0.003 | 0.009 | −0.003 |
| Predicted | 0.009 | 0.013 | 0.005 | 0.006 | 0.006 | 0.004 | −0.002 | 0.016 | 0.012 | 0.008 |
| Predicted | | | 0.012 | 0.007 | 0.006 | 0.003 | 0.004 | 0.016 | 0.009 | 0.003 |
| Demand and time deposits | | | | | | | | | | |
| Actual | 2.3 | 2.7 | 3.6 | 3.5 | 2.8 | 3.6 | 4.3 | 3.6 | 2.4 | 4.8 |
| Predicted | 2.8 | 3.5 | 3.2 | 3.0 | 3.1 | 2.8 | 3.8 | 3.6 | 3.3 | 3.9 |
| Predicted | | | 3.3 | 3.1 | 3.1 | 2.8 | 3.9 | 3.6 | 3.3 | 3.9 |
| Net exports in constant dollars | | | | | | | | | | |
| Actual | 0.9 | 1.4 | 0.3 | −1.6 | −0.1 | 0.1 | −0.8 | 1.5 | 0.0 | −0.7 |
| Predicted | 0.2 | 0.0 | 0.1 | −0.2 | −0.5 | −0.4 | −0.2 | −0.3 | −0.4 | −0.2 |
| Predicted | | | −0.5 | −0.7 | −0.6 | −0.6 | −0.4 | −0.4 | −0.4 | −0.2 |
| Government bonds short-term interest rate | | | | | | | | | | |
| Actual | −0.630 | −0.050 | 0.040 | −0.050 | 0.000 | 0.160 | 0.260 | −0.010 | 0.130 | −0.030 |
| Predicted | −0.441 | −0.383 | 0.196 | 0.098 | 0.039 | 0.041 | −0.133 | 0.240 | 0.192 | −0.470 |
| Predicted | | | 0.043 | 0.081 | 0.068 | −0.137 | −0.336 | 0.204 | 0.068 | −0.458 |
| Unemployment rate | | | | | | | | | | |
| Actual | 0.003 | 0.007 | 0.005 | 0.002 | −0.002 | −0.005 | −0.007 | −0.001 | 0.001 | 0.000 |
| Predicted | 0.001 | 0.001 | 0.000 | 0.000 | 0.000 | −0.001 | −0.002 | −0.001 | 0.000 | 0.001 |
| Predicted | | | 0.001 | −0.003 | −0.004 | −0.004 | −0.003 | 0.000 | 0.001 | 0.002 |

a) For each variable the first row of figures contains the actual first differences and the second and third rows the first differences of complete system solution beginning in 1960:3 and 1961:1, respectively. Monetary variables are in billions of dollars at annual rates. Price indexes are in terms of 1954 = 1.0, interest rates are in percentages and the unemployment rate is a fraction.

increase of real *GNP* rises in the second quarter of 1961, falls in the third quarter, rises to a peak in the fourth quarter, then declines for three quarters and, finally, begins to increase again in the fourth quarter of 1962. Nonetheless, it would be unwise to attach undue significance to this coincidence of movement since *GNP* is a sum of many components. The predicted aggregate may only exhibit a pattern similar to the actual as a consequence of compensating errors in the components. Yet the model passes even this test reasonably well, although certainly far better for total real consumption than for the investment variables.

On the current dollar side of the model, the estimates are derived by multiplying constant dollar quantities by price indexes. Thus, errors in the latter are transmitted directly to the current money value products. Some reasons for the discrepancies in price predictions have been given in chapter 1. Another source of this difficulty in the solution is the output-employment-labor force-unemployment-wages-prices nexus. Overestimates in output lead to overestimates in employment and, given a somewhat sluggish response in the increase of the labor force, underestimates in the rate of unemployment. This last variable enters into the wage rate determination equations (as a distributed lag), thereby resulting in overstatements of increases in compensation per manhour. These, in turn, bias prices upward. Although the errors in predicted unemployment are small, the distributed lag cumulates them and helps to cause a significant wage push in the model in 1962.

In the case of the last set of variables tabulated, those for the financial sector, the predictions of demand and time deposits are quite accurate on a two-quarter basis. With some averaging, interest rate movements are also predicted without undue error.

In addition to the eight-quarter solution described, a ten-quarter solution was also computed. This solution starts with the initial conditions of the second quarter of 1960 (the peak quarter before the 1960–61 recession) and runs through the fourth quarter of 1962. Table 2.1 shows that predicted real *GNP* turns down in the first quarter (1960:3) by nearly the same amount as actual real *GNP*. Then, whereas the actual shows further declines of \$3.1 and \$2.9 billion in the succeeding two quarters, predicted real *GNP* rises slightly by \$0.7 and \$0.8 billion. In other words, the model does predict (given the actual values of exogenous variables) a small decline in real product and a marked slowing down in the rate of growth. From the foregoing, this would be interpreted as a forecast of an impending recession.

In later quarters, 1961:2–1962:4, the results for the ten-quarter solution are much the same as for the eight-quarter solution. The discrepancies between the actual and predicted first differences are somewhat larger, but not substantially so. The patterns of prediction and accuracy of the other variables follow much the same paths as real *GNP*. The failure of predicted total real consumption to fall in the first solution quarter is primarily due to the residual in nondurable food and beverages equations. The propensity for people to continue eating is apparently higher in the model than in the economy.

While the foregoing residuals are not insignificant, it must be borne in mind that the system is three to four times larger than any of its competitors. Moreover, these are only preliminary results which will improve when the structure of the model and some of its parameter estimates are refined. Furthermore, the prediction of economic events for nearly any period is difficult, but the one selected for the initial predictive tests (1961–62) may be more intractable than most. Not only did the economy experience a very minor recession (which, with continuing data revisions, is becoming even smaller), but several structural changes took place. Finally, other models have not been especially successful in their after-the-fact predictions for this period.

## 2.4. *Impact multipliers*

In addition to solutions, the values of the parameters of the system considered as a whole are important. One such set of parameters, impact multipliers, show the ultimate, one-quarter induced change in a current endogenous variable given an initial unit change in that or another variable.

Let $\boldsymbol{A}$ be a vector of equation constant terms; $\boldsymbol{B}$, $\boldsymbol{C}$ and $\boldsymbol{D}$ constant coefficient matrices; and $\boldsymbol{Y}$ and $\boldsymbol{X}$ vectors of current endogenous and exogenous variables, respectively, and $\boldsymbol{Y}_{-i}$ a vector of lagged endogenous variables. Then, linearizing some terms and considering only the "real" part of the system:

$$\boldsymbol{DY} = \boldsymbol{A}+\boldsymbol{BX}+\boldsymbol{CY}_{-i}$$

$$\boldsymbol{Y} = \boldsymbol{D}^{-1}\boldsymbol{A}+\boldsymbol{D}^{-1}\boldsymbol{BX}+\boldsymbol{D}^{-1}\boldsymbol{CY}_{-i}$$

Then, $\boldsymbol{D}^{-1}$ and $\boldsymbol{D}^{-1}\boldsymbol{B}$ are impact multiplier matrices which show the change in $\boldsymbol{Y}$ given a unit change in $\boldsymbol{A}$ or $\boldsymbol{X}$. A sixteen-variable segment of $\boldsymbol{D}^{-1}$ is listed in table 2.2. (The full set of $78\times78$, or 6,864 entries, is too extensive to be tabulated here.) It shows, for example, that an initial exogenous increase of \$1 in real consumption expenditures for automobiles ($C_{DA}^{54}$) results in an increase of \$1.12 in automobile consumption and a \$1.59 increase in real *GNP*.

The impact multipliers reported here are somewhat greater than those customarily estimated. However, most of the other information we have on such multipliers is derived from models which are highly recursive, rather than simultaneous. This high degree of recursion tends to dampen the reaction of the system to shocks during the initial period, that is, it tends to produce low impact multipliers. Solutions of models which are more simultaneous, for example, the Wharton model, tend to yield multipliers which are consistent with the present results.

It should also be emphasized that these are one-quarter impact multipliers; in a system with lags, longer term multipliers tend to be different. For the most part, expenditure multipliers approach a higher asymptotic limit. But where accumulated stocks have a major influence, the multipliers may at first rise and then decline, or simply decline, from their initial values.

More complicated multipliers associated with coefficient parameter changes in the "real" block (such as tax rates, prices, and wage rates) would not be invariant with such parameter shifts. They would have to be determined by solving the system under successively altered conditions and examining the solutions for jointly determined variables. Also, because the system is nonlinear, in both this case and the former (where the "price" block is held constant) the magnitudes of the multipliers depend on the size of the multiplicands. The linear approximations to the nonlinearities would change accordingly.

## *2.5. System simulations*

Pseudo-realistic solutions, such as the foregoing can act as bench marks for simulations with the complete model. Several different kinds of simulation studies might be conducted, with the response of the overall system observed in each case.

(1) Stochastic disturbances drawn from assumed distributions (for example, multivariate normal distributions with mean zero and covariances equal to those of the equations in question) can be introduced into individual equations or blocks of equations.

(2) In addition to error variance characteristics which can be estimated

from the data, these stochastic disturbances can be given assumed serial correlation or covariance properties.

(3) Selected parameters may be incremented.

(4) The initial conditions may be changed.

(5) Shocks can be imposed on certain endogenous or exogenous variables (for example, inventory change might be held to zero or the rate of population growth might be increased).

These tests are of a purely structural nature. Simulations of alterations in government policy parameters such as tax, transfer, expenditure, and monetary rates are of interest as well. Various structural and policy simulations can also be combined. In addition, parameters derived from applying different estimation techniques can be used.

Thus, a wide range of experiments is possible. In each instance the system's solution path (that is, the values of endogenous variables) over time would be computed. Obviously, for stochastic experiments (which by definition involve repeated trials) means, variances, and covariances should be calculated. As appropriate to the experiment, judgments can then be made about the system's stability, parameter sensitivity, and growth path characteristics. For policy experiments, interest centers on impact and dynamic multipliers, the net government cost of policy changes, Phillips curves, and induced rates of inflation.

In addition to observing the outcome of the experiments, it is also feasible to design stabilization policies. These policies might take the form of integral stabilization, formula flexibility, discretionary gap adjustment, or other forms. However, all policies must assume either an explicit or implicit preference function for achieving desired states of a set of target variables. Changes in instrument variables may affect target variables only after some lag; the effects are generally distributed over time once the impact is felt. This must be taken into account as must potential errors in making unconditional forecasts of the economy's movements and conditional forecasts of the effects of policy actions. This class of problems is treated by Henri Theil in his *Economic Forecasts and Policy* (North-Holland, 1961); his method of analysis is yet to be applied to the U.S. economy, a task which should yield useful results.

Analytical techniques used with engineering problems might also be usefully adapted to economic analysis, as the work of Tustin, Phillips, Holt, and May has revealed. The study of large nonlinear dynamic economic systems is relatively new, and insights gained from these applications should be studied.

TABLE 2.2

*Quarterly impact multipliers (Prices, wage rates, and interest rates are assumed to be constant)* [a]).

| Induced change in | Unit change in $C^{54}_{DEA}$ | $C^{54}_{DA}$ | $C^{54}_{NFB}$ | $C^{54}_{NEFB}$ | $C^{54}_{S}$ | $\Delta INV^{54}_{MD}$ | $\Delta INV^{54}_{MN}$ | $\Delta INV^{54}_{T}$ | $\Delta INV^{54}_{0*4}$ | $M^{54}_{FIN}$ | $M^{54}_{EFIN}$ | $TP$ | $TX$ | $TC$ | $TW$ | $V_G$ |
|---|---|---|---|---|---|---|---|---|---|---|---|---|---|---|---|---|
| $C^{54}_{DEA}$ | 1.086 | 0.086 | 0.056 | 0.058 | 0.042 | 0.080 | 0.067 | 0.060 | 0.054 | −0.061 | −0.061 | −0.219 | −0.024 | −0.017 | −0.180 | 0.100 |
| $C^{54}_{DA}$ | 0.125 | 1.121 | 0.079 | 0.081 | 0.058 | 0.112 | 0.079 | 0.086 | 0.074 | −0.088 | −0.088 | −0.095 | −0.018 | −0.007 | −0.078 | 0.078 |
| $C^{54}_{NFB}$ | 0.038 | 0.038 | 1.025 | 0.026 | 0.018 | 0.035 | 0.025 | 0.027 | 0.024 | −0.027 | −0.027 | −0.097 | −0.011 | −0.008 | −0.079 | 0.079 |
| $C^{54}_{NEFB}$ | 0.052 | 0.052 | 0.034 | 1.035 | 0.025 | 0.048 | 0.034 | 0.037 | 0.033 | −0.037 | −0.037 | −0.133 | −0.015 | −0.011 | −0.110 | 0.110 |
| $C^{54}_{S}$ | 0.011 | 0.011 | 0.007 | 0.008 | 1.006 | 0.011 | 0.008 | 0.008 | 0.007 | −0.008 | −0.008 | −0.029 | −0.003 | −0.002 | −0.024 | 0.024 |
| $INV^{54}_{MD}$ | 0.266 | 0.265 | 0.028 | 0.029 | 0.021 | 1.039 | 0.027 | 0.029 | 0.026 | −0.090 | −0.090 | −0.067 | −0.007 | −0.005 | −0.055 | 0.055 |
| $INV^{54}_{MN}$ | 0.001 | 0.001 | 0.021 | 0.021 | 0.001 | 0.001 | 1.001 | 0.001 | 0.001 | −0.008 | −0.008 | −0.004 | −0.001 | −0.000 | −0.003 | 0.003 |
| $INV^{54}_{T}$ | 0.060 | 0.059 | 0.055 | 0.055 | 0.006 | 0.010 | 0.006 | 1.007 | 0.006 | −0.056 | −0.056 | −0.024 | −0.003 | −0.002 | −0.019 | 0.019 |
| $INV^{54}_{0*4}$ | 0.004 | 0.004 | 0.004 | 0.004 | 0.004 | 0.001 | 0.001 | 0.001 | 1.001 | −0.004 | −0.004 | −0.002 | −0.000 | −0.000 | −0.001 | 0.001 |
| $M^{54}_{FIN}$ | 0.012 | 0.012 | 0.008 | 0.008 | 0.006 | 0.011 | 0.008 | 0.009 | 0.008 | 0.991 | −0.009 | −0.031 | −0.003 | −0.002 | −0.025 | 0.025 |
| $M^{54}_{EFIN}$ | 0.038 | 0.036 | 0.019 | 0.022 | 0.006 | 0.059 | 0.052 | 0.050 | 0.041 | −0.023 | 0.977 | −0.013 | −0.001 | −0.001 | −0.010 | 0.010 |
| $TP$ | 0.100 | 0.100 | 0.064 | 0.067 | 0.048 | 0.092 | 0.065 | 0.070 | 0.062 | −0.070 | −0.070 | 0.964 | −0.028 | −0.020 | −0.208 | 0.208 |
| $TX$ | 0.220 | 0.247 | 0.178 | 0.182 | 0.179 | 0.199 | 0.161 | 0.166 | 0.185 | −0.180 | −0.180 | −0.089 | 0.990 | −0.007 | −0.073 | 0.073 |
| $TC$ | 0.383 | 0.489 | 0.371 | 0.384 | 0.436 | 0.340 | 0.308 | 0.307 | 0.406 | −0.352 | −0.352 | −0.171 | −0.472 | 9.987 | −0.141 | 0.141 |
| $TW$ | 0.078 | 0.074 | 0.047 | 0.049 | 0.029 | 0.072 | 0.050 | 0.054 | 0.043 | −0.053 | −0.053 | −0.027 | −0.003 | −0.002 | 0.978 | 0.022 |
| $V_G$ | −0.108 | −0.106 | −0.078 | −0.079 | −0.065 | −0.091 | −0.074 | −0.078 | −0.072 | 0.084 | 0.084 | 0.040 | 0.004 | 0.003 | 0.033 | 0.967 |
| $GNP^{54}$ | 1.593 | 1.590 | 1.282 | 1.286 | 1.168 | 1.266 | 1.177 | 1.197 | 1.175 | −1.347 | −1.347 | −0.626 | −0.068 | −0.049 | −0.515 | 0.515 |

[a]) Each entry in the table represents the induced change in the row item given a unit change in the column item.

Finally, one of the most intriguing simulation applications of the model is the examination of economic history. By varying the movement of exogenous variables and shifting autonomous and other parameters, it is possible to determine the course of the economy under altered conditions. This yields insights into its basic stability and indicates what might have taken place under more favorable circumstances. For example, one experiment might be to superimpose the characteristics of the 1930's depression on the present economic structure to see what magnitude and duration of downturn might occur; for example, plant and equipment investment might be drastically curtailed, prices could be severely depressed, and government expenditures could be cut while maintaining tax receipts.

### 2.5.1. *Simulation experiments*

In this study, eight roughly equivalent simulation experiments were run for the period 1960:3–1962:4. For expenditure increases and income tax reductions the equivalence is in terms of the constant dollar amount of policy change. The "equivalence" for the monetary policy shifts was to set them to yield substantial increments in real *GNP* after ten quarters. The experiments are as follows:

| Amounts (monetary flows in billions of dollars at annual rates) | Current dollars [3] | Constant dollars |
|---|---|---|
| 1. Increase in government durables purchases | $3.8 | $3.2 |
| 2. Increase in government nondurables purchases | 3.3 | 3.2 |
| 3. Increase in government employment (626,000 employees) | 4.0 | 3.2 |
| 4. Increase in government construction expenditures | 3.8 | 3.2 |
| 5. Reduction in personal federal income taxes [4] | 4.0 | 3.5 |
| 6. Reduction in personal federal income taxes plus monetary policy | 4.0 | 3.5 |
| 7. Reduction in reserve requirements on demand deposits from 0.149 to 0.139 | — | — |
| 8. Increase in unborrowed reserves (open market operations) | 1.0 | — |

In each experiment all other exogenous variables except the one to be changed were maintained at the actual values prevailing during the simulation period. The shift in the policy under study was performed in each

[3]) Averages over the period.

[4]) The figures shown are averages over the period with the current dollar amounts deflated by the implicit price deflator for personal consumption expenditures. Quarterly tax reductions were derived by shifting the tax rate parameters from $TP = -21.2849 + 0.1784\ Y_P$ to $TP = -19.7985 + 0.1659\ Y_P$.

quarter beginning with 1960:3. Thus, for example, government durables purchases were increased by 3.2 billion 1954 dollars from their actual levels in 1960:3 through 1962:4. Therefore, the predicted impact of the policy change is the difference between the solutions with and without the expenditures increase.

### *2.5.2. Simulation results*

Summary measures of some of the results of the foregoing experiments are shown in table 2.3. They may also be compared with the excise tax simulations of chapter 4; these comparisons appear in chapter 5.

The largest impacts on real *GNP* after ten quarters are obtained from the increases in government nondurables and construction expenditures, with the effects of higher expenditures on durables and changes in the monetary variables not lagging far behind. However, the increase in government employment and both a straight income tax cut and one combined with an "accommodating" monetary policy (to be defined) have significantly lower real outputs. On an immediate impact basis, in one quarter, the situation is slightly different. The employment policy has an effect approximately comparable to the other expenditure increases, while the monetary factors actually cause a decline in real *GNP* through their influence on interest income. Still, the income tax cuts are not as powerful a stimulant as the expenditure boosts.

As might be expected, the influence of the alternative policy changes varies from one *GNP* expenditure and income component to another. For example, income tax cuts cause the largest spurts in consumption while the monetary variables have the greatest impact on real investment. The employment increase also has a relatively strong consumption impact, especially in the initial quarter. Real investment, in turn, affects the composition of consumption and other expenditure items through relative capacity, productivity, and price effects.

Somewhat surprisingly, all the stimulative policies cause a fall (in relation to the original solution) in the rate of increase of prices, at least for a period of time. The results for the implicit price deflator for *GNP*, in the durable purchases simulation show, for example, that the difference in prices (to the original solution) is about −0.5 index points in the first and second simulation quarters, −0.6 index points in the third and fourth quarters, and −0.5, −0.4, −0.4, −0.2, −0.1, and −0.0 index points in the following consecutive quarters. Prices in both the simulation and original solutions do rise, of course, from

1.146 to 1.228 in the former and from 1.150 to 1.228 in the latter. This type of movement can be largely explained by the surge in output and labor productivity, which produces declining relative unit labor costs, thereby lessening price pressures. The gain in productivity in the short run occurs because of the increasing use of underemployed labor and inertial factors in the employment process. As output continues to grow, however, additional manpower is required and hired, thereby lessening the rate of increase of productivity. This short-run productivity spurt effect tends to die out after three to four quarters, and the rate of increase of labor costs and prices rises at a faster rate from that point. If the simulations were extended beyond ten quarters, prices would probably be higher with the stimulative policies than in the original solution. In fact, this is exactly what occurs in the government employment simulation after nine quarters. Increases in capacity, with output given, also have a depressive effect on prices. This accounts for the favorable price behavior of the monetary policy simulations. (The model provides for no purely monetary influences on prices; all price changes arise from elements in the real or quantity blocks.)

Given the errors in price predictions of the original solutions, these results might be viewed with some skepticism. However, they are not unreasonable theoretically. A priori, it might be expected that the productivity surges associated with spurts in output act as a restraining influence on the rate of price increases. Yet, it is possible that the estimated relative weights of the labor cost (which is the inverse of productivity) and demand terms in the price equations are biased in favor of the cost variables. If this is true, prices will begin to increase earlier than indicated in table 2.3. In any event, the negative price effects are quite small in most instances and statistically may not be significantly different from zero. Thus, the results might be construed as indicating that prices are unaffected for a period of time and then begin to rise.

A review of the impact of the various policies on the balance of payments shows that all of the policies result in a deterioration of the net exports of goods and services account. The largest increase in the importation of finished goods results from the policies which have strong direct effects on consumption, that is, the employment increase and income tax cuts, while the other expenditure policies generate the greatest demand for unfinished imports. All the policies have an approximately equivalent effect on current dollar exports since higher export prices are offset by lower export volumes. Taking the difference between constant dollar exports and imports, it is found that by the end of the period the employment and monetary policies

TABLE 2.3

*Simulation results: impact of government expenditure increases, personal income tax cut, and monetary policy.*

| Solution | Year and quarter | | | | | | | | | |
|---|---|---|---|---|---|---|---|---|---|---|
| | 1960:3 | 1960:4 | 1961:1 | 1961:2 | 1961:3 | 1961:4 | 1962:1 | 1962:2 | 1962:3 | 1962:4 |
| | A. Current dollar *GNP* | | | | | | | | | |
| Original solution | 509.2 | 515.7 | 519.9 | 533.1 | 546.1 | 562.6 | 576.5 | 587.3 | 595.8 | 603.2 |
| Simulations | | | | | | | | | | |
| Government | | | | | | | | | | |
| Durables expenditures | 512.9 | 520.6 | 525.9 | 538.1 | 551.8 | 568.4 | 584.8 | 596.9 | 606.3 | 613.6 |
| Nondurables expenditures | 511.2 | 519.3 | 524.3 | 537.2 | 550.4 | 567.6 | 583.2 | 595.5 | 605.1 | 612.8 |
| Employment | 514.3 | 521.6 | 526.5 | 540.8 | 553.3 | 569.5 | 584.4 | 595.9 | 605.1 | 612.6 |
| Construction expenditures | 512.0 | 520.4 | 525.8 | 538.6 | 552.3 | 569.2 | 585.2 | 597.2 | 606.6 | 614.1 |
| Income tax cut | 510.5 | 517.6 | 522.2 | 535.1 | 548.5 | 565.2 | 579.7 | 591.2 | 600.3 | 608.0 |
| Income tax cut plus monetary policy | 510.5 | 517.6 | 522.3 | 535.4 | 549.0 | 566.1 | 580.9 | 592.7 | 601.9 | 609.9 |
| Reserve requirements reduction | 508.4 | 516.9 | 521.5 | 535.9 | 549.1 | 570.2 | 583.4 | 594.4 | 602.7 | 611.4 |
| Open market operations | 508.4 | 517.0 | 521.6 | 536.0 | 549.2 | 570.5 | 583.5 | 594.4 | 602.6 | 611.4 |
| Simulation less original solution | | | | | | | | | | |
| Government | | | | | | | | | | |
| Durables expenditures | 3.7 | 4.9 | 6.0 | 5.0 | 5.6 | 5.8 | 8.2 | 9.6 | 10.5 | 10.4 |
| Nondurable expenditures | 2.0 | 3.6 | 4.4 | 4.1 | 4.2 | 5.0 | 6.7 | 8.2 | 9.2 | 9.6 |
| Employment | 5.2 | 5.9 | 6.6 | 7.7 | 7.1 | 6.9 | 7.9 | 8.6 | 9.2 | 9.4 |
| Construction expenditures | 2.8 | 4.7 | 5.9 | 5.5 | 6.1 | 6.7 | 8.6 | 9.9 | 10.7 | 10.9 |
| Income tax cut | 1.4 | 1.9 | 2.3 | 2.1 | 2.4 | 2.7 | 3.2 | 3.9 | 4.4 | 4.8 |
| Income tax cut plus monetary policy | 1.3 | 2.0 | 2.4 | 2.3 | 2.8 | 3.5 | 4.4 | 5.4 | 6.1 | 6.7 |
| Reserve requirements reduction | −0.7 | 1.2 | 1.6 | 2.8 | 3.0 | 7.6 | 6.8 | 7.1 | 6.8 | 8.3 |
| Open market operations | −0.8 | 1.3 | 1.6 | 2.9 | 3.1 | 8.0 | 6.9 | 7.1 | 6.8 | 8.2 |

| | | | | | | | | | | |
|---|---|---|---|---|---|---|---|---|---|---|
| | | | | | B. Constant dollar GNP | | | | | |
| Original solution | 440.8 | 442.0 | 443.5 | 452.4 | 459.8 | 471.4 | 481.4 | 485.4 | 487.0 | 490.2 |
| Simulations | | | | | | | | | | |
| Government | | | | | | | | | | |
| Durables expenditures | 446.0 | 448.5 | 451.2 | 459.2 | 466.9 | 478.1 | 490.0 | 494.4 | 496.1 | 498.9 |
| Nondurables expenditures | 445.3 | 448.5 | 451.0 | 460.2 | 467.8 | 479.0 | 490.2 | 494.6 | 496.2 | 499.4 |
| Employment | 446.1 | 448.2 | 450.4 | 459.3 | 466.6 | 476.9 | 487.6 | 491.6 | 493.3 | 490.2 |
| Construction expenditures | 446.0 | 449.1 | 451.7 | 460.2 | 468.0 | 479.3 | 490.7 | 495.0 | 496.4 | 499.4 |
| Income tax cut | 443.3 | 445.3 | 447.3 | 456.2 | 464.0 | 475.6 | 485.7 | 489.9 | 491.6 | 494.9 |
| Income tax cut plus monetary policy | 443.2 | 445.3 | 447.6 | 456.7 | 464.7 | 476.9 | 487.5 | 491.9 | 493.7 | 497.2 |
| Reserve requirements reduction | 439.4 | 444.5 | 446.0 | 456.8 | 464.7 | 482.5 | 490.2 | 494.3 | 495.0 | 499.0 |
| Open market operations | 439.3 | 444.7 | 446.2 | 456.9 | 464.9 | 483.0 | 490.2 | 494.3 | 494.9 | 498.8 |
| Simulation less original solution | | | | | | | | | | |
| Government | | | | | | | | | | |
| Durables expenditures | 5.2 | 6.5 | 7.7 | 6.8 | 7.1 | 6.7 | 8.6 | 9.0 | 9.1 | 8.6 |
| Nondurables expenditures | 4.6 | 6.5 | 7.5 | 7.8 | 8.0 | 7.6 | 8.9 | 9.2 | 9.3 | 9.2 |
| Employment | 5.3 | 6.2 | 6.8 | 6.9 | 6.8 | 5.5 | 6.2 | 6.2 | 6.3 | 6.3 |
| Construction expenditures | 5.3 | 7.1 | 8.1 | 7.8 | 8.2 | 7.9 | 9.4 | 9.6 | 9.4 | 9.2 |
| Income tax cut | 2.5 | 3.3 | 3.8 | 3.8 | 4.2 | 4.2 | 4.4 | 4.5 | 4.6 | 4.7 |
| Income tax cut plus monetary policy | 2.4 | 3.3 | 4.0 | 4.3 | 4.9 | 5.5 | 6.1 | 6.5 | 6.7 | 7.0 |
| Reserve requirements reduction | −1.4 | 2.5 | 2.5 | 4.4 | 4.9 | 11.1 | 8.8 | 8.9 | 8.0 | 8.8 |
| Open market operations | −1.5 | 2.7 | 2.6 | 4.5 | 5.1 | 11.6 | 8.9 | 8.9 | 7.9 | 8.6 |
| | | | | | C. Total real investment | | | | | |
| Original solution | 57.2 | 56.6 | 55.2 | 57.7 | 60.2 | 63.6 | 64.8 | 64.6 | 65.2 | 67.7 |
| Simulations | | | | | | | | | | |
| Government | | | | | | | | | | |
| Durables expenditures | 57.2 | 57.0 | 55.9 | 58.5 | 61.0 | 64.8 | 66.2 | 66.2 | 66.9 | 69.4 |

TABLE 2.3 (Continued)

| Solution | 1960:3 | 1960:4 | 1961:1 | 1961:2 | 1961:3 | 1961:4 | 1962:1 | 1962:2 | 1962:3 | 1962:4 |
|---|---|---|---|---|---|---|---|---|---|---|
| | Year and quarter | | | | | | | | | |
| Nondurables expenditures | 57.2 | 57.1 | 56.0 | 58.6 | 61.1 | 65.3 | 66.7 | 66.7 | 67.4 | 69.9 |
| Employment | 57.2 | 56.8 | 55.5 | 58.0 | 60.5 | 64.0 | 65.1 | 65.1 | 65.7 | 68.2 |
| Construction expenditures | 57.2 | 57.1 | 56.1 | 58.6 | 61.1 | 64.9 | 66.3 | 66.3 | 66.9 | 69.4 |
| Income tax cut | 57.2 | 56.8 | 55.5 | 58.0 | 60.5 | 64.1 | 65.3 | 65.1 | 65.8 | 68.3 |
| Income tax cut plus monetary policy | 57.2 | 56.8 | 55.6 | 58.2 | 60.8 | 64.6 | 66.0 | 65.9 | 66.6 | 69.2 |
| Reserve requirements reduction | 57.2 | 57.3 | 56.3 | 59.5 | 62.3 | 69.1 | 68.0 | 67.8 | 68.5 | 71.0 |
| Open market operations | 57.2 | 57.3 | 56.4 | 59.5 | 62.4 | 69.3 | 68.0 | 67.8 | 68.5 | 70.9 |
| Simulation less original solution | | | | | | | | | | |
| Government | | | | | | | | | | |
| Durables expenditures | 0.0 | 0.4 | 0.7 | 0.8 | 0.8 | 1.2 | 1.4 | 1.7 | 1.7 | 1.7 |
| Nondurables expenditures | 0.0 | 0.5 | 0.7 | 0.9 | 1.0 | 1.7 | 1.9 | 2.2 | 2.2 | 2.2 |
| Employment | 0.0 | 0.2 | 0.3 | 0.3 | 0.4 | 0.4 | 0.4 | 0.5 | 0.5 | 0.5 |
| Construction expenditures | 0.0 | 0.6 | 0.8 | 0.9 | 0.9 | 1.2 | 1.5 | 1.7 | 1.7 | 1.7 |
| Income tax cut | 0.0 | 0.2 | 0.3 | 0.3 | 0.4 | 0.4 | 0.5 | 0.6 | 0.6 | 0.6 |
| Income tax cut plus monetary policy | 0.0 | 0.3 | 0.4 | 0.5 | 0.7 | 1.0 | 1.2 | 1.4 | 1.4 | 1.5 |
| Reserve requirements reduction | 0.0 | 0.7 | 1.1 | 1.8 | 2.2 | 5.4 | 3.2 | 3.3 | 3.3 | 3.3 |
| Open market operations | 0.0 | 0.7 | 1.1 | 1.9 | 2.2 | 5.6 | 3.2 | 3.2 | 3.3 | 3.2 |
| | D. Total real consumption | | | | | | | | | |
| Original solution | 299.6 | 301.2 | 304.0 | 307.4 | 311.3 | 315.4 | 320.7 | 322.9 | 325.3 | 328.1 |
| Simulations | | | | | | | | | | |
| Government | | | | | | | | | | |
| Durables expenditures | 301.1 | 303.1 | 306.5 | 309.8 | 313.9 | 317.9 | 323.8 | 326.2 | 328.6 | 331.5 |

| | | | | | | | | | | |
|---|---|---|---|---|---|---|---|---|---|---|
| Employment | 301.6 | 303.6 | 306.8 | 310.4 | 314.2 | 318.0 | 323.5 | 325.7 | 328.0 | 330.9 |
| Construction expenditures | 300.9 | 303.2 | 306.7 | 310.2 | 314.3 | 318.4 | 324.1 | 326.4 | 328.8 | 331.7 |
| Income tax cut | 302.0 | 303.9 | 307.1 | 310.7 | 314.9 | 319.2 | 324.7 | 327.0 | 329.4 | 332.5 |
| Income tax cut plus monetary policy | 301.9 | 303.9 | 307.2 | 310.9 | 315.2 | 319.7 | 325.4 | 327.9 | 330.5 | 333.6 |
| Reserve requirements reduction | 299.1 | 302.1 | 305.1 | 309.2 | 313.5 | 319.7 | 324.9 | 327.4 | 329.7 | 333.0 |
| Open market operations | 299.1 | 302.2 | 305.1 | 309.3 | 313.6 | 319.9 | 324.9 | 327.4 | 329.7 | 333.0 |
| Simulation less original solution | | | | | | | | | | |
| Government | | | | | | | | | | |
| Durables expenditures | 1.5 | 2.0 | 2.5 | 2.4 | 2.6 | 2.5 | 3.1 | 3.2 | 3.4 | 3.3 |
| Nondurables expenditures | 1.3 | 1.9 | 2.3 | 2.7 | 2.9 | 2.9 | 3.3 | 3.4 | 3.5 | 3.5 |
| Employment | 2.0 | 2.4 | 2.8 | 2.9 | 3.0 | 2.6 | 2.7 | 2.7 | 2.8 | 2.8 |
| Construction expenditures | 1.4 | 2.1 | 2.6 | 2.7 | 3.0 | 3.0 | 3.4 | 3.5 | 3.5 | 3.6 |
| Income tax cut | 2.4 | 2.7 | 3.0 | 3.3 | 3.6 | 3.8 | 3.9 | 4.1 | 4.2 | 4.3 |
| Income tax cut plus monetary policy | 2.4 | 2.7 | 3.1 | 3.5 | 3.9 | 4.3 | 4.7 | 5.0 | 5.2 | 5.5 |
| Reserve requirements reduction | −0.5 | 0.9 | 1.1 | 1.8 | 2.3 | 4.3 | 4.1 | 4.5 | 4.5 | 4.9 |
| Open market operations | −0.5 | 1.0 | 1.1 | 1.9 | 2.4 | 4.5 | 4.2 | 4.5 | 4.5 | 4.8 |
| E. Real consumption of automobiles | | | | | | | | | | |
| Original solution | 13.4 | 13.5 | 13.6 | 13.9 | 14.2 | 14.6 | 15.2 | 15.4 | 15.5 | 15.6 |
| Simulations | | | | | | | | | | |
| Government | | | | | | | | | | |
| Durables expenditures | 13.7 | 13.9 | 14.2 | 14.4 | 14.9 | 15.2 | 15.8 | 16.0 | 16.2 | 16.3 |
| Nondurables expenditures | 13.6 | 13.8 | 14.1 | 14.4 | 14.8 | 15.3 | 15.8 | 16.0 | 16.2 | 16.3 |
| Employment | 13.8 | 14.1 | 14.5 | 14.7 | 15.0 | 15.3 | 15.8 | 16.0 | 16.1 | 16.2 |
| Construction expenditures | 13.7 | 13.9 | 14.2 | 14.5 | 15.0 | 15.3 | 15.9 | 16.1 | 16.3 | 16.3 |
| Income tax cut | 13.7 | 13.8 | 14.1 | 14.4 | 14.8 | 15.2 | 15.8 | 15.9 | 16.1 | 16.1 |
| Income tax cut plus monetary policy | 13.7 | 13.8 | 14.1 | 14.4 | 14.8 | 15.3 | 15.9 | 16.1 | 16.2 | 16.3 |

TABLE 2.3 (Continued)

| Solution | 1960:3 | 1960:4 | 1961:1 | 1961:2 | 1961:3 | 1961:4 | 1962:1 | 1962:2 | 1962:3 | 1962:4 |
|---|---|---|---|---|---|---|---|---|---|---|
| Reserve requirements reduction | 13.3 | 13.6 | 13.7 | 14.1 | 14.6 | 15.3 | 15.9 | 16.1 | 16.2 | 16.2 |
| Open market operations | 13.3 | 13.6 | 13.7 | 14.1 | 14.6 | 15.4 | 15.9 | 16.1 | 16.2 | 16.2 |
| Simulation less original solution | | | | | | | | | | |
| Government | | | | | | | | | | |
| Durables expenditures | 0.3 | 0.4 | 0.6 | 0.6 | 0.6 | 0.6 | 0.6 | 0.7 | 0.7 | 0.7 |
| Nondurables expenditures | 0.2 | 0.3 | 0.5 | 0.6 | 0.6 | 0.6 | 0.6 | 0.6 | 0.7 | 0.7 |
| Employment | 0.4 | 0.7 | 0.8 | 0.9 | 0.8 | 0.7 | 0.6 | 0.6 | 0.6 | 0.7 |
| Construction expenditures | 0.2 | 0.4 | 0.6 | 0.7 | 0.7 | 0.7 | 0.7 | 0.7 | 0.7 | 0.8 |
| Income tax cut | 0.3 | 0.4 | 0.5 | 0.5 | 0.5 | 0.5 | 0.5 | 0.5 | 0.6 | 0.6 |
| Income tax cut plus monetary policy | 0.3 | 0.4 | 0.5 | 0.5 | 0.6 | 0.6 | 0.7 | 0.7 | 0.7 | 0.7 |
| Reserve requirements reduction | —0.1 | 0.1 | 0.1 | 0.3 | 0.4 | 0.7 | 0.7 | 0.7 | 0.7 | 0.6 |
| Open market operations | —0.1 | 0.1 | 0.1 | 0.3 | 0.4 | 0.7 | 0.7 | 0.7 | 0.6 | 0.6 |
| F. Real consumption of durables other than automobiles | | | | | | | | | | |
| Original solution | 28.3 | 28.4 | 28.8 | 29.4 | 30.5 | 31.3 | 32.5 | 32.2 | 32.1 | 32.3 |
| Simulations | | | | | | | | | | |
| Government | | | | | | | | | | |
| Durables expenditures | 29.0 | 29.0 | 29.5 | 30.0 | 31.0 | 31.8 | 33.1 | 32.8 | 32.7 | 32.8 |
| Nondurables expenditures | 28.8 | 29.0 | 29.5 | 30.1 | 31.1 | 31.9 | 33.1 | 32.8 | 32.7 | 32.8 |
| Employment | 29.1 | 29.1 | 29.5 | 30.1 | 31.1 | 31.7 | 33.0 | 32.6 | 32.6 | 32.7 |
| Construction expenditures | 28.9 | 29.1 | 29.6 | 30.1 | 31.1 | 31.9 | 33.2 | 32.8 | 32.7 | 32.8 |
| Income tax cut | 29.3 | 29.4 | 29.8 | 30.3 | 31.4 | 32.2 | 33.3 | 33.0 | 32.9 | 33.0 |
| Income tax cut plus monetary policy | 29.3 | 29.4 | 29.8 | 30.4 | 31.4 | 32.3 | 33.5 | 33.2 | 33.1 | 33.2 |

| | | | | | | | | | | |
|---|---|---|---|---|---|---|---|---|---|---|
| Reserve requirements reduction | 28.1 | 28.7 | 29.0 | 29.9 | 30.9 | 32.5 | 33.2 | 32.9 | 32.7 | 32.9 |
| Open market operations | 28.1 | 28.7 | 29.0 | 29.9 | 30.9 | 32.5 | 33.2 | 32.9 | 32.7 | 32.8 |
| Simulation less original solution | | | | | | | | | | |
| Government | | | | | | | | | | |
| Durables expenditures | 0.6 | 0.7 | 0.7 | 0.6 | 0.6 | 0.5 | 0.7 | 0.6 | 0.6 | 0.5 |
| Nondurables expenditures | 0.5 | 0.6 | 0.7 | 0.7 | 0.6 | 0.5 | 0.6 | 0.6 | 0.6 | 0.5 |
| Employment | 0.7 | 0.7 | 0.7 | 0.7 | 0.6 | 0.4 | 0.5 | 0.5 | 0.4 | 0.4 |
| Construction expenditures | 0.6 | 0.7 | 0.8 | 0.7 | 0.7 | 0.6 | 0.7 | 0.7 | 0.6 | 0.6 |
| Income tax cut | 1.0 | 1.0 | 1.0 | 0.9 | 0.9 | 0.9 | 0.9 | 0.8 | 0.8 | 0.8 |
| Income tax cut plus monetary policy | 1.0 | 1.0 | 1.0 | 1.0 | 1.0 | 1.0 | 1.0 | 1.0 | 1.0 | 1.0 |
| Reserve requirements reduction | −0.2 | 0.3 | 0.2 | 0.4 | 0.5 | 1.1 | 0.7 | 0.7 | 0.5 | 0.6 |
| Open market operations | −0.2 | 0.3 | 0.2 | 0.5 | 0.5 | 1.2 | 0.7 | 0.7 | 0.5 | 0.6 |
| | | | | | G. Real nonfarm residential construction | | | | | |
| Original solution | 18.4 | 18.2 | 18.3 | 20.2 | 21.3 | 21.6 | 21.6 | 21.6 | 21.8 | 21.8 |
| Simulations | | | | | | | | | | |
| Government | | | | | | | | | | |
| Durables expenditures | 18.4 | 18.2 | 18.3 | 20.2 | 21.4 | 21.7 | 21.7 | 21.8 | 22.0 | 21.9 |
| Nondurables expenditures | 18.4 | 18.2 | 18.3 | 20.2 | 21.4 | 21.7 | 21.8 | 21.8 | 22.1 | 22.0 |
| Employment | 18.4 | 18.2 | 18.3 | 20.1 | 21.3 | 21.5 | 21.6 | 21.6 | 21.8 | 21.7 |
| Construction expenditures | 18.4 | 18.3 | 18.4 | 20.3 | 21.4 | 21.7 | 21.7 | 21.7 | 21.9 | 21.9 |
| Income tax cut | 18.4 | 18.2 | 18.3 | 20.1 | 21.2 | 21.5 | 21.5 | 21.6 | 21.8 | 21.7 |
| Income tax cut plus monetary policy | 18.4 | 18.2 | 18.3 | 20.3 | 21.5 | 21.8 | 21.9 | 21.9 | 22.1 | 22.0 |
| Reserve requirements reduction | 18.4 | 18.5 | 19.1 | 21.5 | 22.9 | 23.0 | 22.8 | 22.6 | 22.6 | 22.5 |
| Open market operations | 18.4 | 18.5 | 19.1 | 21.6 | 22.9 | 23.0 | 22.7 | 22.5 | 22.6 | 22.4 |

TABLE 2.3 (Continued)

| Solution | Year and quarter | | | | | | | | | |
|---|---|---|---|---|---|---|---|---|---|---|
| | 1960:3 | 1960:4 | 1961:1 | 1961:2 | 1961:3 | 1961:4 | 1962:1 | 1962:2 | 1962:3 | 1962:4 |
| Simulation less original solution | | | | | | | | | | |
| Government | | | | | | | | | | |
| Durables expenditures | 0 | 0.0 | 0.0 | 0.0 | 0.1 | 0.1 | 0.1 | 0.1 | 0.1 | 0.1 |
| Nondurables expenditures | 0 | 0.0 | 0.0 | 0.1 | 0.1 | 0.2 | 0.2 | 0.2 | 0.2 | 0.3 |
| Employment | 0 | 0.0 | 0.0 | 0.0 | −0.1 | −0.1 | −0.1 | −0.1 | −0.1 | 0.0 |
| Construction expenditures | 0 | 0.0 | 0.1 | 0.1 | 0.1 | 0.1 | 0.1 | 0.1 | 0.1 | 0.1 |
| Income tax cut | 0 | 0.0 | 0.0 | −0.1 | −0.1 | −0.1 | −0.1 | −0.1 | −0.1 | −0.1 |
| Income tax cut plus monetary policy | 0 | 0.0 | 0.0 | 0.1 | 0.1 | 0.2 | 0.2 | 0.2 | 0.2 | 0.2 |
| Reserve requirements reduction | 0 | 0.3 | 0.8 | 1.4 | 1.6 | 1.4 | 1.1 | 1.0 | 0.8 | 0.7 |
| Open market operations | 0 | 0.3 | 0.8 | 1.4 | 1.6 | 1.4 | 1.1 | 1.0 | 0.8 | 0.6 |
| H. Real business investment in plant and equipment | | | | | | | | | | |
| Original solution | 36.1 | 35.6 | 34.2 | 34.7 | 36.0 | 39.2 | 40.2 | 39.9 | 40.3 | 42.8 |
| Simulations | | | | | | | | | | |
| Government | | | | | | | | | | |
| Durables expenditures | 36.1 | 36.1 | 34.8 | 35.5 | 36.7 | 40.2 | 41.5 | 41.4 | 41.7 | 44.2 |
| Nondurables expenditures | 36.1 | 36.1 | 34.9 | 35.5 | 36.8 | 40.6 | 41.9 | 41.8 | 42.2 | 44.6 |
| Employment | 36.1 | 35.8 | 34.5 | 35.1 | 36.4 | 39.6 | 40.6 | 40.4 | 40.8 | 43.2 |
| Construction expenditures | 36.1 | 36.1 | 34.9 | 35.5 | 36.8 | 40.2 | 41.5 | 41.4 | 41.8 | 44.3 |
| Income tax cut | 36.1 | 35.8 | 34.5 | 35.1 | 36.4 | 39.6 | 40.7 | 40.4 | 40.8 | 43.3 |
| Income tax cut plus monetary policy | 36.1 | 35.9 | 34.5 | 35.1 | 36.5 | 39.9 | 41.1 | 40.9 | 41.4 | 43.9 |
| Reserve requirements reduction | 36.1 | 36.1 | 34.5 | 35.1 | 36.6 | 43.2 | 42.3 | 42.2 | 42.8 | 45.3 |
| Open market operations | 36.1 | 36.1 | 34.5 | 35.1 | 36.6 | 43.4 | 42.3 | 42.2 | 42.8 | 45.3 |

| | | | | | | | | | | |
|---|---|---|---|---|---|---|---|---|---|---|
| Government | | | | | | | | | | |
| Durables expenditures | 0 | 0.4 | 0.7 | 0.8 | 0.7 | 1.0 | 1.2 | 1.4 | 1.4 | 1.4 |
| Nondurables expenditures | 0 | 0.5 | 0.7 | 0.8 | 0.8 | 1.4 | 1.7 | 1.9 | 1.9 | 1.9 |
| Employment | 0 | 0.2 | 0.3 | 0.3 | 0.4 | 0.4 | 0.3 | 0.5 | 0.5 | 0.4 |
| Construction expenditures | 0 | 0.5 | 0.7 | 0.8 | 0.8 | 1.1 | 1.3 | 1.5 | 1.5 | 1.5 |
| Income tax cut | 0 | 0.2 | 0.3 | 0.4 | 0.4 | 0.4 | 0.5 | 0.5 | 0.5 | 0.5 |
| Income tax cut plus monetary policy | 0 | 0.2 | 0.4 | 0.4 | 0.4 | 0.7 | 0.9 | 1.0 | 1.0 | 1.1 |
| Reserve requirements reduction | 0 | 0.4 | 0.3 | 0.4 | 0.6 | 4.0 | 2.1 | 2.3 | 2.4 | 2.6 |
| Open market operations | 0 | 0.5 | 0.3 | 0.4 | 0.6 | 4.3 | 2.1 | 2.2 | 2.4 | 2.5 |
| | | | | | I. Real disposable income | | | | | |
| Original solution | 320.8 | 321.2 | 324.2 | 327.9 | 333.7 | 339.1 | 346.6 | 347.3 | 348.8 | 350.8 |
| Simulations | | | | | | | | | | |
| Government | | | | | | | | | | |
| Durables expenditures | 323.6 | 324.7 | 328.3 | 331.6 | 337.6 | 342.7 | 351.1 | 351.9 | 353.4 | 355.1 |
| Nondurables expenditures | 323.4 | 324.6 | 328.2 | 332.2 | 338.1 | 343.2 | 351.3 | 352.0 | 353.5 | 355.3 |
| Employment | 324.3 | 325.1 | 328.3 | 332.1 | 337.8 | 342.5 | 350.4 | 351.0 | 352.5 | 354.3 |
| Construction expenditures | 323.5 | 324.9 | 328.6 | 332.1 | 338.1 | 343.3 | 351.6 | 352.2 | 353.6 | 355.4 |
| Income tax cut | 325.5 | 326.3 | 329.7 | 333.5 | 339.6 | 345.1 | 352.8 | 353.5 | 355.0 | 357.0 |
| Income tax cut plus monetary policy | 325.5 | 326.3 | 329.8 | 333.8 | 340.0 | 345.8 | 353.7 | 354.6 | 356.2 | 358.3 |
| Reserve requirements reduction | 319.9 | 322.5 | 325.5 | 330.2 | 336.4 | 345.2 | 351.5 | 352.2 | 353.2 | 355.4 |
| Open market operations | 319.9 | 322.6 | 325.5 | 330.3 | 336.5 | 345.4 | 351.5 | 352.2 | 353.1 | 355.3 |
| Simulation less original solution | | | | | | | | | | |
| Government | | | | | | | | | | |
| Durables expenditures | 2.8 | 3.5 | 4.2 | 3.8 | 3.9 | 3.5 | 4.5 | 4.6 | 4.6 | 4.3 |
| Nondurables expenditures | 2.6 | 3.4 | 4.0 | 4.3 | 4.4 | 4.1 | 4.7 | 4.7 | 4.6 | 4.5 |
| Employment | 3.5 | 3.9 | 4.1 | 4.2 | 4.1 | 3.4 | 3.8 | 3.7 | 3.6 | 3.6 |
| Construction expenditures | 2.7 | 3.7 | 4.4 | 4.3 | 4.5 | 4.2 | 4.9 | 4.9 | 4.8 | 4.6 |

TABLE 2.3 (Continued)

| Solution | 1960:3 | 1960:4 | 1961:1 | 1961:2 | 1961:3 | 1961:4 | 1962:1 | 1962:2 | 1962:3 | 1962:4 |
|---|---|---|---|---|---|---|---|---|---|---|
| Income tax cut | 4.7 | 5.2 | 5.5 | 5.7 | 6.0 | 6.0 | 6.1 | 6.2 | 6.2 | 6.2 |
| Income tax cut plus monetary policy | 4.7 | 5.2 | 5.7 | 5.9 | 6.3 | 6.7 | 7.1 | 7.3 | 7.4 | 7.5 |
| Reserve requirements reduction | −0.9 | 1.4 | 1.3 | 2.3 | 2.7 | 6.0 | 4.9 | 4.9 | 4.3 | 4.6 |
| Open market operations | −1.0 | 1.5 | 1.3 | 2.4 | 2.8 | 6.3 | 4.9 | 4.8 | 4.2 | 4.5 |
| J. Implicit price deflator for *GNP* | | | | | | | | | | |
| Original solution | 1.150 | 1.161 | 1.169 | 1.174 | 1.183 | 1.188 | 1.193 | 1.206 | 1.220 | 1.228 |
| Simulations | | | | | | | | | | |
| Government | | | | | | | | | | |
| Durables expenditures | 1.146 | 1.156 | 1.162 | 1.168 | 1.177 | 1.184 | 1.189 | 1.204 | 1.219 | 1.228 |
| Nondurables expenditures | 1.145 | 1.154 | 1.160 | 1.165 | 1.174 | 1.181 | 1.187 | 1.202 | 1.218 | 1.226 |
| Employment | 1.148 | 1.158 | 1.166 | 1.171 | 1.181 | 1.189 | 1.194 | 1.208 | 1.223 | 1.231 |
| Construction expenditures | 1.143 | 1.154 | 1.161 | 1.167 | 1.176 | 1.183 | 1.188 | 1.203 | 1.219 | 1.227 |
| Income tax cut | 1.147 | 1.157 | 1.164 | 1.169 | 1.177 | 1.183 | 1.189 | 1.203 | 1.218 | 1.226 |
| Income tax cut plus monetary policy | 1.147 | 1.157 | 1.163 | 1.168 | 1.176 | 1.182 | 1.187 | 1.201 | 1.216 | 1.224 |
| Reserve requirements reduction | 1.152 | 1.157 | 1.166 | 1.169 | 1.177 | 1.176 | 1.186 | 1.198 | 1.214 | 1.222 |
| Open market operations | 1.152 | 1.157 | 1.166 | 1.169 | 1.176 | 1.176 | 1.186 | 1.199 | 1.214 | 1.223 |
| Simulation less original solution | | | | | | | | | | |
| Government | | | | | | | | | | |
| Durables expenditures | −0.005 | −0.005 | −0.006 | −0.006 | −0.005 | −0.004 | −0.004 | −0.002 | −0.001 | 0.000 |
| Nondurables expenditures | −0.005 | −0.007 | −0.008 | −0.009 | −0.009 | −0.007 | −0.006 | −0.004 | −0.002 | −0.001 |
| Employment | −0.002 | −0.003 | −0.003 | −0.003 | −0.002 | 0.001 | 0.001 | 0.002 | 0.003 | 0.003 |
| Construction expenditures | −0.007 | −0.007 | −0.007 | −0.007 | −0.007 | −0.005 | −0.005 | −0.003 | −0.001 | 0.000 |

| | | | | | | | | | | |
|---|---|---|---|---|---|---|---|---|---|---|
| Income tax cut plus monetary policy | −0.003 | −0.004 | −0.005 | −0.006 | −0.006 | −0.006 | −0.006 | −0.005 | −0.004 | −0.004 |
| Reserve requirements reduction | 0.002 | −0.004 | −0.003 | −0.005 | −0.006 | −0.012 | −0.007 | −0.007 | −0.006 | −0.005 |
| Open market operations | 0.002 | −0.004 | −0.003 | −0.005 | −0.006 | −0.012 | −0.007 | −0.007 | −0.006 | −0.005 |
| **K. Wholesale price index: manufacturing durables** | | | | | | | | | | |
| Original solution | 1.221 | 1.223 | 1.235 | 1.241 | 1.247 | 1.253 | 1.261 | 1.283 | 1.304 | 1.312 |
| Simulations | | | | | | | | | | |
| Government | | | | | | | | | | |
| Durables expenditures | 1.209 | 1.216 | 1.227 | 1.238 | 1.242 | 1.250 | 1.256 | 1.281 | 1.303 | 1.313 |
| Nondurables expenditures | 1.217 | 1.218 | 1.229 | 1.234 | 1.240 | 1.247 | 1.256 | 1.280 | 1.303 | 1.313 |
| Employment | 1.218 | 1.220 | 1.232 | 1.239 | 1.246 | 1.255 | 1.263 | 1.287 | 1.309 | 1.317 |
| Construction expenditures | 1.214 | 1.215 | 1.227 | 1.234 | 1.239 | 1.247 | 1.255 | 1.279 | 1.302 | 1.311 |
| Income tax cut | 1.217 | 1.220 | 1.231 | 1.237 | 1.243 | 1.249 | 1.258 | 1.281 | 1.303 | 1.311 |
| Income tax cut plus monetary policy | 1.218 | 1.220 | 1.231 | 1.236 | 1.242 | 1.248 | 1.257 | 1.279 | 1.301 | 1.310 |
| Reserve requirements reduction | 1.224 | 1.217 | 1.235 | 1.236 | 1.243 | 1.240 | 1.259 | 1.277 | 1.302 | 1.309 |
| Open market operations | 1.224 | 1.217 | 1.235 | 1.236 | 1.243 | 1.239 | 1.259 | 1.277 | 1.302 | 1.309 |
| Simulation less original solution | | | | | | | | | | |
| Government | | | | | | | | | | |
| Durables expenditures | −0.012 | −0.006 | −0.009 | −0.003 | −0.005 | −0.003 | −0.006 | −0.002 | −0.002 | −0.001 |
| Nondurables expenditures | −0.004 | −0.005 | −0.007 | −0.007 | −0.007 | −0.006 | −0.006 | −0.003 | −0.001 | 0.001 |
| Employment | −0.003 | −0.003 | −0.003 | −0.002 | −0.001 | 0.002 | 0.002 | 0.004 | 0.005 | 0.005 |
| Construction expenditures | −0.008 | −0.007 | −0.009 | −0.007 | −0.007 | −0.006 | −0.006 | −0.004 | −0.002 | −0.001 |
| Income tax cut | −0.004 | −0.003 | −0.004 | −0.004 | −0.004 | −0.004 | −0.003 | −0.002 | −0.002 | −0.001 |
| Income tax cut plus monetary policy | −0.004 | −0.003 | −0.005 | −0.004 | −0.005 | −0.005 | −0.005 | −0.004 | −0.003 | −0.002 |
| Reserve requirements reduction | 0.002 | −0.005 | −0.001 | −0.005 | −0.004 | −0.013 | −0.003 | −0.006 | −0.002 | −0.003 |
| Open market operations | 0.002 | −0.006 | −0.001 | −0.005 | −0.004 | −0.014 | −0.002 | −0.006 | −0.002 | −0.003 |

TABLE 2.3 (Continued)

| Solutions | Year and quarter | | | | | | | | | |
|---|---|---|---|---|---|---|---|---|---|---|
| | 1960:3 | 1960:4 | 1961:1 | 1961:2 | 1961:3 | 1961:4 | 1962:1 | 1962:2 | 1962:3 | 1962:4 |
| | L. Consumer price index | | | | | | | | | |
| Original solution | 1.111 | 1.123 | 1.128 | 1.135 | 1.141 | 1.146 | 1.143 | 1.160 | 1.172 | 1.180 |
| Simulations | | | | | | | | | | |
| Government | | | | | | | | | | |
| Durables expenditures | 1.105 | 1.116 | 1.120 | 1.126 | 1.134 | 1.140 | 1.138 | 1.156 | 1.169 | 1.178 |
| Nondurables expenditures | 1.104 | 1.114 | 1.118 | 1.123 | 1.130 | 1.136 | 1.134 | 1.153 | 1.167 | 1.176 |
| Employment | 1.108 | 1.119 | 1.124 | 1.131 | 1.138 | 1.146 | 1.143 | 1.161 | 1.174 | 1.182 |
| Construction expenditures | 1.105 | 1.115 | 1.119 | 1.125 | 1.132 | 1.139 | 1.137 | 1.155 | 1.169 | 1.177 |
| Income tax cut | 1.107 | 1.118 | 1.122 | 1.128 | 1.135 | 1.140 | 1.138 | 1.156 | 1.169 | 1.177 |
| Income tax cut plus monetary policy | 1.107 | 1.118 | 1.122 | 1.128 | 1.134 | 1.138 | 1.136 | 1.153 | 1.166 | 1.174 |
| Reserve requirements reduction | 1.113 | 1.119 | 1.125 | 1.129 | 1.134 | 1.132 | 1.133 | 1.149 | 1.163 | 1.172 |
| Open market operations | 1.113 | 1.119 | 1.125 | 1.129 | 1.134 | 1.131 | 1.133 | 1.149 | 1.163 | 1.172 |
| Simulation less original solution | | | | | | | | | | |
| Government | | | | | | | | | | |
| Durables expenditures | −0.006 | −0.007 | −0.008 | −0.008 | −0.008 | −0.005 | −0.006 | −0.004 | −0.002 | −0.001 |
| Nondurables expenditures | −0.007 | −0.009 | −0.011 | −0.012 | −0.012 | −0.009 | −0.009 | −0.007 | −0.005 | −0.004 |
| Employment | −0.003 | −0.004 | −0.004 | −0.004 | −0.003 | −0.000 | −0.000 | 0.001 | 0.002 | 0.002 |
| Construction expenditures | −0.006 | −0.008 | −0.009 | −0.010 | −0.009 | −0.007 | −0.007 | −0.005 | −0.003 | −0.002 |
| Income tax cut | −0.004 | −0.005 | −0.006 | −0.007 | −0.007 | −0.006 | −0.005 | −0.004 | −0.003 | −0.003 |
| Income tax cut plus monetary policy | −0.004 | −0.005 | −0.006 | −0.007 | −0.008 | −0.008 | −0.007 | −0.006 | −0.006 | −0.005 |
| Reserve requirements reduction | 0.002 | −0.004 | −0.003 | −0.006 | −0.007 | −0.014 | −0.010 | −0.010 | −0.008 | −0.008 |
| Open market operations | 0.002 | −0.004 | −0.003 | −0.006 | −0.007 | −0.014 | −0.010 | −0.010 | −0.008 | −0.007 |

| | | | | | | | | | | |
|---|---|---|---|---|---|---|---|---|---|---|
| Original solution | 1.357 | 1.348 | 1.390 | 1.177 | 0.695 | 0.257 | −0.035 | −0.036 | −0.763 | −0.957 |
| Simulations | | | | | | | | | | |
| Government | | | | | | | | | | |
| Durables expenditures | 1.232 | 1.097 | 1.035 | 0.825 | 0.333 | −0.114 | −0.489 | −0.888 | −1.338 | −1.539 |
| Nondurables expenditures | 1.270 | 1.138 | 1.100 | 0.861 | 0.371 | −0.062 | −0.387 | −0.764 | −1.208 | −1.430 |
| Employment | 1.244 | 1.136 | 1.102 | 0.848 | 0.339 | −0.093 | −0.402 | −0.755 | −1.185 | −1.396 |
| Construction expenditures | 1.249 | 1.112 | 1.061 | 0.830 | 0.322 | −0.143 | −0.498 | −0.877 | −1.308 | −1.511 |
| Income tax cut | 1.207 | 1.078 | 1.037 | 0.789 | 0.278 | −0.178 | −0.492 | −0.845 | −1.270 | −1.486 |
| Income tax cut plus monetary policy | 1.211 | 1.080 | 1.034 | 0.777 | 0.255 | −0.221 | −0.558 | −0.930 | −1.365 | −1.590 |
| Reserve requirements reduction | 1.415 | 1.311 | 1.310 | 1.030 | 0.516 | −0.105 | −0.462 | −0.801 | −1.155 | −1.366 |
| Open market operations | 1.419 | 1.308 | 1.304 | 1.023 | 0.510 | −0.120 | −0.472 | −0.805 | −1.152 | −1.360 |
| Simulation less original solution | | | | | | | | | | |
| Government | | | | | | | | | | |
| Durables expenditures | −0.125 | −0.251 | −0.355 | −0.352 | −0.362 | −0.372 | −0.454 | −0.525 | −0.574 | −0.582 |
| Nondurables expenditures | −0.087 | −0.210 | −0.290 | −0.316 | −0.325 | −0.319 | −0.352 | −0.401 | −0.444 | −0.472 |
| Employment | −0.113 | −0.212 | −0.288 | −0.329 | −0.356 | −0.350 | −0.367 | −0.392 | −0.422 | −0.439 |
| Construction expenditures | −0.109 | −0.236 | −0.329 | −0.347 | −0.374 | −0.400 | −0.463 | −0.514 | −0.545 | −0.554 |
| Income tax cut | −0.150 | −0.270 | −0.353 | −0.388 | −0.417 | −0.435 | −0.458 | −0.482 | −0.507 | −0.529 |
| Income tax cut plus monetary policy | −0.147 | −0.269 | −0.356 | −0.400 | −0.441 | −0.478 | −0.524 | −0.567 | −0.602 | −0.633 |
| Reserve requirements reduction | 0.058 | −0.037 | −0.080 | −0.147 | −0.179 | −0.362 | −0.427 | −0.438 | −0.392 | −0.409 |
| Open market operations | 0.061 | −0.041 | −0.086 | −0.154 | −0.186 | −0.377 | −0.438 | −0.442 | −0.388 | −0.402 |
| | | | | | N. Unemployment rate | | | | | |
| Original solution | 0.055 | 0.056 | 0.055 | 0.055 | 0.055 | 0.054 | 0.051 | 0.049 | 0.049 | 0.049 |
| Simulations | | | | | | | | | | |
| Government | | | | | | | | | | |
| Durables expenditures | 0.053 | 0.053 | 0.051 | 0.050 | 0.050 | 0.049 | 0.047 | 0.045 | 0.043 | 0.044 |

TABLE 2.3 (Continued)

| Solution | Year and quarter | | | | | | | | | |
|---|---|---|---|---|---|---|---|---|---|---|
| | 1960:3 | 1960:4 | 1961:1 | 1961:2 | 1961:3 | 1961:4 | 1962:1 | 1962:2 | 1962:3 | 1962:4 |
| Nondurables expenditures | 0.054 | 0.054 | 0.052 | 0.051 | 0.050 | 0.049 | 0.047 | 0.045 | 0.044 | 0.044 |
| Employment | 0.052 | 0.051 | 0.048 | 0.048 | 0.048 | 0.048 | 0.046 | 0.045 | 0.044 | 0.044 |
| Construction expenditures | 0.053 | 0.053 | 0.051 | 0.050 | 0.050 | 0.049 | 0.046 | 0.044 | 0.043 | 0.043 |
| Income tax cut | 0.054 | 0.055 | 0.053 | 0.053 | 0.052 | 0.051 | 0.049 | 0.047 | 0.046 | 0.046 |
| Income tax cut plus monetary policy | 0.054 | 0.055 | 0.053 | 0.053 | 0.052 | 0.051 | 0.048 | 0.046 | 0.045 | 0.045 |
| Reserve requirements reduction | 0.055 | 0.055 | 0.054 | 0.053 | 0.052 | 0.050 | 0.046 | 0.044 | 0.043 | 0.044 |
| Open market operations | 0.055 | 0.055 | 0.054 | 0.053 | 0.052 | 0.050 | 0.046 | 0.044 | 0.043 | 0.044 |
| Simulation less original solution (calculated with unrounded levels) | | | | | | | | | | |
| Government | | | | | | | | | | |
| Durables expenditures | −0.001 | −0.002 | −0.004 | −0.004 | −0.005 | −0.004 | −0.004 | −0.005 | −0.005 | −0.005 |
| Nondurables expenditures | −0.001 | −0.002 | −0.003 | −0.004 | −0.005 | −0.005 | −0.004 | −0.005 | −0.005 | −0.005 |
| Employment | −0.002 | −0.005 | −0.007 | −0.007 | −0.007 | −0.006 | −0.005 | −0.004 | −0.005 | −0.005 |
| Construction expenditures | −0.001 | −0.002 | −0.004 | −0.005 | −0.005 | −0.005 | −0.005 | −0.005 | −0.005 | −0.006 |
| Income tax cut | 0.000 | −0.001 | −0.002 | −0.002 | −0.002 | −0.002 | −0.002 | −0.002 | −0.002 | −0.003 |
| Income tax cut plus monetary policy | 0.000 | −0.001 | −0.002 | −0.002 | −0.003 | −0.003 | −0.003 | −0.003 | −0.004 | −0.004 |
| Reserve requirements reduction | 0.000 | 0.000 | −0.001 | −0.002 | −0.002 | −0.004 | −0.005 | −0.005 | −0.005 | −0.005 |
| Open market operations | 0.000 | 0.000 | −0.001 | −0.002 | −0.002 | −0.004 | −0.005 | −0.005 | −0.005 | −0.005 |
| O. All government tax receipts | | | | | | | | | | |
| Original solution | 140.8 | 143.3 | 144.6 | 149.9 | 155.4 | 162.8 | 166.7 | 171.0 | 174.0 | 175.7 |
| Simulations | | | | | | | | | | |
| Government | | | | | | | | | | |
| [illegible] | [illegible] | [illegible] | [illegible] | [illegible] | [illegible] | [illegible] | [illegible] | [illegible] | [illegible] | [illegible] |

| | | | | | | | | | | |
|---|---|---|---|---|---|---|---|---|---|---|
| Employment | 142.7 | 145.5 | 147.0 | 152.8 | 158.0 | 165.3 | 169.5 | 174.1 | 177.3 | 179.0 |
| Construction expenditures | 141.9 | 145.3 | 147.0 | 152.0 | 157.8 | 165.4 | 170.0 | 174.9 | 178.0 | 179.8 |
| Income tax cut | 137.8 | 140.5 | 141.8 | 146.9 | 152.4 | 159.8 | 163.7 | 168.2 | 171.3 | 173.0 |
| Income tax cut plus monetary policy | 137.8 | 140.5 | 141.8 | 147.0 | 152.6 | 160.1 | 164.2 | 168.8 | 171.9 | 173.7 |
| Reserve requirements reduction | 140.5 | 143.8 | 145.1 | 150.9 | 156.6 | 165.9 | 169.3 | 173.7 | 176.4 | 178.7 |
| Open market operations | 140.5 | 143.8 | 145.1 | 151.0 | 156.6 | 166.0 | 169.4 | 173.7 | 176.4 | 178.7 |
| Simulation less original solution | | | | | | | | | | |
| Government | | | | | | | | | | |
| Durables expenditures | 1.6 | 2.1 | 2.5 | 2.0 | 2.2 | 2.2 | 3.2 | 3.7 | 4.0 | 3.9 |
| Nondurables expenditures | 0.8 | 1.5 | 1.8 | 1.7 | 1.6 | 1.9 | 2.5 | 3.1 | 3.5 | 3.6 |
| Employment | 1.9 | 2.2 | 2.4 | 3.0 | 2.6 | 2.4 | 2.8 | 3.1 | 3.3 | 3.4 |
| Construction expenditures | 1.1 | 2.0 | 2.4 | 2.2 | 2.4 | 2.6 | 3.3 | 3.8 | 4.1 | 4.1 |
| Income tax cut | −3.0 | −2.8 | −2.8 | −3.0 | −3.0 | −3.0 | −3.0 | −2.8 | −2.7 | −2.6 |
| Income tax cut plus monetary policy | −3.0 | −2.8 | −2.7 | −2.9 | −2.8 | −2.7 | −2.5 | −2.2 | −2.1 | −1.9 |
| Reserve requirements reduction | −0.3 | 0.4 | 0.6 | 1.1 | 1.1 | 3.1 | 2.7 | 2.7 | 2.5 | 3.0 |
| Open market operations | −0.3 | 0.5 | 0.6 | 1.1 | 1.2 | 3.2 | 2.7 | 2.7 | 2.5 | 3.0 |
| | | | | | P. Government surplus | | | | | |
| Original solution | 3.8 | 4.2 | 1.9 | 3.8 | 7.1 | 8.3 | 9.2 | 11.2 | 13.0 | 11.7 |
| Simulations | | | | | | | | | | |
| Government | | | | | | | | | | |
| Durables expenditures | 2.0 | 2.9 | 1.2 | 2.7 | 6.2 | 8.3 | 9.4 | 11.9 | 13.9 | 12.4 |
| Nondurables expenditures | 1.1 | 2.4 | 0.6 | 2.5 | 5.8 | 8.2 | 8.9 | 11.5 | 13.5 | 12.2 |
| Employment | 2.1 | 3.0 | 1.0 | 3.6 | 6.4 | 8.2 | 8.6 | 10.8 | 12.7 | 11.5 |
| Construction expenditures | 1.7 | 3.0 | 1.3 | 3.1 | 6.6 | 8.8 | 9.7 | 12.1 | 14.1 | 12.7 |
| Income tax cut | 1.0 | 1.7 | −0.5 | 1.3 | 4.7 | 5.9 | 6.9 | 9.1 | 10.9 | 9.7 |
| Income tax cut plus monetary policy | 1.0 | 1.7 | −0.4 | 1.5 | 4.9 | 6.4 | 7.6 | 9.9 | 11.9 | 10.7 |

TABLE 2.3 (Continued)

| Solution | Year and quarter | | | | | | | | | |
|---|---|---|---|---|---|---|---|---|---|---|
| | 1960:3 | 1960:4 | 1961:1 | 1961:2 | 1961:3 | 1961:4 | 1962:1 | 1962:2 | 1962:3 | 1962:4 |
| Reserve requirements reduction | 3.4 | 4.9 | 2.7 | 5.5 | 8.9 | 12.8 | 13.0 | 15.2 | 16.7 | 15.9 |
| Open market operations | 3.4 | 5.0 | 2.8 | 5.5 | 9.0 | 13.0 | 13.0 | 15.2 | 16.6 | 15.9 |
| Simulation less original solution | | | | | | | | | | |
| Government | | | | | | | | | | |
| Durables expenditures | −1.8 | −1.2 | −0.6 | −1.1 | −0.8 | 0.0 | 0.2 | 0.6 | 0.9 | 0.8 |
| Nondurables expenditures | −2.7 | −1.8 | −1.3 | −1.3 | −1.3 | −0.1 | −0.3 | 0.2 | 0.5 | 0.6 |
| Employment | −1.7 | −1.2 | −0.8 | −0.2 | −0.7 | −0.1 | −0.6 | −0.4 | −0.2 | −0.2 |
| Construction | −2.1 | −1.1 | −0.5 | −0.7 | −0.5 | 0.5 | 0.4 | 0.9 | 1.1 | 1.1 |
| Income tax cut | −2.8 | −2.5 | −2.3 | −2.4 | −2.4 | −2.4 | −2.3 | −2.2 | −2.1 | −2.0 |
| Income tax cut plus monetary policy | −2.8 | −2.5 | −2.2 | −2.3 | −2.1 | −1.9 | −1.6 | −1.3 | −1.1 | −1.0 |
| Reserve requirements reduction | −0.3 | 0.8 | 0.9 | 1.7 | 1.9 | 4.5 | 3.8 | 3.9 | 3.7 | 4.3 |
| Open market operations | −0.3 | 0.8 | 0.9 | 1.7 | 1.9 | 4.7 | 3.8 | 3.9 | 3.6 | 4.2 |
| | Q. Demand deposits plus time deposits | | | | | | | | | |
| Original Solution | 181.6 | 184.9 | 188.1 | 191.0 | 194.1 | 196.7 | 200.4 | 203.9 | 207.2 | 211.2 |
| Simulations | | | | | | | | | | |
| Government | | | | | | | | | | |
| Durables expenditures | 181.6 | 185.1 | 188.3 | 191.2 | 194.3 | 196.9 | 200.6 | 204.1 | 207.5 | 211.5 |
| Nondurables expenditures | 181.6 | 185.0 | 188.2 | 191.1 | 194.1 | 196.7 | 200.3 | 203.9 | 207.2 | 211.2 |
| Employment | 181.7 | 185.2 | 188.5 | 191.5 | 194.6 | 197.3 | 201.0 | 204.6 | 208.0 | 212.0 |
| Construction expenditures | 181.7 | 185.1 | 188.3 | 191.2 | 194.3 | 196.9 | 200.6 | 204.2 | 207.5 | 211.5 |
| Income tax cut | 181.7 | 185.3 | 188.6 | 191.7 | 194.8 | 197.6 | 201.3 | 204.9 | 208.3 | 212.3 |
| Income tax cut plus monetary | | | | | | | | | | |

| | | | | | | | | | | |
|---|---|---|---|---|---|---|---|---|---|---|
| Reserve requirements reduction | 184.6 | 188.4 | 192.1 | 195.5 | 199.0 | 201.7 | 205.6 | 209.3 | 212.7 | 216.7 |
| Open market operations | 184.8 | 188.6 | 192.2 | 195.6 | 199.0 | 201.6 | 205.5 | 209.2 | 212.5 | 216.5 |
| Simulation less original solution | | | | | | | | | | |
| Government | | | | | | | | | | |
| Durables expenditures | 0.1 | 0.1 | 0.2 | 0.2 | 0.2 | 0.2 | 0.2 | 0.2 | 0.2 | 0.3 |
| Nondurables expenditures | 0.0 | 0.1 | 0.1 | 0.1 | 0.1 | 0.0 | 0.0 | −0.1 | −0.1 | 0.0 |
| Employment | 0.1 | 0.3 | 0.4 | 0.5 | 0.6 | 0.6 | 0.6 | 0.7 | 0.7 | 0.8 |
| Construction expenditures | 0.1 | 0.2 | 0.2 | 0.2 | 0.2 | 0.2 | 0.2 | 0.2 | 0.2 | 0.3 |
| Income tax cut | 0.1 | 0.3 | 0.5 | 0.7 | 0.8 | 0.9 | 0.9 | 1.0 | 1.1 | 1.1 |
| Income tax cut plus monetary policy | 0.3 | 0.7 | 1.1 | 1.5 | 1.8 | 2.0 | 2.2 | 2.5 | 2.6 | 2.8 |
| Reserve requirements reduction | 3.0 | 3.5 | 4.0 | 4.5 | 4.9 | 5.0 | 5.2 | 5.4 | 5.5 | 5.5 |
| Open market operations | 3.2 | 3.6 | 4.1 | 4.6 | 5.0 | 4.9 | 5.1 | 5.2 | 5.3 | 5.3 |

R. Government bond short-term interest rate

| | | | | | | | | | | |
|---|---|---|---|---|---|---|---|---|---|---|
| Original solution | 2.422 | 2.028 | 2.247 | 2.332 | 2.417 | 2.421 | 2.262 | 2.514 | 2.717 | 2.251 |
| Simulations | | | | | | | | | | |
| Government | | | | | | | | | | |
| Durables expenditures | 2.461 | 2.065 | 2.282 | 2.350 | 2.431 | 2.412 | 2.255 | 2.502 | 2.707 | 2.234 |
| Nondurables expenditures | 2.445 | 2.045 | 2.258 | 2.334 | 2.413 | 2.380 | 2.209 | 2.453 | 2.655 | 2.185 |
| Employment | 2.477 | 2.115 | 2.336 | 2.418 | 2.499 | 2.492 | 2.335 | 2.478 | 2.777 | 2.307 |
| Construction expenditures | 2.472 | 2.071 | 2.284 | 2.355 | 2.436 | 2.423 | 2.258 | 2.501 | 2.703 | 2.230 |
| Income tax cut | 2.497 | 2.150 | 2.379 | 2.465 | 2.552 | 2.556 | 2.397 | 2.648 | 2.852 | 2.389 |
| Income tax cut plus monetary policy | 2.422 | 2.208 | 2.247 | 2.332 | 2.417 | 2.421 | 2.262 | 2.514 | 2.717 | 2.251 |
| Reserve requirements reduction | 1.028 | 1.451 | 1.753 | 1.912 | 2.012 | 1.892 | 1.850 | 2.100 | 2.297 | 1.845 |
| Open market operations | 0.941 | 1.451 | 1.768 | 1.917 | 2.032 | 1.919 | 1.871 | 2.118 | 2.321 | 1.869 |

TABLE 2.3 (Continued)

| Solution | Year and quarter | | | | | | | | | |
|---|---|---|---|---|---|---|---|---|---|---|
| | 1960:3 | 1960:4 | 1961:1 | 1961:2 | 1961:3 | 1961:4 | 1962:1 | 1962:2 | 1962:3 | 1962:4 |
| Simulation less original solution | | | | | | | | | | |
| Government | | | | | | | | | | |
| Durables expenditures | 0.039 | 0.037 | 0.035 | 0.018 | 0.014 | −0.008 | −0.006 | −0.011 | −0.010 | −0.017 |
| Nondurables expenditures | 0.023 | 0.017 | 0.012 | 0.002 | −0.004 | −0.041 | −0.053 | −0.061 | −0.062 | −0.066 |
| Employment | 0.055 | 0.087 | 0.089 | 0.086 | 0.082 | 0.071 | 0.073 | −0.036 | 0.060 | 0.056 |
| Construction expenditures | 0.050 | 0.043 | 0.037 | 0.024 | 0.019 | 0.002 | −0.004 | −0.012 | −0.014 | −0.021 |
| Income tax cut | 0.075 | 0.122 | 0.132 | 0.133 | 0.135 | 0.135 | 0.136 | 0.134 | 0.135 | 0.138 |
| Income tax cut plus monetary policy | 0 | 0 | 0 | 0 | 0 | 0 | 0 | 0 | 0 | 0 |
| Reserve requirements reduction | −1.394 | −0.577 | −0.493 | −0.420 | −0.405 | −0.528 | −0.412 | −0.414 | −0.419 | −0.406 |
| Open market operations | −1.481 | −0.576 | −0.479 | −0.415 | −0.385 | −0.502 | −0.391 | −0.396 | −0.395 | −0.382 |

*Note*: Simulation less original solution detail may not reconcile precisely with simulation solutions due to rounding.

result in the least decline in the U.S. net trade position, although not by an appreciable amount. The situation is much the same for current dollars, although here these policies have less advantage over their rivals. However, because the monetary policies cause a decline in interest rates, their balance of payments effects are understated if only net export accounts are considered. If short-term capital flows were included, these policies would clearly reveal a severe drain on U.S. reserves.

Because the final levels of real output of all the policies (except the income tax cuts and the employment increase) lie within a $1 billion range, their 1962:4 unemployment rates are practically identical. All of the policies reduce unemployment by about 10 per cent, lowering the rate from the 4.9 per cent in the original solution to about 4.4 per cent. The income tax reductions produce less of an increase in output and consequently experience more unemployment than the other policies. Although the government employment policy causes a smaller rise in real output, it produces about the same decrease in unemployment as the other expenditure policies. This is due in large measure to the nature of the policy and only partially to its stimulus.

Finally, in the area of government tax receipts and surplus on income and product account, the largest revenues are produced by the expenditure policies, but the largest surpluses are generated by the monetary policies. (Receipts include all income and other taxes and contributions for social insurance, while the surplus is this quantity less expenditures, interest and transfer payments, and subsidies less current surplus of government enterprises.) As might be expected, income tax cuts fare poorly on both grounds, and still have deficits of $2.0 and $1.0 billion (at annual rates) after ten quarters.

Table 2.4 gives a summary of the impact of the different simulation policies. For each of the selected variables shown, the policies are ranked in ascending order of largest increase after ten quarters. For example, a rise in government durables expenditures produces the highest consumption of automobiles in 1962:4.

Strictly speaking, the monetary policies should not be contrasted directly with the fiscal policies because the exogenous changes themselves are not comparable [5]). However, the monetary policies do have an appreciable effect on the economy, especially in the area of business investment and

---

[5]) A method of translating exogenous monetary policy shifts into equivalent fiscal outlays is presented in chapter 5.

TABLE 2.4

*Ranking of simulation effects after ten quarters (ranked in order of largest increase unless otherwise indicated)* [a].

| | $GNP^{54}$ | $C^{54}$ | $C^{54}_{DA}$ | $Y^{54}_{D}$ | $I^{54}-\Delta INV^{54}$ | $I^{54}_{BUS}$ | Smallest $P_{GNP}$ | Smallest $RU$ | $EX^{54}-M^{54}$ | $T$ | $T-G-V_G-SUB-INT_G$ | $DD+DT$ |
|---|---|---|---|---|---|---|---|---|---|---|---|---|
| $\Delta G_{CD}$ | 4 | 7 | 1 | 7 | 4 | 5 | 7 | 2 | 2 | 2 | 4 | 6 |
| $\Delta G_{CN}$ | 1 | 5 | 1 | 5 | 3 | 3 | 4 | 2 | 5 | 3 | 5 | 8 |
| $\Delta E_G$ | 8 | 8 | 5 | 8 | 8 | 8 | 8 | 2 | 6 | 4 | 6 | 5 |
| $\Delta G_{IC}$ | 1 | 5 | 1 | 3 | 4 | 4 | 6 | 1 | 3 | 1 | 3 | 6 |
| $\Delta Y_D$ | 7 | 4 | 8 | 2 | 7 | 7 | 4 | 8 | 4 | 8 | 8 | 4 |
| $\Delta Y_D+MP$ [b]) | 6 | 1 | 1 | 1 | 6 | 6 | 3 | 7 | 1 | 7 | 7 | 3 |
| $\Delta RRR_{DD}$ | 3 | 2 | 5 | 3 | 1 | 1 | 1 | 2 | 7 | 5 | 1 | 1 |
| $\Delta RES_{NB}$ | 5 | 2 | 5 | 5 | 2 | 1 | 2 | 2 | 8 | 5 | 1 | 2 |

a) For a list of symbols, see appendix A.

b) Here, *MP* denotes monetary policy.

TABLE 2.5

*Dynamic multipliers*

Increases in real gross national product per constant dollar of expenditure increase or tax reduction [a]).

| | Multipliers | | | | | | | | | |
|---|---|---|---|---|---|---|---|---|---|---|
| | 1960:3 | 1960:4 | 1961:1 | 1961:2 | 1961:3 | 1961:4 | 1962:1 | 1962:2 | 1962:3 | 1962:4 |
| $\Delta G^{54}_{CD}$ | 1.6 | 2.0 | 2.4 | 2.1 | 2.2 | 2.1 | 2.7 | 2.8 | 2.8 | 2.7 |
| $\Delta G^{54}_{CN}$ | 1.4 | 2.0 | 2.3 | 2.4 | 2.5 | 2.4 | 2.8 | 2.9 | 2.9 | 2.9 |
| $\Delta E_G$ | 1.7 | 1.9 | 2.1 | 2.1 | 2.1 | 1.7 | 1.9 | 1.9 | 2.0 | 2.0 |
| $\Delta G^{54}_{IC}$ | 1.6 | 2.2 | 2.5 | 2.4 | 2.6 | 2.5 | 2.9 | 3.0 | 3.0 | 2.9 |
| $\Delta Y^{54}_{D}$ | 0.8 | 1.0 | 1.2 | 1.1 | 1.2 | 1.2 | 1.2 | 1.2 | 1.2 | 1.2 |
| $\Delta Y^{54}_{D}+MP$ | 0.8 | 1.0 | 1.2 | 1.3 | 1.4 | 1.5 | 1.7 | 1.8 | 1.8 | 1.8 |

a) For a list of symbols, see appendix A.

residential construction. The lag before an impact is felt does not last very long; an increase in output occurs in the first quarter after the policy change (see table 2.3). It is possible, of course, that the interest elasticity of expenditures is overstated in the model's investment functions. On the other hand, no account is taken of credit effects in the consumer durables equations. Recent research for the model by Michael Evans and Avram Kisselgoff shows that the response of consumer durables demand to relaxation of credit terms is strong [6]). Finally, in interpreting the impact of the monetary policies it should be recognized that the exogenous shifts introduced are large (—0.01 in demand deposit reserve requirements and +\$1.0 billion in unborrowed reserves). One member of the staff of the Federal Reserve Board has estimated that the greatest net decrease in reserve requirements that took place in the postwar period (net, after offsetting open market operations) was 0.005. Thus, one insight gained from the simulations is that monetary policy shifts must be substantial if the course of the economy is to be changed, at least in a recessionary situation.

### *2.5.3. Dynamic multipliers*

One method of analyzing the effect of the fiscal policies is to examine a set of dynamic multipliers [7]). Table 2.5 shows, by quarter, the increase in real gross national product over the original solution divided by the constant increase in real expenditures. For the tax cuts, the amount of the reduction is taken as the difference in tax rates multiplied by the personal income tax base before the change, divided by the implicit price deflator for personal consumption expenditures. The reduction varies from quarter to quarter, rising from \$3.2 billion in 1906:3 to \$3.8 billion in 1962:4, both in 1954 dollars.

The results show that, per dollar of expenditure increase or tax reduction, additional government employment is most effective and personal income tax cuts least effective in stimulating real *GNP* in the first quarter. By the second quarter, all the expenditure policies have nearly equivalent effects

---

[6]) Michael K. Evans and Avram Kisselgoff, "Demand for Consumer Instalment Credit and its Effects on Consumption," in *The Brookings Model: Some Further Results* (Rand McNally-North Holland, 1968).

[7]) Dynamic multipliers are period-by-period response rates of endogenous variables to exogenous shifts in levels, flows, or parameters. That is, they measure the response along the transient path to final equilibrium positions. This is in contrast to static multipliers which give the equilibrium responses of the endogenous variables to exogenous changes.

while the tax cut policies are even further behind. At the end of ten quarters, most of the lag influences have had their major impact and the multipliers should be nearly at their "equilibrium" values. However, this is not strictly true of the income tax policies. Here, the reductions increase over time and, because of lagged adjustments in the system, the indicated multipliers are probably biased downwards. That is, the true tax cut multipliers are probably somewhat larger than those computed by dividing current period increases in real *GNP* by current period reductions in tax liabilities.

Moreover, because of various factors (including the impact of initial conditions), not too much emphasis should be given to the exact time path of increase of the various multipliers. A complex, dynamic, difference equation system is likely to have roots that produce fluctuating responses to any stepped changes in its forcing functions (exogenous inputs). Such a model is also likely to be influenced by specification choices and the techniques used to estimate parameters. Consequently, the dynamic multipliers fluctuate.

Notwithstanding these fluctuations, examination of the increases in real gross product per constant dollar of expenditure increase over the period indicates that the government durables, nondurables, and construction multipliers are approximately 2.8 to 3.0, while the employment expenditure multiplier is significantly lower, at about 2.0. This difference may be explained by the greater impact of the former expenditures on business investment. While the employment policy has a greater direct effect on the rate of unemployment, which is beneficial to consumption, this is not sufficient to override this investment advantage. The nonemployment policies would fare even better were it not for the greater leakages of their expenditures into corporate profits (and, therefore retained earnings and taxes).

Income tax multipliers would theoretically be expected to be less than expenditure multipliers. For simple, linear, income determination models, equal absolute amounts of ex post tax and expenditure increase, that is, a balanced government budget increment of zero, produce a multiplier of 1.0 [7]). For the same models, with an increase in tax *rates* yielding a balanced budget with the original ex ante tax base, the multiplier would be greater than 1.0 because of the growth in the tax base under the stimulus of higher government expenditures. Nevertheless, this type of growth is insufficient to explain the foregoing discrepancies between the "pure" (without an

[7]) The classic example may be found in Paul A. Samuelson, "The Simple Mathematics of Income Determination", in *Money, Trade, and Economic Growth; Essays in Honor of John Henry Williams* (Macmillan, 1951).

accommodating monetary policy) income tax multiplier of 1.2 and those on expenditures of about 3.0.

Examination of the detailed simulation results indicates that many of these discrepancies were due to the complex, nonlinear nature of the model and, in particular, to the behavior of long-term interest rates. For the "pure" income tax rise, equilibrium interest rates rose (thereby depressing investment), while for expenditures they were largely unchanged. This can be explained by the fact that direct impact of the tax reduction was larger than that of the expenditure increases on personal disposable income. The higher such income, the greater the desire of consumers to hold demand deposits and, with fixed bank reserves, the greater the pressure on interest rates. (Higher business income also tends to create such pressures; but higher business income, and cash flow, enables greater investment in plant and equipment, an offsetting influence to deposit demands.) In other words, for an income tax reduction to be fully effective, an accommodating monetary policy which allows for an expansion in bank reserves and the money supply must also be undertaken. Such a monetary policy might be defined as one which maintains interest rates as they would have been without the income tax reduction. This, in fact, is the simulation of an income tax cut with monetary policy that is reported in the foregoing tables. With it, the ten-quarter multiplier is 1.8, which gives about the expected difference between tax rate and expenditure policies.

Judging the various fiscal policies on their relative efficiency in producing real *GNP* increases, it appears, although the matter is not clear cut, that the nonemployment government expenditure policies might be preferred. However, certain cautions should be observed. In a non-linear system the magnitude of the effects do not vary in fixed proportions with policy changes. Thus, for larger increases in expenditures or tax reductions than were introduced in the foregoing simulations, the multipliers will be greater and the relative differences in impact may change. Also, it is likely that initial conditions play a key role in the size of the multipliers. For example, with more initial excess capacity, investment expenditures are not as strongly stimulated and multipliers are lower. In addition, due to stock effects, ratchets, and other asymmetrical responses, the multipliers are probably not reversible. That is, in curbing inflation and excess demand, the relative effectiveness of alternative policies is likely to differ from their effectiveness in preventing or curing a recession.

Further comments on these matters and additional comparisons of the different policies, including excise tax reductions, appear in chapter 5.

# 3

## ANALYSIS OF EXCISE TAX CHANGES

### *3.1. Excise taxes as a policy instrument*

Expenditures, income taxes, and monetary policy variables and parameters are powerful instruments used by governments to influence cyclical stability and growth. But they are not the only tools available for this purpose. Certainly excise tax changes deserve consideration as an alternative or complementary device whenever major shifts in government economic policy are contemplated. This is especially true because excise taxes directly impinge on relative and absolute levels of prices, an important consideration whenever balance of payments and price stability are primary social goals.

Additionally, evaluation of the impact of excise tax changes is of interest because a major shift in such taxes was recently enacted. On June 21, 1965, President Johnson signed into law a bill which markedly altered the excise tax structure of the United States. A large number of excises were eliminated as of June 22, 1965 (the tax on air conditioners was eliminated retroactively to May 15, 1965, while the tax on automobiles was modified retroactively to May 15). A few other excises were to be reduced in phases from June 22 until January 1, 1969 [1]). By the latter date, the law will require a 1 per cent tax on automobiles and more substantial taxes on the sumptuary items, liquor, beer, tobacco, and "use" taxes on gasoline, trucks, tires, air travel, and fishing rods. Items which will no longer be taxed include refrigerators, freezers, records, air conditioners, gas and electric appliances, musical instruments, business machines, safe deposit boxes, telephone calls, jewelry, and matches. The tax cut on an item-by-item basis is significant as the *ad valorem* rates were mainly 5 or 10 per cent (although not necessarily on the retail price). By 1969, the tax cut is predicted to be approximately \$4.5 billion per year, while for 1965 it is about \$1.75 billion, at annual rates.

The change in the law was enacted for two main reasons. First, the excise tax system, as constructed, was somewhat illogical (for example, washing

---

[1]) Scheduled reductions of some of these excises were postponed in 1966 for fiscal policy reasons.

machines were not taxed although every other major gas and electric appliance was), and it resulted in misallocation of resources. Second, the measure was advocated to insure the continuation of the then current economic boom.

The use of excise tax cuts as a fiscal policy device to maintain an economic boom raises many questions. It is necessary to know how expansionary excise cuts are, that is, what is their comparative static multiplier. Also, does the economy follow a monotonic time path in reaching the new comparative static or equilibrium solution, and how long does it take to reach equilibrium solutions? In addition, ignoring the beneficial side effects on resource allocation, is this particular fiscal policy the best one in terms of having the largest long-run multipliers or the quickest speed of response? If the entire tax cut is not reflected in price reductions, what are the consequences? Since the remaining excises probably cannot or will not be used for fiscal policy purposes, it is questionable if the results have anything more than historical meaning [2]). However, they do have current significance, because recently proposed employment taxes (employer tax payments based on wages and salaries) are similar in nature to *ad valorem* excises.

This study answers a number of the foregoing questions. This chapter describes some general elements in the analysis of excise tax changes. It also contains the particular approximations and shifts in coefficients required to simulate the 1965 excise reductions with the Brookings econometric model. Because of data limitations, the simulations could only be run as if equivalent changes had taken place in 1960–62. Chapter 4 contains the simulation results.

## *3.2. Excise changes and disposable income*

The Brookings model consists of three interdependent sectors: (1) a real sector including such factors as consumption, employment, and investment functions; (2) a price sector consisting of some behavioral wage and price equations, plus conversion or transformation routines; and (3) a revenue sector which uses data generated by the other two sectors in combination with some legal and institutional characteristics.

---

[2]) While the postponement of reductions in early 1966 left room for additional excise cuts in later years which could be used as fiscal stimulants, it is doubtful (for political reasons) that when these taxes are totally eliminated that they can be reimposed as peacetime inflationary deterrents.

Obviously, the revenue sector of the model will be altered by the tax cut. Before considering this sector, it is necessary to discuss the manner in which the excise cut enters the other two sectors.

One possibility is to say that an excise cut of $1.75 billion is equivalent to adding the same amount to current dollar disposable income. Thus, the monetary value of the excise cut could be added to disposable income and deflated by prices before the excise reduction, and the model could be solved or simulated for as long a period as desired. The problems with this approach are: (1) the amount of equivalent purchasing power varies over time if the economy is in disequilibrium, growing, or if the mix between taxed and nontaxed goods alters cyclically (excluding any tax change induced substitution); (2) no direct Pigou effect resulting from the cuts is taken into account; and (3) to obtain all other tax revenues, the real quantities must be converted into current dollar amounts, requiring an adjustment for the effect of the elimination or lowering of excises on prices.

Therefore, a more valid solution can be obtained by introducing the excise cuts through the price mechanism, and then letting them affect real disposable income, assets, etc., by means of deflators. Since the excises enter the system in a different manner than a personal income tax cut which would be added directly to current dollar disposable income, the results of initial equivalent excise and personal income tax cuts could be quite dissimilar. (The two taxes are compared in chapter 5.)

## *3.3. Translation of excise reductions into price changes*

In considering the translation of excise tax rate changes into price changes, economic theory is almost too helpful to the econometrician. Different assumptions about firms' behavioral patterns and shapes of supply and demand curves yield widely different conclusions about tax incidence and resulting prices [3]). While the Brookings model uses a form of markup determination for its price equations, these equations are only assumptions about or approximations to reality [4]). Moreover, a markup scheme can be consistent with a number of different price effects.

---

[3]) R. Musgrave, *Theory of Public Finance* (McGraw-Hill, 1959), p. 259–299, and P. Taubman, "The Effects of Ad Valorem and Specific Taxes on Prices," *Quarterly Journal of Economics*, November 1965.

[4]) C. L. Schultze and J. L. Tryon, "Prices and Wages", in *The Brookings Quarterly Econometric Model of the United States*, op. cit., pp. 280–333.

### *3.3.1. Markup mechanisms*

If it is assumed that firms use a markup pricing mechanism and, if a *specific* tax (that is, the tax is a fixed amount per unit independent of the price) is considered part of cost, it is easy to demonstrate that for a specific tax $P = (1+k)\,(C+T)$ where $P$ is price, $k$ is the markup factor, $C$ the cost base other than tax per unit, and $T$ is the specific tax amount per unit which is considered part of the cost base. The ultimate effect on prices of final goods depends on the stage of production at which the tax is imposed since the tax can be marked up at each stage [5]).

However, this is not the only possible result for a markup system since if $T$ is not considered part of the cost base, $P$ could equal $[(1+k)C+T]$. This form also implies some tax pyramiding (that is, the ultimate change in price depends on where the tax is imposed) if $T$ is imposed on any level other than retail trade. It is also possible for $T$ to be kept separate at all levels of production and for no pyramiding to take place.

*Ad valorem* taxes in which the amount is a percentage of the price must be treated somewhat differently. For instance, it can be shown that pyramiding depends in part on the input-output relations at each stage of production. In determining $P$ at any stage of production, $P$ could equal $(1+k)\ C(1+r)$ where $r$ is the *ad valorem* rate imposed at one stage of production only. Another possibility is $P = (1+k+r)\,C$. Under the first alternative, if $C$ is the only element in the cost base, then $P$ at each stage is arrived at by multiplying each previous price by one, plus the relevant markup. Here no pyramiding occurs since $(1+k_1)\ (1+k_2)\ (1+r)\ C$ is the same regardless of order of arrangement [6]).

### *3.3.2. Changes in the price structure*

Even if a markup formulation is accepted, there are still a number of possible ways to change the price structure. In this instance, the most plausible method is that for *ad valorem* rates: the price before tax, $P_B$, is multiplied by $(1+r)$ to set the price after tax, $P$. (Only two minor specific taxes were changed, and they will be ignored.) Appendix C contains some data which were analyzed for conformity with this hypothesis. Unfortunately, the analysis really tests a joint hypothesis which consists of the one given and one that states that all tax changes are fully passed along. Rejection of the

---

[5]) See Taubman, *op. cit.*, p. 651.

[6]) See Taubman, *ibid.*, p. 653.

joint hypothesis would not imply which part is wrong. The foregoing assumption of the manner in which excises are reflected in prices coincides with the Council of Economic Advisers view which defines a 100 per cent pass-along as occurring when $P_1/P_2 = (1+r_1)/(1+r_2)$, where $P_1$ is the price after the tax cut and $P_2$ the price before the tax cut. This definition of 100 per cent pass-along suggests how excise cuts might be allowed to alter the structure of the price sector.

As mentioned, the Brookings model uses markup equations to determine prices in a behavioral or structural sense. The dependent variable in these functions is value-added prices for six industry groups: durable manufacturing, nondurable manufacturing, construction, regulated industries, wholesale and retail trade, and other (agriculture, which is exogenous, is not considered). Suppose that for *ad valorem* taxes the equation is written as:

$$PV_{i_t} = (1+r_1)(a_i + b_i W_{i_t} + c_i Y_{i_t}) + u_{i_t} \qquad (3.1)$$

$PV_{i_t}$ = value added price of the *i*th good; $r_1$ = the rax rate; $W_1$ = the long-run per unit labor cost of the *i* good; $Y_1$ are other price determinants of this good; $u_1$ is an error term which satisfies the least square requirements; $a$, $b$, and $c$ are constants, $t$ refers to time [7]).

If equation 3.1 were fitted during a period in which $r_1$ is constant, and as a result ignored, then the expected value of each coefficient would be multiplied by $(1+r_i)$. In fact, the equations were fitted from the end of 1953 through 1960. Most *ad valorem* rates that had a change in that period experienced it in the second quarter of 1954; thus, the present coefficients are not exactly $(1+r_i)\,b$, etc., but are treated as such.

It has been suggested that equation 3.1 cannot be a completely valid description unless the tax cut is fully passed along in price decreases. If firms retain part of the tax for instance, $m$ per cent, how should equation 3.1 be altered at the date of the cut? Suppose that when excise rates $r_i$ fall to $\bar{r}_i$, prices fall to:

$$\frac{\bar{P}_i}{P_i} = 1 - m\left[\frac{(r_i - \bar{r}_i)}{1+r_i}\right] \qquad (3.2)$$

[7]) Because output determination in the Brookings model is cast in value added terms (or, synonymously, output originating) the *ad valorem* tax imposed here is on value added. The usual situation in the United States is for such excises to be imposed on sales (the case is the opposite in many other countries). Assuming that sales bear a relatively constant relationship to value added, the analysis is unaffected except that higher implicit *ad valorem* tax rates on value added must be used rather than the explicit legislated rates that apply to sales.

rather than

$$\frac{\bar{P}_i}{P_i} = 1 - \left[\frac{(r_i - \bar{r}_i)}{1 + r_i}\right]. \tag{3.3}$$

One adjustment possibility is to multiply each coefficient in equation 3.1 by

$$\frac{1 + \bar{r}_i + (1-m)(r_i - \bar{r}_i)}{(1 + r_i)}. \tag{3.4}$$

This method adjusts all coefficients proportionately and results in an increased profit share, that is, the method is equivalent to an increase in the markup factor $b_i$.

Another adjustment method is to multiply through by $(1+\bar{r}_i)/(1+r_i)$ and then adjust $a$ so that $PV_{it}$ will be at its new level. This method leaves the markup factor, $b_i$, constant.

The first alternative is preferred since it seems likely that once firms have been able to increase their profit share, they will fight to keep this "historically" determined norm and avoid a profit squeeze.

### 3.3.3. *Implicit excise tax rate estimates*

The commodities or products within each of the six groupings for which structural equations were computed were not all taxed at the same rate. Therefore, it was necessary to construct implicit tax rates of the form:

$$R_{j_t} = \frac{\sum_k TX_{kj_t}}{\sum_k X_{kj_t}}. \tag{3.5}$$

$R_{j_t}$ is the implicit rate for the $j$th sector ($j = 1, \ldots 6$) which is obtained by dividing the sum of tax collections, $TX$, from the $k$ subsectors (including those not taxed) by the sum of current dollar gross output originating, $X_{kj}$, in the same subsectors. Because it was desirable to make the rate change calculations over time independent of shifts in the mix of consumption of the taxed commodities, the actual procedure used was slightly more complicated. Implicit rates were calculated for each of the $k$ subsectors and these were then combined with fixed, fiscal 1960 relative output originating weights. Changes in the subsector rates were made proportionate to those legislated in the June 1965 tax law. Current dollars are used because the rates apply on this basis.

In table 3.1 column (2) shows that the two producing sectors bearing the "heaviest" tax load prior to the 1965 reduction were durables and regulated [8]). Also, the biggest potential price reductions of 1.7 and 1.5 per cent were in the same two sectors. During 1965, however, only durable manufacturing shows significant potential price reductions (see column 6) because telephone rates were not scheduled to be reduced until 1966. The word "potential" means the result that would follow if producers cut prices by the ratio of the index numbers. If, however, prices are cut on the average by 80 per cent and equation 3.4 is used, the durables figures change in columns 6 and 7 from 1.012 to 1.010 and 1.017 to 1.014, while for the regulated sector, the 1.003 changes to 1.001 and the 1.015 becomes 1.013. The durable manufacturing reduction is small, less than 2 per cent, because the sector includes producers' and consumers' durables and the former are not taxed (except for business machines such as computers).

TABLE 3.1

*Markup factors for ad valorem tax rates and value-added prices: 1965–67* [a])

| (1) Sector | (2) 1-1-65 | (3) 7-1-65 | (4) 1-1-66 | (5) 1-1-67 | (6) (2)/(3) | (7) (2)/(5) |
|---|---|---|---|---|---|---|
| Durable manufacturing | 1.027 | 1.015 | 1.013 | 1.010 | 1.012 | 1.017 |
| Nondurable manufacturing | 1.000 | 1.000 | 1.000 | 1.000 | 1.000 | 1.000 |
| Trade | 1.004 | 1.000 | 1.000 | 1.000 | 1.004 | 1.004 |
| Regulated | 1.022 | 1.019 | 1.007 | 1.006 | 1.003 | 1.015 |
| Construction | 1.000 | 1.000 | 1.000 | 1.000 | 1.000 | 1.000 |
| Residual industries | 1.000 | 1.000 | 1.000 | 1.000 | 1.000 | 1.000 |

[a]) *Source*: *Markup factor* = $(1+R_{j_t})$. Based on 1960 relative importance weights, gross output data for sectors, Brookings Institution. Fiscal 1960 tax revenues, *Annual Report*, Commissioner of Internal Revenue, Tables 2 and 3. Items assigned to sectors on basis of Standard Industrial Classification Index.

Given the tax markup factors, new levels of prices for the producing sectors can be computed. If factors which assume less than full shifting are used, it is also possible to calculate the increased profit share of business.

[8]) Regulated sector includes the telephone and transportation industries.

## *3.4. Nonlinear considerations*

With the exception of certain special problems, which are discussed in appendix D, this largely concludes the consideration of the price effects of excise reductions. However, further adjustments were necessary since it was impossible to obtain sufficient data to simulate and evaluate the 1966 version of the Brookings model for 1965 and later years. Therefore, the results calculated and given in chapter 4 indicate what would have happened in 1960–62 if the tax changes effective July 1965 had gone into effect beginning in July 1960. To arrive at these results, the Brookings model was solved assuming no excise tax changes and then resolved with the tax reductions included. For any variable at any point in time, the difference between the two solutions can be calculated. This difference is attributable to the tax change.

At first it would seem that since both the solution obtained assuming no excise tax changes and that obtained with the tax reductions included contain the same exogenous and endogenous variables and conditions (with the exception of excises), there is no cause to worry about different values of exogenous variables when generalizing the results (in percentage but not absolute terms). However, this conclusion is only valid for completely linear models. For instance, in a macro model of the usual LS–IM type, the change in output, prices, and employment that occurs with any change in government fiscal policy depends upon the initial starting point, for example, in the liquidity trap, or on the inflationary escalator. In other words, an important consideration in making generalizations based on a nonlinear model may be how far the system is from capacity or full employment output at every point during the simulation period as contrasted to other periods to which the results are being applied.

A related problem occurs if any structural shifts have taken place between the simulation and the generalization periods. In the present case, the major known changes are personal and corporate income tax cuts in 1964, and the Vietnam situation. A lower income tax schedule implies lower leakages on each expenditure round (provided government spending is not affected) and a larger multiplier than the model would predict. In terms of government revenues, the model may tend to overstate the recapture of income via the corporate and personal income tax. (For a proportional income tax, it is easy to show that the higher the tax rate, the more government income tax revenues increase for any exogenous change.)

A final difficulty is the determination of the size of the excise cut in periods after the rate reduction. The initial amount of taxes relinquished can be calculated, as well as the multipliers based on this amount. But lowering excise tax rates reduces government revenues from what they would otherwise be as the economy grows in response to population increases, technological advances, export demands, and other exogenous variables. That is, exogenous growth in tax bases implies additional amounts of taxes given up in the future. If the alternative to an excise rate reduction is a government expenditure increase, the expenditures must increase over time [9]). For comparative fiscal policy purposes, increases in revenues foregone should be included in the multiplier, which would then be defined somewhat differently from the traditional concept. Nevertheless, the latter concept can be measured far more readily and therefore will be used in most comparisons.

With the foregoing as background, it is now possible to discuss the results.

---

[9]) Such an expenditure policy may be hard to implement because the information to calculate the increases in tax bases is difficult to predict.

# 4

## EXCISE TAX REDUCTIONS: SIMULATION RESULTS

The empirical results of simulations with the Brookings model of changes in the excise tax structure indicate what might have happened during the period from mid 1960 through 1962 if the excise tax reductions enacted by Congress in July 1965 had gone into effect beginning July 1960. The results presented concentrate on twelve different aspects of the economy for two different amounts of tax cut, with three sets of assumptions about how much of the tax change initially shows up in price changes.

### *4.1. Input*

The initial size of the tax cut is determined by taking the original solution, that is, the solution applying to the period with the excise law as it existed in mid 1960–62, and multiplying each of the relevant tax bases in the third quarter of 1960 by the appropriate change in tax rates. For the smaller cut, the change in rates is that which took place in mid 1965; this change yields an equivalent 1960:3 excise reduction of $1.6 billion. For the larger cut the change in rates is the difference in excise rates between January 1, 1967 and those in effect before July 1, 1965 (that is, the total 1965–67 rate change is collapsed to a single date); here the equivalent 1960:3 reduction is $2.7 billion. (The size of the reductions grows over time as the tax bases increase. Thus, computed for the fourth quarter of 1962, the figures become $1.9 and $3.3 billion, respectively.) The equivalent 1960:3 reductions appear out of proportion to the official figures given for the 1965–67 cuts, that is, $1.75 and $4.0 billion. This phenomenon is caused by two factors: first, new car purchases are much higher now than in 1960:3 (this affects the level of both reductions and their relative difference); second, the levels of the 1960:3 cut are somewhat too large for that quarter because the original solution to some extent overestimates consumption and production. Also, in calculating the larger equivalent 1960:3 cut, no account was taken of the stage reduction in automobile parts excises. These difficulties are not insurmountable, however, since the primary purpose of this analysis is to show the effect of excise tax reductions in general rather than the effect of the 1965 cut in particular.

For each of the two different size cuts three assumptions were made concerning how tax changes affected prices initially. In the 100 per cent *pass-along* assumption all tax decreases are reflected in equivalent price reductions (the amusement tax is treated as an exception; prices here are assumed to be unaffected by the removal of the taxes). The 80 per cent *pass-along* assumption differs from the first in that prices initially fall by 80 per cent of the tax change for automobiles, other consumer durables, and the manufacturing durables sectors. Under the 50 per cent *pass-along* assumption, the prices for the three sectors involved initially fall by 50 per cent of the tax change.

## *4.2. Results*

### *4.2.1. Absolute impact on GNP*

Table 4.1 presents the results for the control solution and for each of the experiments on different tax sizes and pass-along assumptions for the following variables: real *GNP* (in 1954 dollars), real investment, real consumption, unemployment rate, employment, *WPI* in manufacturing durables, implicit price deflator for *GNP*, profits before taxes, government revenues, government transfers, and real disposable income. The table also shows the difference between each of the tax cuts and the original solution. These differences are the primary focus of attention in this chapter, although some attention is given to multipliers. A full discussion of multipliers is postponed to the next chapter because of the many conceptual problems involved.

Probably the most comprehensive single summary measure of the state of the economy and indicator of the impact of the tax cut is *GNP* in constant dollars. The results for real *GNP* are given in table 4.1. This table also shows the difference between each of the excise combinations and the original solution. Consider first the three assumptions under the smaller tax cut, that is, the \$1.6 billion initial equivalent reduction. For the first quarter, the change in real *GNP* is \$0.9 billion for the 50 per cent assumption, \$1.4 billion for the 80 per cent assumption, and \$1.6 billion for the 100 per cent assumption. These three *GNP* figures highlight the importance of whether or not firms fully pass along the tax decrease, since the range of increase in real output is 40 per cent of the 100 per cent solution.

### 4.2.2. Multipliers

At this point, it is necessary to consider multipliers. One type of multiplier can be obtained by dividing the increase in *real GNP* by the amount of *current* dollar revenue foregone; this might be called a fiscal policy effectiveness multiplier. If a deflated value were used in the denominator, the same deflator would be employed for all calculations; therefore, the results would be proportional to the multipliers given, and rankings of policies would be identical. The first quarter impact multipliers of the \$1.6 billion tax cut are 1.0, 0.85, and 0.55 for the 100, 80, and 50 per cent assumptions, respectively [2]).

In addition to impact multipliers, it is possible to solve the system for the ten-quarter time response path of real *GNP*. For the smaller tax reduction the multipliers increase irregularly, with a hesitation in the middle period, until the eighth quarter and then decline. By ten quarters, the *GNP* increments for the 100, 80, and 50 per cent assumptions are \$2.2, \$1.9, and \$1.3 billion, respectively. The difference of \$0.9 billion or 40 per cent in real *GNP* between the 100 and 50 per cent assumptions is substantial [3]). The ten-quarter multipliers are 1.35, 1.15, and 0.80 if the initial tax cut of \$1.6 billion is used as the denominator. However, since this initial cut increases to \$1.9 billion by the fourth quarter of 1962, an alternative calculation (with \$1.9 billion in the denominator) would yield multipliers of 1.15, 1.00, and 0.70, respectively. The true answer lies somewhere between these two estimates. The first set of figures may be of interest to the Congress, since in passing the tax legislation it might believe it is giving up only \$1.6 billion in revenues.

For the larger cut, the results on the surface appear similar to the smaller cut. The first quarter effect on real *GNP* is \$2.5, \$1.9, and \$1.5 billion. The

---

[1]) This may seem an unusual way to compute a multiplier, but it will be shown in chapter 5 that no method is ideal. This multiplier measures the fiscal policy return on Congressional action.

[2]) However, if the extra profit and profit taxes of the less than 100 per cent pass-along are treated as an expected reduction in the size of the fiscal program, different multipliers result (see chapter 5).

[3]) Inasmuch as investment depends on sales, not profits, the true difference between the two simulations might be somewhat less. Yet, since the impact on investment is small in any event (about \$0.4 billion under the 100 per cent assumption), the gap would not be appreciably narrowed.

TABLE 4.1

*Simulation results: impact of excise tax reductions.*[a])

| Solution | Year and quarter | | | | | | | | | |
|---|---|---|---|---|---|---|---|---|---|---|
| | 1960:3 | 1960:4 | 1961:1 | 1961:2 | 1961:3 | 1961:4 | 1962:1 | 1962:2 | 1962:3 | 1962:4 |
| | | | | | A. Real gross national product | | | | | |
| Original solution | 440.8 | 442.0 | 443.5 | 452.4 | 459.8 | 471.4 | 481.4 | 485.4 | 487.0 | 490.2 |
| Simulations | | | | | | | | | | |
| $1.6 billion cut | | | | | | | | | | |
| 100 per cent pass along | 442.4 | 443.9 | 445.6 | 454.3 | 461.8 | 473.8 | 484.0 | 488.0 | 489.4 | 492.5 |
| 80 per cent pass along | 442.2 | 443.6 | 445.4 | 454.0 | 461.6 | 473.5 | 483.6 | 487.6 | 489.1 | 492.1 |
| 50 per cent pass along | 441.7 | 443.1 | 444.8 | 453.6 | 461.1 | 472.9 | 482.9 | 487.0 | 488.4 | 491.5 |
| $2.7 billion cut | | | | | | | | | | |
| 100 per cent pass along | 443.3 | 445.2 | 447.3 | 456.1 | 464.1 | 476.6 | 487.4 | 491.7 | 493.4 | 496.7 |
| 80 per cent pass along | 442.7 | 444.5 | 446.6 | 455.5 | 463.4 | 475.8 | 486.4 | 490.8 | 492.5 | 495.9 |
| 50 per cent pass along | 442.3 | 444.0 | 446.0 | 455.0 | 462.8 | 475.1 | 485.6 | 489.9 | 491.6 | 495.0 |
| Simulation less original solution | | | | | | | | | | |
| $1.6 billion cut | | | | | | | | | | |
| 100 per cent pass along | 1.6 | 1.9 | 2.1 | 1.8 | 2.0 | 2.4 | 2.6 | 2.6 | 2.4 | 2.2 |
| 80 per cent pass along | 1.4 | 1.6 | 1.8 | 1.6 | 1.7 | 2.1 | 2.3 | 2.3 | 2.1 | 1.9 |
| 50 per cent pass along | 0.9 | 1.1 | 1.3 | 1.2 | 1.3 | 1.5 | 1.6 | 1.6 | 1.4 | 1.3 |
| $2.7 billion cut | | | | | | | | | | |
| 100 per cent pass along | 2.5 | 3.2 | 3.8 | 3.7 | 4.3 | 5.2 | 6.0 | 6.4 | 6.4 | 6.4 |
| 80 per cent pass along | 1.9 | 2.5 | 3.1 | 3.1 | 3.6 | 4.4 | 5.1 | 5.4 | 5.5 | 5.6 |
| 50 per cent pass along | 1.6 | 2.0 | 2.5 | 2.5 | 3.0 | 3.7 | 4.3 | 4.6 | 4.7 | 4.8 |
| | | | | | B. Real consumption | | | | | |
| Original solution | 299.6 | 301.2 | 304.0 | 307.4 | 311.3 | 315.4 | 320.7 | 322.9 | 325.3 | 328.1 |

| Simulations | | | | | | | | | | |
|---|---|---|---|---|---|---|---|---|---|---|
| $1.6 billion cut | | | | | | | | | | |
| 100 per cent pass along | 301.1 | 302.7 | 305.6 | 309.0 | 312.8 | 317.1 | 322.5 | 324.7 | 327.0 | 329.9 |
| 80 per cent pass along | 300.9 | 302.5 | 305.4 | 308.8 | 312.6 | 316.9 | 322.3 | 324.5 | 326.8 | 329.7 |
| 50 per cent pass along | 300.5 | 302.1 | 305.0 | 308.4 | 312.2 | 316.5 | 321.8 | 324.1 | 326.4 | 329.3 |
| $2.7 billion cut | | | | | | | | | | |
| 100 per cent pass along | 302.0 | 303.9 | 307.0 | 310.6 | 314.7 | 319.2 | 324.9 | 327.3 | 329.8 | 332.9 |
| 80 per cent pass along | 301.4 | 303.3 | 306.5 | 310.1 | 314.2 | 318.7 | 324.3 | 326.8 | 329.3 | 332.4 |
| 50 per cent pass along | 301.1 | 302.9 | 306.0 | 309.6 | 313.7 | 318.2 | 323.8 | 326.2 | 328.7 | 331.8 |
| Simulation less original solution | | | | | | | | | | |
| $1.6 billion cut | | | | | | | | | | |
| 100 per cent pass along | 1.5 | 1.6 | 1.6 | 1.5 | 1.6 | 1.7 | 1.8 | 1.8 | 1.8 | 1.8 |
| 80 per cent pass along | 1.3 | 1.4 | 1.4 | 1.3 | 1.4 | 1.5 | 1.5 | 1.5 | 1.6 | 1.5 |
| 50 per cent pass along | 0.9 | 0.9 | 1.0 | 0.9 | 1.0 | 1.1 | 1.1 | 1.1 | 1.1 | 1.1 |
| $2.7 billion cut | | | | | | | | | | |
| 100 per cent pass along | 2.4 | 2.7 | 3.0 | 3.2 | 3.5 | 3.8 | 4.2 | 4.4 | 4.6 | 4.8 |
| 80 per cent pass along | 1.8 | 2.1 | 2.4 | 2.6 | 2.9 | 3.3 | 3.6 | 3.8 | 4.0 | 4.2 |
| 50 per cent pass along | 1.5 | 1.8 | 2.0 | 2.2 | 2.4 | 2.8 | 3.0 | 3.2 | 3.4 | 3.6 |
| C. Real disposable income | | | | | | | | | | |
| Original solution | 320.8 | 321.2 | 324.2 | 327.9 | 333.7 | 339.1 | 346.6 | 347.3 | 348.8 | 350.8 |
| Simulations | | | | | | | | | | |
| $1.6 billion cut | | | | | | | | | | |
| 100 per cent pass along | 323.1 | 323.5 | 326.5 | 330.0 | 335.8 | 341.4 | 349.0 | 349.6 | 351.0 | 352.9 |
| 80 per cent pass along | 322.8 | 323.2 | 326.3 | 329.8 | 335.6 | 341.2 | 348.7 | 349.3 | 350.8 | 352.6 |
| 50 per cent pass along | 322.3 | 322.6 | 325.7 | 329.3 | 335.1 | 340.7 | 348.2 | 348.9 | 350.4 | 352.2 |
| $2.7 billion cut | | | | | | | | | | |
| 100 per cent pass along | 324.7 | 325.4 | 328.8 | 332.6 | 338.7 | 344.6 | 352.4 | 353.1 | 354.7 | 356.7 |
| 80 per cent pass along | 323.9 | 324.6 | 328.0 | 331.9 | 338.0 | 343.9 | 351.7 | 352.5 | 354.1 | 356.1 |
| 50 per cent pass along | 323.5 | 324.2 | 327.5 | 331.4 | 337.5 | 343.3 | 351.1 | 351.9 | 353.5 | 355.5 |

TABLE 4.1 (Continued).

| Solution | 1960:3 | 1960:4 | 1961:1 | 1961:2 | 1961:3 | 1961:4 | 1962:1 | 1962:2 | 1962:3 | 1962:4 |
|---|---|---|---|---|---|---|---|---|---|---|
| | Year and quarter | | | | | | | | | |
| Simulation less original solution | | | | | | | | | | |
| $1.6 billion cut | | | | | | | | | | |
| 100 per cent pass along | 2.3 | 2.3 | 2.3 | 2.2 | 2.1 | 2.3 | 2.3 | 2.3 | 2.2 | 2.1 |
| 80 per cent pass along | 2.0 | 2.0 | 2.1 | 1.9 | 1.9 | 2.0 | 2.1 | 2.0 | 2.0 | 1.9 |
| 50 per cent pass along | 1.4 | 1.5 | 1.5 | 1.4 | 1.4 | 1.5 | 1.6 | 1.5 | 1.5 | 1.4 |
| $2.7 billion cut | | | | | | | | | | |
| 100 per cent pass along | 3.9 | 4.3 | 4.6 | 4.7 | 5.0 | 5.4 | 5.8 | 5.8 | 5.9 | 5.9 |
| 80 per cent pass along | 3.1 | 3.5 | 3.8 | 4.0 | 4.3 | 4.7 | 5.1 | 5.2 | 5.2 | 5.3 |
| 50 per cent pass along | 2.7 | 3.0 | 3.3 | 3.5 | 3.8 | 4.1 | 4.5 | 4.6 | 4.6 | 4.8 |
| | | | | | D. Total real investment | | | | | |
| Original solution | 57.2 | 56.6 | 55.2 | 57.7 | 60.2 | 63.6 | 64.8 | 64.6 | 65.2 | 67.7 |
| Simulations | | | | | | | | | | |
| $1.6 billion cut | | | | | | | | | | |
| 100 per cent pass along | 57.2 | 56.7 | 55.5 | 58.0 | 60.5 | 64.1 | 65.3 | 65.1 | 65.7 | 68.1 |
| 80 per cent pass along | 57.2 | 56.7 | 55.4 | 57.9 | 60.4 | 64.0 | 65.2 | 65.0 | 65.6 | 68.1 |
| 50 per cent pass along | 57.2 | 56.7 | 55.4 | 57.9 | 60.3 | 63.9 | 65.1 | 64.9 | 65.5 | 67.9 |
| $2.7 billion cut | | | | | | | | | | |
| 100 per cent pass along | 57.2 | 56.8 | 55.6 | 58.2 | 60.8 | 64.5 | 65.9 | 65.9 | 66.5 | 69.0 |
| 80 per cent pass along | 57.2 | 56.8 | 55.5 | 58.1 | 60.7 | 64.4 | 65.7 | 65.6 | 66.3 | 68.8 |
| 50 per cent pass along | 57.2 | 56.7 | 55.5 | 58.0 | 60.6 | 64.2 | 65.6 | 65.5 | 66.2 | 68.7 |
| Simulation less original solution | | | | | | | | | | |
| $1.6 billion cut | | | | | | | | | | |
| 100 per cent pass along | 0 | 0.2 | 0.2 | 0.3 | 0.3 | 0.4 | 0.5 | 0.6 | 0.5 | 0.5 |
| 80 per cent pass along | 0 | 0.1 | 0.2 | 0.2 | 0.3 | 0.4 | 0.5 | 0.5 | 0.4 | 0.4 |
| 50 per cent pass along | 0 | 0.1 | 0.1 | 0.2 | 0.2 | 0.3 | 0.3 | 0.3 | 0.3 | 0.2 |

| | | | | | | | | | | |
|---|---|---|---|---|---|---|---|---|---|---|
| $2.7 billion cut | | | | | | | | | | |
| 100 per cent pass along | 0 | 0.2 | 0.4 | 0.5 | 0.6 | 0.9 | 1.2 | 1.3 | 1.3 | 1.3 |
| 80 per cent pass along | 0 | 0.2 | 0.3 | 0.4 | 0.5 | 0.7 | 0.9 | 1.1 | 1.1 | 1.1 |
| 50 per cent pass along | 0 | 0.2 | 0.3 | 0.3 | 0.4 | 0.6 | 0.8 | 0.9 | 0.9 | 1.0 |
| E. Profits before taxes | | | | | | | | | | |
| Original solution | 44.6 | 44.6 | 42.6 | 45.4 | 46.7 | 52.0 | 50.5 | 52.1 | 51.8 | 49.8 |
| Simulations | | | | | | | | | | |
| $1.6 billion cut | | | | | | | | | | |
| 100 per cent pass along | 43.8 | 45.1 | 43.2 | 46.2 | 47.9 | 53.8 | 52.7 | 54.6 | 54.4 | 52.4 |
| 80 per cent pass along | 43.9 | 45.1 | 43.2 | 46.3 | 48.0 | 53.8 | 52.7 | 54.6 | 54.4 | 52.5 |
| 50 per cent pass along | 44.1 | 45.3 | 43.4 | 46.5 | 48.2 | 53.9 | 52.8 | 54.7 | 54.5 | 52.5 |
| $2.7 billion cut | | | | | | | | | | |
| 100 per cent pass along | 44.2 | 45.4 | 43.5 | 46.5 | 48.2 | 54.1 | 53.2 | 55.3 | 55.1 | 53.2 |
| 80 per cent pass along | 44.5 | 45.7 | 43.8 | 46.7 | 48.4 | 54.3 | 53.3 | 55.3 | 55.2 | 53.3 |
| 50 per cent pass along | 44.6 | 45.8 | 43.9 | 46.9 | 48.6 | 54.4 | 53.4 | 55.4 | 55.3 | 53.3 |
| Simulation less original solution | | | | | | | | | | |
| $1.6 billion cut | | | | | | | | | | |
| 100 per cent pass along | 0.2 | 0.5 | 0.6 | 0.8 | 1.2 | 1.7 | 2.1 | 2.5 | 2.6 | 2.7 |
| 80 per cent pass along | 0.3 | 0.6 | 0.7 | 0.9 | 1.3 | 1.8 | 2.2 | 2.5 | 2.6 | 2.7 |
| 50 per cent pass along | 0.5 | 0.8 | 0.8 | 1.1 | 1.4 | 1.9 | 2.3 | 2.5 | 2.7 | 2.8 |
| $2.7 billion cut | | | | | | | | | | |
| 100 per cent pass along | 0.5 | 0.8 | 0.9 | 1.0 | 1.5 | 2.1 | 2.6 | 3.1 | 3.3 | 3.4 |
| 80 per cent pass along | 0.9 | 1.1 | 1.2 | 1.3 | 1.7 | 2.3 | 2.8 | 3.2 | 3.4 | 3.5 |
| 50 per cent pass along | 1.0 | 1.2 | 1.3 | 1.4 | 1.8 | 2.4 | 2.8 | 3.2 | 3.5 | 3.6 |
| F. *GNP* implicit price deflator | | | | | | | | | | |
| Original solution | 1.150 | 1.161 | 1.169 | 1.174 | 1.183 | 1.188 | 1.193 | 1.206 | 1.220 | 1.228 |

TABLE 4.1 (Continued)

| Solution | Year and quarter | | | | | | | | | |
|---|---|---|---|---|---|---|---|---|---|---|
| | 1960:3 | 1960:4 | 1961:1 | 1961:2 | 1961:3 | 1961:4 | 1962:1 | 1962:2 | 1962:3 | 1962:4 |
| Simulations | | | | | | | | | | |
| $1.6 billion cut | | | | | | | | | | |
| 100 per cent pass along | 1.144 | 1.155 | 1.162 | 1.168 | 1.178 | 1.184 | 1.190 | 1.205 | 1.220 | 1.228 |
| 80 per cent pass along | 1.145 | 1.155 | 1.163 | 1.169 | 1.179 | 1.185 | 1.191 | 1.205 | 1.220 | 1.228 |
| 50 per cent pass along | 1.147 | 1.157 | 1.165 | 1.171 | 1.181 | 1.187 | 1.192 | 1.207 | 1.221 | 1.229 |
| $2.7 billion cut | | | | | | | | | | |
| 100 per cent pass along | 1.140 | 1.149 | 1.155 | 1.158 | 1.167 | 1.172 | 1.179 | 1.194 | 1.209 | 1.217 |
| 80 per cent pass along | 1.142 | 1.151 | 1.157 | 1.161 | 1.169 | 1.175 | 1.181 | 1.195 | 1.210 | 1.218 |
| 50 per cent pass along | 1.143 | 1.153 | 1.159 | 1.163 | 1.171 | 1.177 | 1.183 | 1.197 | 1.212 | 1.220 |
| Simulation less original solution | | | | | | | | | | |
| $1.6 billion cut | | | | | | | | | | |
| 100 per cent pass along | −0.006 | −0.006 | −0.006 | −0.006 | −0.005 | −0.004 | −0.003 | −0.001 | 0.000 | 0.000 |
| 80 per cent pass along | −0.005 | −0.005 | −0.005 | −0.005 | −0.004 | −0.003 | −0.002 | 0.000 | 0.000 | 0.001 |
| 50 per cent pass along | −0.004 | −0.004 | −0.003 | −0.003 | −0.002 | −0.001 | 0.000 | 0.001 | 0.001 | 0.002 |
| $2.7 billion cut | | | | | | | | | | |
| 100 per cent pass along | −0.010 | −0.012 | −0.014 | −0.016 | −0.016 | −0.016 | −0.014 | −0.012 | −0.011 | −0.011 |
| 80 per cent pass along | −0.008 | −0.009 | −0.011 | −0.013 | −0.013 | −0.013 | −0.012 | −0.011 | −0.010 | −0.009 |
| 50 per cent pass along | −0.007 | −0.008 | −0.010 | −0.011 | −0.011 | −0.011 | −0.010 | −0.009 | −0.008 | −0.008 |
| G. *WPI* manufacturing durables | | | | | | | | | | |
| Original solution | 1.221 | 1.223 | 1.235 | 1.241 | 1.247 | 1.253 | 1.261 | 1.283 | 1.304 | 1.312 |
| Simulations | | | | | | | | | | |
| $1.6 billion cut | | | | | | | | | | |
| 100 per cent pass along | 1.217 | 1.219 | 1.230 | 1.236 | 1.242 | 1.249 | 1.259 | 1.283 | 1.305 | 1.315 |
| 80 per cent pass along | 1.218 | 1.220 | 1.231 | 1.237 | 1.244 | 1.251 | 1.261 | 1.285 | 1.307 | 1.316 |
| 50 per cent pass along | 1.219 | 1.221 | 1.233 | 1.239 | 1.246 | 1.253 | 1.263 | 1.287 | 1.309 | 1.318 |

| | | | | | | | | | | |
|---|---|---|---|---|---|---|---|---|---|---|
| $2.7 billion cut | | | | | | | | | | |
| 100 per cent pass along | 1.215 | 1.216 | 1.225 | 1.229 | 1.235 | 1.241 | 1.251 | 1.275 | 1.298 | 1.308 |
| 80 per cent pass along | 1.216 | 1.218 | 1.228 | 1.232 | 1.237 | 1.244 | 1.253 | 1.277 | 1.299 | 1.309 |
| 50 per cent pass along | 1.217 | 1.219 | 1.229 | 1.234 | 1.240 | 1.247 | 1.257 | 1.280 | 1.303 | 1.312 |
| Simulation less original solution | | | | | | | | | | |
| $1.6 billion cut | | | | | | | | | | |
| 100 per cent pass along | −0.004 | −0.003 | −0.005 | −0.005 | −0.004 | −0.003 | −0.002 | 0.000 | 0.001 | 0.003 |
| 80 per cent pass along | −0.004 | −0.003 | −0.004 | −0.004 | −0.003 | −0.002 | −0.001 | 0.001 | 0.002 | 0.004 |
| 50 per cent pass along | −0.002 | −0.002 | −0.002 | −0.002 | −0.001 | 0.000 | 0.002 | 0.003 | 0.004 | 0.006 |
| $2.7 billion cut | | | | | | | | | | |
| 100 per cent pass along | −0.007 | −0.006 | −0.010 | −0.001 | −0.012 | −0.012 | −0.010 | −0.008 | −0.006 | −0.005 |
| 80 per cent pass along | −0.005 | −0.005 | −0.008 | −0.009 | −0.009 | −0.009 | −0.008 | −0.006 | −0.005 | −0.003 |
| 50 per cent pass along | −0.004 | −0.004 | −0.006 | −0.007 | −0.007 | −0.006 | −0.005 | −0.003 | −0.001 | 0.000 |
| H. Federal, state, and local government revenues | | | | | | | | | | |
| Original solution | 140.8 | 143.3 | 144.6 | 149.9 | 155.4 | 162.8 | 166.7 | 171.0 | 174.0 | 175.7 |
| Simulations | | | | | | | | | | |
| $1.6 billion cut | | | | | | | | | | |
| 100 per cent pass along | 139.7 | 142.2 | 143.5 | 148.5 | 154.2 | 161.7 | 165.8 | 170.3 | 173.2 | 174.9 |
| 80 per cent pass along | 139.7 | 142.3 | 143.6 | 148.6 | 154.2 | 161.7 | 165.8 | 170.3 | 173.1 | 174.8 |
| 50 per cent pass along | 139.9 | 142.4 | 143.7 | 148.8 | 154.4 | 161.9 | 165.8 | 170.2 | 173.1 | 174.8 |
| $2.7 billion cut | | | | | | | | | | |
| 100 per cent pass along | 138.7 | 141.1 | 142.2 | 146.9 | 152.5 | 160.1 | 164.3 | 169.1 | 172.1 | 173.8 |
| 80 per cent pass along | 138.8 | 141.3 | 142.4 | 147.2 | 152.7 | 160.2 | 164.3 | 169.0 | 172.0 | 173.7 |
| 50 per cent pass along | 138.9 | 141.3 | 142.4 | 147.3 | 152.8 | 160.3 | 164.4 | 169.0 | 171.9 | 173.7 |
| Simulation less original solution | | | | | | | | | | |
| $1.6 billion cut | | | | | | | | | | |
| 100 per cent pass along | −1.1 | −1.1 | −1.0 | −1.4 | −1.2 | −1.1 | −0.9 | −0.7 | −0.8 | −0.8 |
| 80 per cent pass along | −1.1 | −1.0 | −1.0 | −1.3 | −1.2 | −1.1 | −0.9 | −0.8 | −0.8 | −0.8 |
| 50 per cent pass along | −0.9 | −0.9 | −0.9 | −1.1 | −1.0 | −1.0 | −0.9 | −0.8 | −0.8 | −0.9 |

TABLE 4.1 (Continued)

| Solution | Year and quarter | | | | | | | | | |
|---|---|---|---|---|---|---|---|---|---|---|
| | 1960:3 | 1960:4 | 1961:1 | 1961:2 | 1961:3 | 1961:4 | 1962:1 | 1962:2 | 1962:3 | 1962:4 |
| $2.7 billion cut | | | | | | | | | | |
| 100 per cent pass along | −2.1 | −2.2 | −2.3 | −3.0 | −2.9 | −2.7 | −2.4 | −2.0 | −1.9 | −1.9 |
| 80 per cent pass along | −2.0 | −2.1 | −2.2 | −2.7 | −2.7 | −2.6 | −2.4 | −2.1 | −2.0 | −2.0 |
| 50 per cent pass along | −1.9 | −2.0 | −2.1 | −2.6 | −2.6 | −2.5 | −2.3 | −2.1 | −2.0 | −2.0 |
| I. Government transfers | | | | | | | | | | |
| Original solution | 27.8 | 28.6 | 29.3 | 29.8 | 30.3 | 30.6 | 30.8 | 31.2 | 31.8 | 32.5 |
| Simulations | | | | | | | | | | |
| $1.6 billion cut | | | | | | | | | | |
| 100 per cent pass along | 27.7 | 28.4 | 29.1 | 29.6 | 30.1 | 30.3 | 30.5 | 31.0 | 31.5 | 32.2 |
| 80 per cent pass along | 27.7 | 28.5 | 29.1 | 29.6 | 30.1 | 30.4 | 30.6 | 31.0 | 31.6 | 32.2 |
| 50 per cent pass along | 27.7 | 28.5 | 29.2 | 29.6 | 30.1 | 30.4 | 30.6 | 31.1 | 31.7 | 32.3 |
| $2.7 billion cut | | | | | | | | | | |
| 100 per cent pass along | 27.7 | 28.4 | 29.0 | 29.4 | 29.9 | 30.1 | 30.2 | 30.6 | 31.1 | 31.7 |
| 80 per cent pass along | 27.7 | 28.4 | 29.1 | 29.5 | 29.9 | 30.2 | 30.3 | 30.7 | 31.2 | 31.8 |
| 50 per cent pass along | 27.7 | 28.4 | 29.1 | 29.5 | 30.0 | 30.2 | 30.4 | 30.8 | 31.3 | 31.9 |
| Simulation less original solution | | | | | | | | | | |
| $1.6 billion cut | | | | | | | | | | |
| 100 per cent pass along | −0.1 | −0.1 | −0.2 | −0.2 | −0.2 | −0.2 | −0.3 | −0.3 | −0.3 | −0.3 |
| 80 per cent pass along | −0.1 | −0.1 | −0.1 | −0.2 | −0.2 | −0.2 | −0.2 | −0.2 | −0.3 | −0.3 |
| 50 per cent pass along | 0.0 | −0.1 | −0.1 | −0.1 | −0.1 | −0.1 | −0.2 | −0.2 | −0.2 | −0.2 |
| $2.7 billion cut | | | | | | | | | | |
| 100 per cent pass along | −0.1 | −0.2 | −0.3 | −0.3 | −0.4 | −0.5 | −0.6 | −0.6 | −0.7 | −0.8 |
| 80 per cent pass along | −0.1 | −0.2 | −0.2 | −0.3 | −0.3 | −0.4 | −0.5 | −0.5 | −0.6 | −0.7 |
| 50 per cent pass along | −0.1 | −0.1 | −0.2 | −0.2 | −0.3 | −0.3 | −0.4 | −0.4 | −0.5 | −0.6 |

| | | | | | | | | | | |
|---|---|---|---|---|---|---|---|---|---|---|
| | | | | | J. Total employment (thousands of persons) | | | | | |
| Original solution | 67.1 | 67.4 | 67.9 | 67.9 | 68.1 | 68.8 | 69.6 | 69.7 | 70.1 | 70.3 |
| Simulations | | | | | | | | | | |
| $1.6 billion cut | | | | | | | | | | |
| 100 per cent pass along | 67.2 | 67.5 | 68.0 | 68.0 | 68.3 | 69.0 | 69.8 | 70.0 | 70.4 | 70.6 |
| 80 per cent pass along | 67.2 | 67.5 | 68.0 | 68.0 | 68.3 | 69.0 | 69.8 | 70.0 | 70.3 | 70.5 |
| 50 per cent pass along | 67.2 | 67.5 | 68.0 | 68.0 | 68.2 | 69.0 | 69.7 | 70.0 | 70.3 | 70.5 |
| $2.7 billion cut | | | | | | | | | | |
| 100 per cent pass along | 67.2 | 67.6 | 68.1 | 68.2 | 68.5 | 69.2 | 70.1 | 70.3 | 70.7 | 70.9 |
| 80 per cent pass along | 67.2 | 67.5 | 68.1 | 68.1 | 68.4 | 69.1 | 70.0 | 70.2 | 70.6 | 70.9 |
| 50 per cent pass along | 67.2 | 67.5 | 68.0 | 68.1 | 68.4 | 69.0 | 70.0 | 70.1 | 70.5 | 70.8 |
| Simulation less original solution | | | | | | | | | | |
| $1.6 billion cut | | | | | | | | | | |
| 100 per cent pass along | 0.1 | 0.1 | 0.2 | 0.2 | 0.3 | 0.3 | 0.3 | 0.4 | 0.4 | 0.3 |
| 80 per cent pass along | 0.1 | 0.1 | 0.2 | 0.2 | 0.2 | 0.3 | 0.3 | 0.3 | 0.3 | 0.3 |
| 50 per cent pass along | 0.0 | 0.1 | 0.1 | 0.1 | 0.2 | 0.2 | 0.2 | 0.2 | 0.2 | 0.2 |
| $2.7 billion cut | | | | | | | | | | |
| 100 per cent pass along | 0.1 | 0.2 | 0.4 | 0.4 | 0.5 | 0.6 | 0.7 | 0.8 | 0.9 | 0.9 |
| 80 per cent pass along | 0.1 | 0.2 | 0.3 | 0.4 | 0.4 | 0.5 | 0.6 | 0.7 | 0.7 | 0.8 |
| 50 per cent pass along | 0.1 | 0.1 | 0.3 | 0.3 | 0.3 | 0.4 | 0.5 | 0.6 | 0.6 | 0.6 |
| | | | | | K. Unemployment rate [b]) | | | | | |
| Original solution | 0.055 | 0.056 | 0.055 | 0.055 | 0.055 | 0.054 | 0.051 | 0.049 | 0.049 | 0.049 |
| Simultations | | | | | | | | | | |
| $1.6 billion cut | | | | | | | | | | |
| 100 per cent pass along | 0.054 | 0.055 | 0.054 | 0.054 | 0.053 | 0.052 | 0.050 | 0.048 | 0.047 | 0.047 |
| 80 per cent pass along | 0.054 | 0.055 | 0.054 | 0.054 | 0.054 | 0.053 | 0.050 | 0.048 | 0.047 | 0.048 |
| 50 per cent pass along | 0.054 | 0.055 | 0.055 | 0.054 | 0.054 | 0.053 | 0.050 | 0.049 | 0.048 | 0.048 |

TABLE 4.1 (Continued)

| Solution | Year and quarter | | | | | | | | | |
|---|---|---|---|---|---|---|---|---|---|---|
| | 1960:3 | 1960:4 | 1961:1 | 1961:2 | 1961:3 | 1961:4 | 1962:1 | 1962:2 | 1962:3 | 1962:4 |
| $2.7 billion cut | | | | | | | | | | |
| 100 per cent pass along | 0.054 | 0.055 | 0.053 | 0.053 | 0.052 | 0.051 | 0.048 | 0.046 | 0.045 | 0.045 |
| 80 per cent pass along | 0.054 | 0.055 | 0.054 | 0.053 | 0.053 | 0.052 | 0.049 | 0.047 | 0.046 | 0.046 |
| 50 per cent pass along | 0.054 | 0.055 | 0.054 | 0.053 | 0.053 | 0.052 | 0.049 | 0.047 | 0.046 | 0.046 |
| Simulation less original solution | | | | | | | | | | |
| $1.6 billion cut | | | | | | | | | | |
| 100 per cent pass along | 0.000 | −0.001 | −0.001 | −0.001 | −0.001 | −0.001 | −0.001 | −0.001 | −0.002 | −0.002 |
| 80 per cent pass along | 0.000 | −0.001 | −0.001 | −0.001 | −0.001 | −0.001 | −0.001 | −0.001 | −0.001 | −0.001 |
| 50 per cent pass along | 0.000 | 0.000 | −0.001 | −0.001 | −0.001 | −0.001 | −0.001 | −0.001 | −0.001 | −0.001 |
| $2.7 billion cut | | | | | | | | | | |
| 100 per cent pass along | −0.001 | −0.001 | −0.002 | −0.002 | −0.002 | −0.003 | −0.003 | −0.003 | −0.004 | −0.004 |
| 80 per cent pass along | 0.000 | −0.001 | −0.001 | −0.002 | −0.002 | −0.002 | −0.002 | −0.003 | −0.003 | −0.003 |
| 50 per cent pass along | 0.000 | −0.001 | −0.001 | −0.001 | −0.002 | −0.002 | −0.002 | −0.002 | −0.002 | −0.003 |

[a]) Unless otherwise specified, monetary magnitudes are in billions of current dollars (real variables are in billions of 1954 dollars), seasonally adjusted at annual rates; price indexes are 1954 = 1.00.

[b]) Proportion of civilian labor force unemployed.

*Note*: Simulation less original solution detail may not reconcile precisely with simulation solutions due to rounding.

extra $1.1 billion cut increases real *GNP* by $0.9, $0.6, and $0.6 billion for the 100, 80, and 50 per cent assumptions. The impact multipliers are 0.95, 0.75, and 0.55, which are reasonably close to those obtained for the smaller cut. The time path of real *GNP* increases irregularly (without a peak in the eighth quarter) and in 1962:4 is $6.4, $5.6, and $4.8 billion. But at the end of the period the difference between the 100 and 50 per cent assumptions is almost $1.7 billion, or 25 per cent of the $6.4 billion. The 80 per cent figure is $0.8 billion less than the 100 per cent figure. The multipliers using the $2.7 initial reduction are 2.40, 2.10, and 1.80; while using the $3.3 billion final reduction they are 1.90, 1.70, and 1.30. As before, the "true" multipliers lie somewhere between the two calculations which use either of the extremes, $2.7 or $3.3 billion as the divisor.

### *4.2.3. Economics of scale in excise effects*

It should be remembered that the ten-quarter multipliers for the smaller tax cut of $1.6–$1.9 billion under the 100 per cent pass-along assumption were 1.15–1.35, substantially less than the figures for the larger reduction. Thus, the *expansionary effects* of the *larger* tax cut are proportionately *greater* than the smaller cut, or there are *increasing returns* to *excise* tax *reductions*. This conclusion calls for explanation. [4])

Consider figure 4.1 with employment, *E*, along the horizontal axis and consumption (in money rather than real terms), *PQ*, on the vertical axis. It is possible to construct a supply curve, *Z*, which shows the amount of revenue businessmen want (expect) a given amount of real output (not shown) to yield. With given technology and capital stock (these are relatively fixed in the short run) it is possible to translate this output into employment. Similarly, by knowing market prices, income distributions, and demand functions, it is possible to show the amount of current dollar demand at every employment level. Let $D_0$ and $Z_0$ be the curves before the excise cut.

When excises fall, market prices decrease. However, for producers, a cost (the tax) declines by at least as much, if not more, than the price drop. The total amount of proceeds needed to produce any level of *E* will be less. Therefore, $Z_0$ will shift down to $Z_1$. At the same time, prices are lower so the quantity of consumption will increase (ignoring income distribution

---

[4]) The explanation is an adaption of the work of S. Weintraub in *An Approach to the Theory of Income Distribution* (Chilton, 1958). See also P. Davidson, "Rolph on the Aggregate Effects of a General Excise Tax," *Southern Economic Journal*, July 1960.

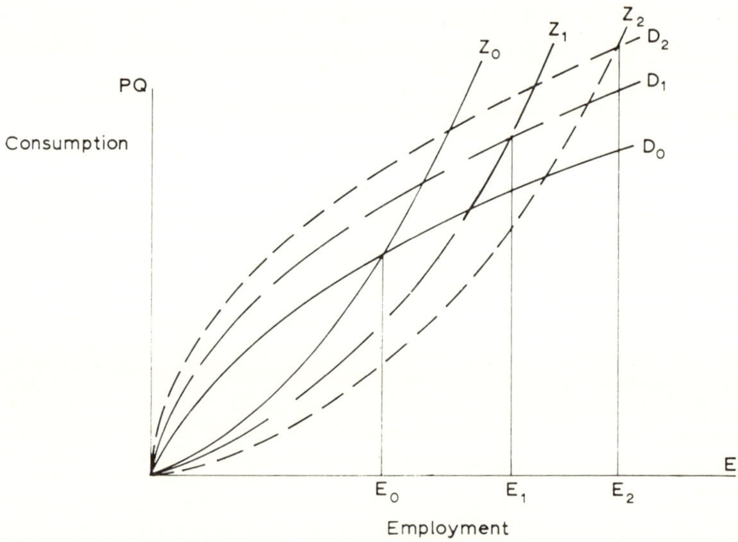


*Figure 4.1. Consumption and employment effects of excise tax reductions.*

changes), although it is not certain what will happen to *PQ* at every level of employment. The new equilibrium is at $E_1$, which will be to the right of $E_0$ unless $Z$ is vertical, which is unlikely, or $D$ slopes downward in the range of the cut, which is theoretically possible [5]), or $D$ is markedly shifted downward by price elasticities of demand substantially less than unity.

A bigger tax cut causes shifts to $Z_2$, $D_2$, and $E_2$. Thus, a good explanation of the "increasing returns" is that the price cut operates on the supply side by shifting the curve down. With a nonlinear model, larger tax reductions give rise to disproportionately greater downward shifts of the supply function. However, these shifts do not become apparent for several quarters because the initial nonlinearities are small and the upward shift of the demand curve (due to price effects) is gradual. Moreover, the larger the tax cut, the smaller the coefficients in the price determination equations; therefore, price and wage movements are more damped. This results in larger increases in real disposable income, both because of lower personal taxes and because of real income gains of fixed income recipients. Concerning the absolute size of the multipliers, the excise tax reductions directly affect both industry supply and consumer demand functions. Consequently, they

[5]) Weintraub, op. cit., p. 31—45.

can be more effective than government tax or expenditure policies which directly affect only one of the curves.

Translating employment back into output leaves the increasing returns conclusions unchanged, even assuming many different production functions and price decision models. Those unfamiliar with the requisite procedures may find it helpful to consider the effects of differential decreases in monopoly power on employment in the context of a supply and demand model. (This analogy was suggested by E. Cary Brown.) Having examined some propositions on the real *GNP* outcomes, we shall now return to some additional results.

### *4.2.4. Impact on other variables*

*Consumption.* Real consumption responds with a distributed lag to changes in real *GNP*. The gains build up gradually for both size cuts, but in the 100 per cent pass-along cases the smaller one has about 85 per cent of the ten-quarter impact in the first quarter while the larger one has 50 per cent. This occurs because real disposable income grows much more rapidly for the larger tax reduction. (The effect of business decisions concerning how much of the cuts to pass along is also significant. The increase in real disposable income in 1962:4 for the 50 per cent pass-along assumption is about 30 per cent less for the smaller, and 20 per cent less for the larger, tax reduction of that achieved if 100 per cent of the cut is passed along.)

*Disposable income.* In the first quarter, the $1.6 billion tax reduction adds from $1.4 to $2.3 billion (depending on the pass-along assumption) in real disposable income, or not quite one half of the amounts added for the larger cuts. After ten quarters, however, the real disposable income under the lesser fiscal stimulus has remained approximately constant, while the larger cut shows a growth slightly in excess of $2 billion. That is, after ten quarters the larger cut has added two and one-half to three times as much real disposable income as the smaller tax decrease. The superior performance of the larger cut is a direct consequence of the differences in price performance and real *GNP* growth.

The increase in real consumption and income may also be related. Dividing the increase in real consumption of the simulation less the original solution in any quarter by the corresponding tax cut effect on real disposable income yields a "marginal propensity to consume." For the fourth quarter of 1962 this figure is 0.75 to 0.80. The shorter run propensity is approximately 0.60.

*Wage rates.* Initially, the larger excise tax cut reduces prices more, but it also makes the system less responsive in passing along higher costs induced by an expanding economy. These reactions, along with the fact that wage rate changes tend to lag behind price changes, are important for income determination. Thus, in the case of the smaller tax cut, when prices begin to return to their initial level after three quarters (they achieve it after seven to nine quarters), the rate of increase of real compensation per man-hour and real wages and salaries declines. For the larger cut, prices continue to fall for several more quarters. While prices rise eventually, by the end of ten quarters they are still below the levels experienced immediately after the initial reductions. Consequently, real wage rates and fixed incomes have higher values than for the smaller cut.

*Investment.* That there is no impact on real investment in the first quarter is expected, since all the determinants of investment are lagged. For later quarters, again the differences in the pass-along assumptions are important. However, sales and not profits are the determinants of investment in the model; therefore, the differences in the investment outcomes are upper bounds. The ratio between the results for the larger and smaller tax cuts after eight quarters conforms to changes in real *GNP* previously given; for example, 2.2/6.4 is approximately 0.8/2.2. This coincidence is a result of the modified accelerator employed in the model. Because of the magnitude of the accelerator, the tax induced expansion in real investment in percentage terms, although roughly equal, is slightly greater than the increases in real *GNP*, for example 2.25 per cent versus 1.5 per cent for the larger cut (under the 100 per cent pass-along assumption).

*Profits.* The movements of profits before taxes and before inventory valuation adjustments are somewhat unusual. Profits rise smoothly for each of the experiments, even in the ninth and tenth quarters when real *GNP* is falling. This reflects the increases in prices from their lows. One result is that the extra output associated with the larger pass-along assumptions substantially offsets the higher markups of the lower pass-along assumptions. Another result is that at the end of 1962 the larger cut has profits of only \$0.4 billion higher than the smaller cut, while at the beginning the differences are \$0.2 billion (in percentage terms the smaller cut is creeping up). This seems unusual since the larger tax cut reaps increasing returns in terms of the rise in real *GNP*. The primary cause of this result is that the lower level (or relative rate of increase) in prices induced by the larger excise cut is sufficient so that, even after ten quarters, *GNP* in money terms is greater for the $1.6 billion tax reduction than for the $2.7 billion decrease. This might be interpreted as a profits squeeze. However, profits resulting from the larger tax cut enjoy higher purchasing power than those resulting from the lesser reduction in excises. Or, in terms of income shares, profits as a per cent of current dollar *GNP* in the fourth quarter of 1962 equal 8.3 per cent in the original solution, 8.6 per cent with the $1.6 billion tax cut, and 8.8 per cent with the $2.7 billion reduction (both of the latter are under the 100 per cent pass-along assumption). Thus, no squeeze has developed because the profit share is higher with the larger tax cut.

*Prices.* The behavior of the implicit price deflator for *GNP* also changes. For the smaller tax decrease, the level of prices (in comparison to the original solution) declines in the first quarter, then remains constant for two to four quarters with higher productivity offsetting wage increments, and then rises so that the level of prices in the simulation equals or exceeds that in the original solution by the end of the period. Of course, throughout the two years, prices are lowest for the 100 per cent pass-along assumption.

When the reduction is $2.7 billion, a more attenuated pattern occurs. In relation to the original solution, prices continue to decline for four quarters and do not rise until the seventh quarter. The largest (negative) differences between the simulation and original solution, experienced in the sixth quarter, are from 50 to 60 per cent greater than in the initial period. In the seventh quarter prices begin to rise, but by the end of ten quarters (under either of the three pass-along assumptions), they are still further away from the original solution than in the first quarter. This difference in price behavior with the alternative tax reductions, which is a reflection of non-linearities in the model and the greater dampening of the price equations with the larger cut, is instrumental in explaining the difference in the growth of real *GNP* and disposable income. The data for the wholesale price index for manufacturing durables and other prices show similar movements.

*Government deficit.* To this point the $1.6 and $2.7 billion figures have been used as the measures of revenue lost through the tax cuts. However, the federal government recoups a good deal of this revenue from the expansion of the economy, which increases tax bases (especially profits) and reduces transfer payments. Important offsets to this impetus to revenue generation are the price reductions accompanying the excise tax cuts; these reductions are followed by a diminuation in the growth of state and local sales tax receipts and federal tax bases measured in current dollars (as in the foregoing profits case). Another factor is that, given the "normal" growth of the economy and tax bases in the absence of stimulative policies, a reduction in excise tax rates involves an increasingly greater revenue loss over time. The combined effect of all these elements in the case of the \$1.6 billion initial excise tax change (with a 100 per cent pass-along assumption) is that over the ten quarters the government loses an average of only \$650 million in taxes and pays out \$230 million less in transfers (for a net loss of \$420 million) per quarter (at annual rates). As might be anticipated, of the four taxes involved, corporate, personal, employment, and indirect, receipts from the first three are higher in the simulation than in the original solution at the end of ten quarters, but the last is \$3 billion lower. Similar results hold for the larger tax cut. The loss of taxes is \$1.5 billion while transfers fall by \$400 million, for a net loss of \$1.1 billion rather than \$2.7 billion. For both cuts, the loss in revenue reaches a maximum after four quarters and in general seems to correlate well with the movements in the implicit price deflator for *GNP*.

*Unemployment.* Finally, the larger excise cut increases employment and decreases unemployment about two or three times as much as the smaller excise reductions. The greater employment response for the larger cut could be expected as a consequence of the greater growth in real *GNP*.

## *4.3. Summary*

In summary, the excise tax cut, working through the price equations, expands real output by impressive amounts. An increase of up to \$2.4 in real *GNP* is obtained for every dollar given up in tax revenue. In the range of the reductions investigated, the greater the tax cut, the larger the ten-quarter real *GNP* multiplier. The extent that tax cuts show up in lower prices is important, with the difference in real *GNP* between the 50 and 100 per cent pass-along assumption being equal to 30 to 40 of the 100 per cent assumption. Finally, prices fall initially; but, eventually, economic expansion pushes them back towards the original solution.

# 5

## EVALUATION OF ALTERNATIVE POLICIES

What is obvious is not necessarily best and what is best is not generally obvious, or simple. In the formulation and evaluation of economic policies the problems of the policymaker are complicated by the fact that the currently available rules and criteria for judging the merits of alternative policies are few in number, of limited scope, uncoordinated, and sometimes even contradictory. In the preceding chapters various simple comparisons between different policies were made. For example, policies were ranked on the basis of their effects on many variables after ten quarters. This method for judging policies is obviously crude, as are related techniques of asking what kinds and magnitudes of changes result from a policy action or can be feasibly brought about. Such measures include no efficiency criterion, except perhaps a comparison of gross government expenditure with costs. This chapter examines more sophisticated criteria in order to give increased understanding of the merits of the simulated policies. Attention is first given to some traditional concepts.

### *5.1. Derivation of real input multipliers*

In the post-Keynesian era, alternative policies are often viewed in the light of their impact on real gross national product in a time dimensionless sense. Frequently they are compared on the basis of static "equilibrium" multipliers, the increase in real *GNP* flow achieved per constant or current dollar of expenditure increase or tax reduction flow (or unit change in some other variable) after all transitional effects have subsided. Aside from difficulties arising from policies for which comparable multipliers cannot readily be calculated (for example, monetary measures such as shifts in the discount rate or margin requirements), there are many other problems associated with using this type of indicator. However, these multipliers can provide some valuable information.

First, there is what might be called a *real input multiplier*: the increase in real output flow realized per constant dollar of additional resource input. Defined in the long run with both output and input flows taken on a steady state basis, it corresponds to the traditional "equilibrium" multiplier. On a short-run basis with a constant input flow and with varying output, it has generally been termed a "dynamic" or "impact" multiplier. However, if the structure of the economic system is nonlinear, then even at a given point in time there is no single multiplier for changes in a variable but a whole spectrum of multipliers, one for every change. (Analogously, the slope and point elasticities of demand are only equal in the case of a loglinear function.)

### *5.1.1. Government expenditures*

For government expenditure increases, real input multipliers may be readily calculated; they are simply $\Delta GNP^{54}/\Delta G^{54}$ where $\Delta$ pertains to differences between values of the variable with and without the policy change. The same holds true for individual income tax reductions of fixed constant dollar amounts, $\Delta GNP^{54}/\Delta TP^{54}$. This change in taxes can be viewed as a shift in the constant term of a tax function.

### *5.1.2. Income taxes*

The case of reductions in income tax *rates* is slightly more complicated. Here, the amounts increase over time as the tax base grows, making the definition of a real input multiplier somewhat arbitrary. The most reasonable definition of this multiplier seems to be:

$$\Delta GNP^{54}/(TP-TP')/P_C \tag{5.1}$$

where $TP$ and $TP'$ are the revenues collected from the *original tax base* at the old and the new rates, and their differences is deflated by the implicit price deflator for personal consumption expenditures before the reduction. After several quarters, the rates of increase of $\Delta GNP^{54}$ and $(TP-TP')/P_C$ stabilize, yielding constant multipliers as in the expenditure cases [1]). This result is not conditional on the particular model or tax function used here and should be expected in any stable system. Input multipliers computed using actual tax payments after the rate reduction (for $TP'$) do not have this

---

[1]) This is a biased estimate of the real multiplier, however, because the current increase in real *GNP* is divided by the *current* real tax reduction when in fact the denominator should be a distributed lag. Nevertheless, unless the weights on distant periods are large in relation to those on the current period and the tax reduction grows rapidly, the bias is small.

characteristic and in fact turn negative (assuming that the economy is not initially at full employment). This effect results from the stimulus to *GNP* and the tax base caused by the tax decrease.

### *5.1.3. Excise taxes*

The derivation of real input multipliers for excise tax reductions is similar to their derivation for personal income taxes, as the taxes foregone are calculated and deflated as previously described. However, one additional factor is involved: the degree to which the tax savings are passed along to consumers. These amounts may be deflated by the implicit price deflator for personal consumption expenditures to obtain constant dollar inputs. The selection of a deflator for the amounts not passed along but retained by business is more arbitrary. One fraction of the higher profits is subject to income tax, another is invested, and the remainder is paid out in dividends. The fraction paid in taxes can be treated as an instant offset rather than an induced effect and deducted from the amount of the cut. Then, the real input equivalent of the rest may be obtained by deflating the assumed additional dividends by the consumption deflator and the added retained earnings by the business investment deflator.

Stated algebraically, and assuming that excises not passed along are withheld in the corporate sector, the input equals:

$$\beta\left[\frac{TX-TX'}{P_C}\right]-(1-\beta)(RZ_G)(TX-TX') \\ +(1-\beta)(1-RZ_G)(RDIV)\left[\frac{TX-TX'}{P_C}\right] \\ +(1-\beta)(1-RZ_G)(1-RDIV)\left[\frac{TX-TX'}{P_{IBUS}}\right] \qquad (5.2)$$

where

$\beta$ = pass-along percentage
$TX$ = original excise tax collections
$TX'$ = excise tax collections at new rates applied to original base
$P_C$ = original implicit price deflator for personal consumption expenditures
$RZ_G$ = marginal rate of taxation on corporate profits
$RDIV$ = marginal rate of dividend payout on corporate profits after taxes
$P_{IBUS}$ = implicit price deflator for business fixed investment expenditures.

The first term of this expression is for the amount passed along to consumers; the second, for the amount not passed along that is taxed; the third, for the amount not passed along that is paid out in dividends; and the fourth, the amount retained by business. (The comments on bias in the estimate resulting from use of the *current* period real reduction rather than a distributed lag also apply here.) Although no simulations of corporate income tax reductions were run for this study, the determination of real input multipliers for such changes is identical to that for excise tax cuts.

### *5.1.4. Monetary policies*

For monetary policy shifts, "multipliers" may be calculated showing the increase in real *GNP* per percentage point change in the discount rate, the maximum rate payable on time deposits, stock margin loan limits, and bank reserve requirements, or per billion dollars of open market operations. Since the units of measurement of these ratios differ from one another and from those of the foregoing real input multipliers, they should not be termed "multipliers" and should not be compared directly. For example, it is not useful to say that the real input multiplier on real *GNP* with respect to government expenditures is substantially less than the real *GNP* "multiplier" with respect to the discount rate. A translation of monetary policy changes into real resource equivalents is needed so that the multipliers will be comparable.

Such a translation presents difficulties. While most monetary policies impinge directly on the financial sector and are aimed at achieving targets in terms of the size and distribution of bank liabilities and asset portfolios, the broader objective (leaving aside technical corrections of financial structure) is to influence private spending decisions. Thus, the direct effects of monetary policies on the real sector (defined by partial derivatives of real expenditures with respect to monetary variables) can be taken as a measure of real inputs for the multiplier calculation. For those components of real expenditures directly affected by a given monetary policy, it is possible to ask what exogenous increments in the autonomous components of these expenditures are necessary to produce the monetary policy's change in real *GNP*. Or, alternatively, what is the weighted average real input multiplier of the autonomous components of variables directly affected by monetary policy? The weights are the relative amounts (to the total autonomous change) each of the real variables is directly affected.

This definition of the equivalent real input multiplier is arbitrary. Autonomous real resource inputs are calculated for *all* expenditures which are *directly* affected by monetary policy (through financial variables). The inputs for expenditures that are indirectly affected could be computed. Also, a subset of the directly affected expenditures might be selected. However, in either of these last two cases the procedure is tantamount to dropping the financial terms from those equations which are directly affected but do not enter the input computation. This clearly tends to destroy the notion of "equivalence" to autonomous inputs for expenditure policies. In mathematical terms the monetary policy equivalent real input multiplier is:

$$\frac{\sum_i \frac{dGNP^{54}}{d\bar{C}_j^{54}} \frac{\partial \bar{C}_i^{54}}{\partial MV} \frac{\partial MV}{\partial MP} + \sum_j \frac{dGNP^{54}}{d\bar{I}_j^{54}} \frac{\partial \bar{I}_j^{54}}{\partial MV} \frac{\partial MV}{\partial MP} + \dots}{\sum_i \frac{\partial \bar{C}_i^{54}}{\partial MV} \frac{\partial MV}{\partial MP} + \sum_j \frac{\partial \bar{I}_j^{54}}{\partial MV} \frac{\partial MV}{\partial MP} + \dots} \tag{5.3}$$

where $\bar{C}_i^{54}$ and $\bar{I}_j^{54}$ are the autonomous components (denoted by the "bar" over the symbol) of real consumption and investment, respectively; $MV$ is a vector of financial variables such as the long-term government bond rate ($RM_{\text{GBL}}$), the bill rate ($RM_{\text{GBS3}}$), private demand and time deposits ($DD+DT$), and so forth; and $MP$ is a monetary policy variable (for example, the discount rate, $RM_{\text{FRB}}$). The ... continuation in the numerator and denominator refer to all other real expenditures directly affected by monetary policy. The first product term under each summation sign is the multiplier on the autonomous component; the second product term is the partial derivative of the autonomous component with respect to the financial variables in its explanatory equation; and the third term is the partial derivative of the financial variables with respect to monetary policy in the absence of income and expenditure feedback effects.

For a diagrammatic exposition of a simplified model, consider an increase in the discount rate and the following (incomplete) equation system:

$$\begin{aligned}
RM_{\text{GBL}} &= f(RM_{\text{FRB}}, GNP^{54}) \\
I^{54} &= f(RM_{\text{GBL}}, GNP^{54}) \\
GNP^{54} &= f(I^{54}, C^{54}) \\
C^{54} &= f(GNP^{54}, DD^{54}+DT^{54}) \\
DD^{54}+DT^{54} &= f(GNP^{54}, RM_{\text{FRB}})
\end{aligned} \tag{5.4}$$

where the symbols are as defined previously and $DD^{54}$ and $DT^{54}$ are demand and time deposits deflated by the implicit price deflator for personal consumption expenditures. In figure 5.1 showing the relationships of this model, solid lines represent the initial situation, short dashed lines the solution in response to autonomous investment shifts caused by the increase in the discount rate, and the long dashed lines the final "equilibrium" solution after all reactions (note the deposit term in the consumption function) have taken place. The transition from the initial to "equilibrium" situation is not shown.

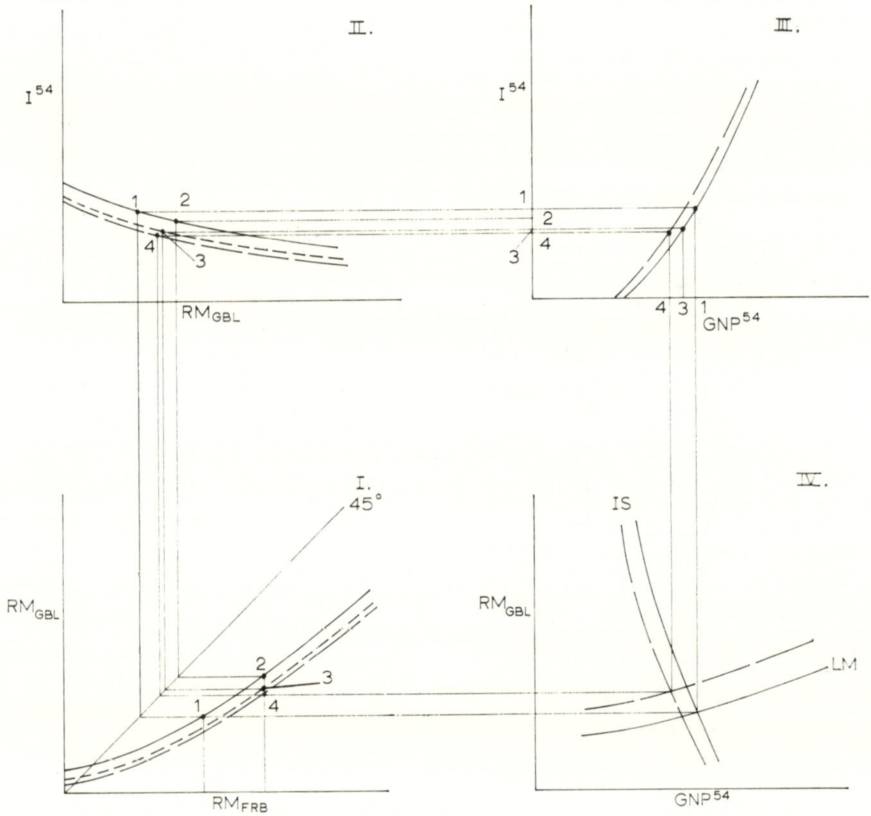


*Figure 5.1. Derivation of equivalent real input multipliers for monetary policies.*

The first equation, in which the government bond rate is a positive function of the discount rate, corresponds to $\partial MV/\partial MP$ and is shown in panel I of the figure. The upward slope of the curves (each of which applies to a different but fixed income level) reflects banks' and other investors' financial portfolio adjustments—of free reserves, government bonds, currency, deposits, and other securities—as borrowing costs are raised by higher discount rates to banks. The original solution to the system is at 1. After the rate increase the initial position is 2, but with the resultant decline in income ($GNP^{54}$) the schedule shifts downward (due to lesser demand for funds) and the final solution is at 4. Point 3 shows the effect of the autonomous investment shift alone.

The second equation's relationship between real gross private domestic investment and the government bond rate (which here is a proxy for a spectrum of capital costs, $\partial \bar{I}^{54}/\partial MV = \partial \bar{I}^{54}/\partial RM_{\text{GBL}}$) at the original and final levels of real $GNP$ may be found in panel II. The points 1, 2, 3 and 4 correspond to those in panel I. The difference between 1 and 2 is the decrease in autonomous investment equivalent to the discount rate increase neglecting monetary terms in the consumption function, that is, $[(\partial \bar{I}^{54}/\partial RM_{\text{GBL}})(\partial RM_{\text{GBL}}/\partial RM_{\text{FRB}})]$, before any income adjustments take place. The difference between 3 and 4 is the additional induced decline in investment generated by the monetary terms in the consumption function.

These terms cause the shift in the investment—$GNP$ schedule of panel III, which is not the identity of $GNP$ equaling the sum of its expenditure components but rather a relationship reflecting induced effects. Therefore, it is invalid to connect point 2 to one of the curves, since it is only the initial autonomous investment amount. The curves have a positive intercept on the abscissa because real $GNP$ will be positive even when real investment is zero (or slightly negative) since consumption can never be negative. They are also concave to the ordinate, to reflect decreasing returns of real $GNP$ to real investment as the latter rises (for example, because of increasing fiscal drag or a greater income elasticity of imports than exports). All points with an identical savings ratio lie on the same curve. Thus, 3 is on the original schedule and the decline in real $GNP$ resulting from the equivalent autonomous decline in real investment $(I_1^{54} - I_2^{54})$ is $(GNP_1^{54} - GNP_3^{54})$. The ratio of these two differences is the unweighted autonomous investment contribution to the equivalent real input multiplier of the discount rate.

The autonomous consumption contribution to this multiplier is $(GNP_3 - GNP_4)$ divided by the decrease in real autonomous consumption (not shown) [2]. In panel III, $GNP_4$ lies on the dashed line, which represents a

[2]) Two panels can be added to the figure. The first, on level with panel I, plot $RM_{\text{GBL}}$ (on the ordinate) and $DD^{54}+DT^{54}$. These curves, one for each income level, are convex to the origin with lower incomes producing shifts to the left. The second panel which lies above the first, has $C^{54}$ on the ordinate and real deposits on the abscissa with the function having a positive intercept and slope and lower incomes generating clockwise twists.

higher savings ratio than the original. This shift occurs because the increase in the discount rate causes bond yields to rise, resulting in substitution of bonds for deposits in asset portfolios. The decline in deposits is reinforced by the drop in income resulting from the equivalent decrease in autonomous investment. Since consumption is positively related to deposits, consumption falls, and the savings ratio (to income) rises. Consequently, when monetary policy is restrictive, the influence of financial factors on consumption requires greater investment at any desired level of real *GNP* than if these factors did not directly impinge on consumers.

Finally, panel IV summarizes all the phenomena previously cited in the well known Hicksian diagram [3]). The monetary and real sectors are in equilibrium at a term structure of interest rates (here $RM_{GBL}$ is a proxy), with savings equaling investment and the demand for funds equaling the supply.

To calculate the equivalent real input multipliers from the diagram the following formula is applied:

$$\left[\frac{GNP_1^{54}-GNP_3^{54}}{I_1^{54}-I_2^{54}} \cdot \frac{I_1^{54}-I_2^{54}}{(I_1^{54}-I_2^{54})+(C_1^{54}-C_2^{54})}\right] + \left[\frac{GNP_3^{54}-GNP_4^{54}}{C_1^{54}-C_2^{54}} \cdot \frac{C_1^{54}-C_2^{54}}{(I_1^{54}-I_2^{54})+(C_1^{54}-C_2^{54})}\right]$$

or

$$\frac{GNP_1^{54}-GNP_4^{54}}{(I_1^{54}-I_2^{54})+(C_1^{54}-C_2^{54})} \tag{5.5}$$

Of course, with an equation system one would evaluate the derivatives shown on page 85. In a nonlinear system, these derivatives would not be constant but would vary with initial conditions and the amount of exogenous policy change. Numerical estimates of real input multipliers for the various policies are presented after a discussion of some additional multiplier concepts.

## *5.2. Real input multipliers for distributive shares*

The use of real input multipliers on real *GNP* as the sole criterion to judge the desirability of alternative policies requires that: (1) the maximum

---

[3]) John R. Hicks, "Mr. Keynes and the 'Classics'; A Suggested Interpretation," *Econometrica*, Vol. 5, No. 2 (1937), pp. 147–159.

increase in total real output be the only desideratum, or (2) that the movement of other variables be perfectly correlated with real *GNP* so that the policy with the highest output clearly dominates all others. The first condition assumes that society is interested only in the quantitative total of its material well-being, without considering the character of its distribution. The second conditions assumes that the real world can be characterized by a system that is linear in variables and parameters and in the reduced form has the same policy elements in all equations in which they appear. Both assumptions are unlikely. There is national concern about the distribution of total product among consumption, investment, and government expenditure and between individuals and corporations, as is shown by publications such as Galbraith's *Affluent Society*, numerous Congressional hearings, and government programs such as the war on poverty. Furthermore, the structure of the economy is nonlinear, and it responds asymmetrically to different policy changes [4]).

Thus, in evaluating alternative policies it is relevant to examine real input multipliers for real disposable income, real personal consumption expenditures, real residential construction, employment, unemployment, and other variables relating to individuals. A real input multiplier for corporate profits deflated by a price index for investment goods can be taken as an indicator of a policy's impact on industry. Real business investment is of interest not for its own sake but because, under the assumption that it embodies some fraction of technical progress, it raises the potential output of the economy, enabling additional policy actions to reap even greater income gains. The same type of reasoning applies to the balance of payments and net exports (in current dollars), where increasing deficits may involve future restrictions to curtail gold outflows and domestic production.

Since government expenditures to a large degree are truly exogenous (and in the present model are wholly exogenous), one cannot speak of a real input multiplier for this variable. In cases where expenditures are increased, the multiplier would be unity and in other instances, zero. With such values, the multiplier is not very useful, and other ways of taking social preferences for higher public expenditures into account must be found.

For government revenue, only tax rates and not tax yields are set exogenously. Therefore, it is possible to examine the increase in real government debt which results from an increase in real resource inputs, that is, a real input multiplier for real debt may be computed. This multiplier can also be

---

[4]) J. K. Galbraith, *The Affluent Society*, (Houghton Mifflin, 1958).

calculated when non-fiscal policy alternatives are compared. The choice of deflators to obtain real from current dollar debt requires assumptions about the marginal distribution of the additional tax burden to meet higher interest charges or to retire the debt. The following formula offers a reasonable first approximation:

$$P_{\mathrm{DBT}} = P_{\mathrm{IBUS}} \frac{TC}{T} + P_{\mathrm{C}} \frac{T-TC}{T} \tag{5.6}$$

where the prices and tax ratios are those existing after the policy change.

The increase in debt is of concern because it involves redistribution of income between taxpayers and bondholders and because, as in the case of other variables (for example, business investment), there are potential consequences for future actions. Excessive government debt–*GNP* ratios may severely hamper future efforts to obtain governmental revenues for desired programs (certainly this is true at the state and local levels) and also cause social strains due to the redistributional elements of deficit financing. Even if there are no absolute limits to the extent that transfers can be made between taxpayers and bondholders (which in itself is doubtful), there are sure to be political repercussions and reductions in output as production incentives are diminished by high marginal tax rates to meet debt servicing costs.

This is not the place to discuss trade offs between deficit and tax financing of government expenditures under varying conditions such as employment, monetary ease, or balance of payments difficulties. Nor is it necessary to consider the alternatives of sales of securities to the central monetary authority, commercial banks, or the non-bank public. It must merely be recognized that: (1) while some debt is necessary for monetary policy open market operations, in peacetime this amount is normally small in relation to *GNP*; and (2) *other things being equal*, that policy should be preferred which results in the smallest increase in the debt. While other things are rarely equal, it would be inconsistent to prefer the low debt policy in cases when they were equal and to ignore debt when they were not. In deciding on the merits of a policy, its debt implications should be considered along with other factors. Such an approach does not imply that deficit financing should not be undertaken in a recession to put idle resources to work. However, against the gains of higher output, there are costs of income redistribution and potential limitations on future actions (the latter need not be absolute and can take the form of an increased marginal cost of funds). While these are second order effects, they are not necessarily negligible [5]).

## *5.3. Fiscal multipliers*

An additional set of multipliers of particular interest to legislative and administration policymakers can be calculated. These current input or *fiscal multipliers* represent the change in the objective variables, such as constant dollar *GNP* or unemployment, divided by the current dollar change in the fiscal policy variables (for example, the excise tax cuts). Their special advantage is that, unlike the real input multipliers, they are expressed in terms the politician can identify. Furthermore, they are useful for federal budget benefit-cost analyses (for example, so much of an increase in employment per dollar of income tax reduction or per dollar of excise tax reduction or per dollar of government expenditure increase). The use of these multipliers is based on the assumption that for stabilization purposes, from the viewpoint of the government generally and from the Treasury in particular, a dollar is a dollar whatever it buys in real terms. However, given their dependence on the current price level, these multipliers are not fixed in magnitude (even with an unchanging economic structure). Thus, they are only relevant to a comparison of policy alternatives at a given point in time or over a brief interval.

If relative or absolute levels of prices change over time, then an initial stabilization program in current dollars will not buy the same amount of goods and services at some future date. Price level relationships imply that the impact of such a program on real *GNP* will be different in the future than at present. Abstracting from the influence of nonlinearities and exogenous conditions, the use of real values in the denominator yields more stable results. However, real input multipliers reveal nothing about fiscal policy in current dollars. Therefore, neither multiplier is completely satisfactory, and

---

[5]) For several years a controversy has raged through the economic literature on whether domestically held debt is a burden and can be transferred between generations. See the collection of articles compiled by James M. Ferguson, *Public Debt and Future Generations* (University of North Carolina Press, 1964) and its review by James Tobin in the *Journal of Finance*, Vol. XX, No. 4, December 1965, pp. 679–82. Whether the debt does or does not involve burdens of the types cited in the Ferguson volume need not concern us here. If it does, then this merely increases the weight accorded the debt in a social preference function.

both the fiscal effectiveness and real input multipliers are necessary for the formulation of desired policies. After considering one additional difficulty in interpreting multiplier results, numerical estimates of these multipliers for various policies will be presented.

## *5.4. Response path considerations*

A common feature of the real world and of econometric models is that reactions to changes are not instantaneous but are stretched out over periods of time. Not all policies have the same time response functions. Therefore, knowledge of long-run or "equilibrium" multipliers is not sufficient for deciding on the relative merits of different policies even when only a single variable is being used as the criterion for the judgment. (The importance of properly defining and estimating distributed lags, must not be underestimated, see chapter 1.) For example, given equal real resource inputs, two policies, A and B, might yield a growth in real *GNP* over time similar to that shown in figure 5.2. Policy B would be preferred until $t_0$, A until $t_1$, and B thereafter.

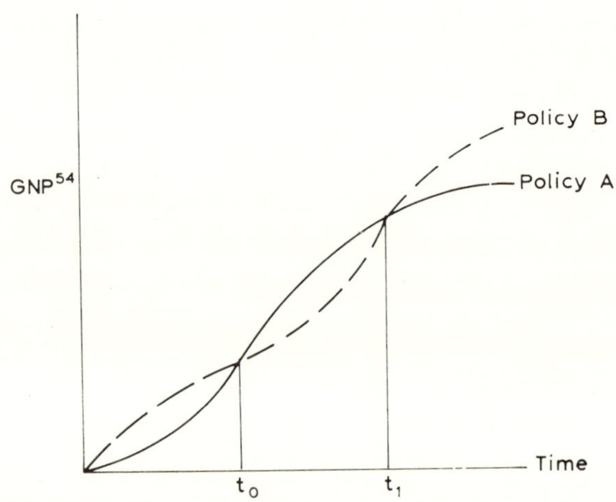


*Figure 5.2. Policy response paths.*

If the policy choices are exclusive (that is either A or B must be chosen and it is impossible to switch from one to the other at $t_0$ or $t_1$), whether A or B should be chosen depends on the relative superiority of each in every period and the social rate of time preference (a time discount factor). The policy with the higher discounted real *GNP* should be selected. Most policy choices are not exclusive in the initial period; a combination can be used. However, for a given total amount of actual or equivalent input, the use of discounted values as the basis for the combination still tends to indicate the correct answer as long as the policies are not too interdependent. That is, total real *GNP* in every period from the combined policies is roughly the weighted sum of the outputs of the policies if adopted separately. Similar behavior is probably true of policies of the same type, such as increases in government expenditures or an easing of monetary policy.

Consequently, the multiplier results of the previous chapters are now presented in two forms: (1) a quarter-by-quarter dynamic path, and (2) a discounted basis.

## 5.5. *Multiplier results*

### 5.5.1. *Actual or equivalent incremental inputs*

Table 5.1 contains the constant and current dollar actual or equivalent incremental inputs used for these multiplier calculations. For the government durable, nondurable, employment, and construction policies the current dollar inputs are derived by multiplying the constant dollar amounts introduced as exogenous stimulants in the simulations by the actual implicit price deflators for the respective expenditures [6]). For the income tax cut, the equivalent input is calculated as described in the beginning of this chapter. The equivalent constant dollar input for the income tax cut plus monetary policy is the sum of the pure income tax cut input and the incremental real *GNP* caused by the combination in policy with the tax cut less that increment divided by the pure income tax cut real input multiplier for real *GNP*. The current dollar input is simply the constant dollar input multiplied by the original solution implicit deflator for personal consumption expenditures.

[6]) Only the overall implicit price deflator for government purchases of goods and services (and not its components) is generated in the model. By the end of the period (1962:4) the original solution value of this deflator is approximately 1.2 per cent greater than the actual value. Thus, using actual rather than simulation values for the component prices causes a very slight downward bias in the current dollar input estimates.

TABLE 5.1

*Constant and current dollar actual or equivalent incremental inputs.*

| | Year and quarter | | | | | | | | | |
|---|---|---|---|---|---|---|---|---|---|---|
| | 1960:3 | 1960:4 | 1961:1 | 1961:2 | 1961:3 | 1961:4 | 1962:1 | 1962:2 | 1962:3 | 1962:4 |
| | Constant dollar inputs (billions of 1954 dollars) | | | | | | | | | |
| Government durables, non-durables, employment and construction | 3.2 | 3.2 | 3.2 | 3.2 | 3.2 | 3.2 | 3.2 | 3.2 | 3.2 | 3.2 |
| Income tax cut | 3.2 | 3.3 | 3.3 | 3.4 | 3.5 | 3.6 | 3.7 | 3.7 | 3.7 | 3.8 |
| Income tax cut plus monetary policy | 3.3 | 3.3 | 3.3 | 3.4 | 3.6 | 3.8 | 3.9 | 4.1 | 4.1 | 4.2 |
| Reserve requirements reduction | −1.1 | 1.0 | 1.9 | 2.8 | 3.6 | 7.6 | 7.1 | 6.6 | 6.3 | 6.0 |
| Open market operations | −1.1 | 1.0 | 1.9 | 2.9 | 3.7 | 7.6 | 7.1 | 6.6 | 6.3 | 5.9 |
| Excise tax cut 1 (small) | | | | | | | | | | |
| 100 per cent pass along | 1.5 | 1.4 | 1.5 | 1.5 | 1.5 | 1.6 | 1.6 | 1.6 | 1.6 | 1.7 |
| 80 per cent pass along | 1.3 | 1.3 | 1.3 | 1.3 | 1.4 | 1.4 | 1.5 | 1.5 | 1.5 | 1.5 |
| 50 per cent pass along | 1.1 | 1.1 | 1.1 | 1.1 | 1.1 | 1.2 | 1.2 | 1.2 | 1.2 | 1.2 |
| Excise tax cut 2 (large) | | | | | | | | | | |
| 100 per cent pass along | 2.5 | 2.5 | 2.5 | 2.5 | 2.6 | 2.7 | 2.7 | 2.8 | 2.8 | 2.8 |
| 80 per cent pass along | 2.2 | 2.2 | 2.2 | 2.3 | 2.3 | 2.4 | 2.5 | 2.5 | 2.5 | 2.5 |
| 50 per cent pass along | 1.8 | 1.8 | 1.8 | 1.9 | 1.9 | 2.0 | 2.0 | 2.0 | 2.0 | 2.1 |
| | Current dollar inputs (billions of current dollars) | | | | | | | | | |
| Government durables expenditures | 3.8 | 3.8 | 3.8 | 3.8 | 3.9 | 3.9 | 3.9 | 3.9 | 3.9 | 3.9 |
| Government nondurables expenditures | 3.1 | 3.3 | 3.5 | 3.4 | 3.1 | 3.4 | 3.3 | 3.4 | 3.4 | 3.3 |
| Government employment | 3.9 | 3.9 | 4.0 | 4.0 | 4.0 | 4.1 | 4.1 | 4.1 | 4.1 | 4.1 |
| Government construction | 3.8 | 3.8 | 3.9 | 3.8 | 3.7 | 3.8 | 3.8 | 3.8 | 3.9 | 3.9 |
| Income tax cut | 3.6 | 3.6 | 3.7 | 3.8 | 3.9 | 4.1 | 4.2 | 4.3 | 4.4 | 4.4 |
| Income tax cut plus monetary policy | 3.6 | 3.6 | 3.8 | 3.9 | 4.1 | 4.3 | 4.5 | 4.7 | 4.8 | 4.9 |
| Reserve requirements reduction | −1.4 | 1.2 | 2.2 | 3.4 | 4.3 | 9.3 | 8.9 | 8.4 | 8.0 | 7.6 |
| Open market operations | −1.4 | 1.2 | 2.2 | 3.4 | 4.4 | 9.4 | 8.9 | 8.3 | 8.0 | 7.5 |
| Excise tax cut 1 (small) | | | | | | | | | | |
| 100 per cent pass along | 1.6 | 1.6 | 1.7 | 1.7 | 1.8 | 1.8 | 1.9 | 1.9 | 1.9 | 1.9 |
| 80 per cent pass along | 1.5 | 1.5 | 1.5 | 1.5 | 1.6 | 1.6 | 1.7 | 1.7 | 1.7 | 1.8 |
| 50 per cent pass along | 1.2 | 1.2 | 1.3 | 1.3 | 1.3 | 1.4 | 1.4 | 1.4 | 1.4 | 1.5 |
| Excise tax cut 2 (large) | | | | | | | | | | |
| 100 per cent pass along | 2.7 | 2.8 | 2.8 | 2.9 | 3.0 | 3.0 | 3.1 | 3.2 | 3.2 | 3.3 |
| 80 per cent pass along | 2.5 | 2.5 | 2.5 | 2.6 | 2.7 | 2.7 | 2.8 | 2.9 | 2.9 | 3.0 |
| 50 per cent pass along | 2.0 | 2.1 | 2.1 | 2.1 | 2.2 | 2.3 | 2.3 | 2.4 | 2.4 | 2.5 |

For the monetary policies, the derivation of real equivalent inputs might have been undertaken as previously outlined. The financial simultaneous equation subsector could have been solved analytically for its semi-reduced form (treating non-financial variables exogenously), and then the various derivatives could have been evaluated. This is a simple matter if the lags are suppressed and the solution is cast in long-run equilibrium terms. However, this method understates the equivalent input because it ignores the transient response which arises from the difference equation structure of the subsystem. For example, a decrease in reserve requirements causes an initial rapid downward movement in interest rates, which subsequently rise as the system absorbs the increased reserves created by the policy shift. If such movements are to be taken into account, the solution must be derived on a quarter-by-quarter basis resulting in a set of highly complex analytical expressions.

Fortunately, it is not necessary to pursue this complicated procedure. The financial subsystem can be solved numerically simply by suppressing the rest of the system and using for the non-financial variables the values of the original solution and for the policy variables the levels after the exogenous shift. The difference between this solution and the original solution is the pure (without income feedbacks) financial sector response to the policy changes. This pure response is then fed into the partial derivatives of those real expenditure functions which have financial terms to obtain the set of equivalent real inputs. When summed, the latter yield the total constant dollar equivalent input. When multiplied by their respective original solution prices and summed, the current dollar equivalent input results.

For excise taxes, real inputs are derived by the formula shown on page 83. Current dollar inputs are calculated by deleting the price terms.

### *5.5.2. Dynamic multipliers*

Based on these inputs, real input and fiscal multipliers were computed for real *GNP* and real consumption; these are given at the end of one, four, seven, and ten quarters in table 5.2. Before examining the results, a word of caution on their interpretation is needed. All the multipliers in the table are calculated with outputs and inputs on a current quarter basis. Thus, particularly in the initial quarters, distributed lagged response terms have not had an opportunity to impart their full effect. Even by the end of the period this is true to some extent. Therefore, the final multipliers may be slightly biased downward. Furthermore, because different policies involve

TABLE 5.2

*Dynamic multipliers for real gross national product and real consumption.*

| | Real input multipliers | | | | Fiscal multipliers | | | |
|---|---|---|---|---|---|---|---|---|
| Final quarter a) | 1960:3 | 1961:2 | 1962:1 | 1962:4 | 1960:3 | 1961:2 | 1962:1 | 1962:4 |
| Number of quarters | 1 | 4 | 7 | 10 | 1 | 4 | 7 | 10 |
| | Dynamic multipliers for real gross national product | | | | | | | |
| Government | | | | | | | | |
| Durables expenditures | 1.6 | 2.1 | 2.7 | 2.7 | 1.4 | 1.8 | 2.2 | 2.2 |
| Nondurables expenditures | 1.4 | 2.4 | 2.8 | 2.9 | 1.5 | 2.3 | 2.6 | 2.8 |
| Employment | 1.7 | 2.1 | 1.9 | 2.0 | 1.9 | 1.7 | 1.5 | 1.5 |
| Construction | 1.6 | 2.4 | 2.9 | 2.9 | 1.4 | 2.1 | 2.5 | 2.3 |
| Income tax cut | 0.8 | 1.1 | 1.2 | 1.2 | 0.7 | 1.0 | 1.0 | 1.1 |
| Income tax cut plus monetary policy with tax cut input | 0.8 | 1.3 | 1.7 | 1.8 | 0.7 | 1.1 | 1.5 | 1.6 |
| Income tax cut plus monetary policy with equivalent input | 0.7 | 1.3 | 1.5 | 1.7 | 0.7 | 1.1 | 1.4 | 1.4 |
| Reserve requirements reduction | 1.3 | 1.5 | 1.2 | 1.5 | 1.0 | 1.3 | 1.0 | 1.2 |
| Open market operations | 1.3 | 1.6 | 1.2 | 1.5 | 1.1 | 1.3 | 1.0 | 1.1 |
| Excise tax cut 1 (small) | | | | | | | | |
| 100 per cent pass along | 1.1 | 1.2 | 1.6 | 1.3 | 1.0 | 1.1 | 1.4 | 1.1 |
| 80 per cent pass along | 1.1 | 1.2 | 1.5 | 1.3 | 0.9 | 1.1 | 1.3 | 1.1 |
| 50 per cent pass along | 0.9 | 1.0 | 1.3 | 1.1 | 0.8 | 0.9 | 1.1 | 0.9 |
| Excise tax cut 2 (large) | | | | | | | | |
| 100 per cent pass along | 1.0 | 1.5 | 2.2 | 2.3 | 0.9 | 1.3 | 1.9 | 2.0 |
| 80 per cent pass along | 0.9 | 1.4 | 2.1 | 2.2 | 0.8 | 1.2 | 1.8 | 1.9 |
| 50 per cent pass along | 0.9 | 1.4 | 2.1 | 2.3 | 0.8 | 1.2 | 1.8 | 1.9 |
| | Dynamic multipliers for real consumption | | | | | | | |
| Government | | | | | | | | |
| Durables expenditures | 0.5 | 0.8 | 1.0 | 1.0 | 0.4 | 0.6 | 0.8 | 0.9 |
| Nondurables expenditures | 0.4 | 0.8 | 1.0 | 1.1 | 0.4 | 0.8 | 1.0 | 1.1 |
| Employment | 0.6 | 0.9 | 0.9 | 0.9 | 0.5 | 0.7 | 0.7 | 0.7 |
| Construction | 0.4 | 0.9 | 1.1 | 1.1 | 0.4 | 0.7 | 0.9 | 0.9 |
| Income tax cut | 0.7 | 1.0 | 1.1 | 1.1 | 0.7 | 0.9 | 0.9 | 1.0 |
| Income tax cut plus monetary policy with tax cut input | 0.7 | 1.0 | 1.3 | 1.5 | 0.7 | 0.9 | 1.1 | 1.2 |
| Income tax cut plus monetary policy with equivalent input | 0.7 | 1.0 | 1.2 | 1.3 | 0.7 | 0.9 | 1.0 | 1.1 |
| Reserve requirements reduction | 0.4 | 0.6 | 0.6 | 0.8 | 0.3 | 0.5 | 0.5 | 0.6 |
| Open market operations | 0.4 | 0.7 | 0.6 | 0.8 | 0.4 | 0.6 | 0.5 | 0.6 |
| Excise tax cut 1 (small) | | | | | | | | |
| 100 per cent pass along | 1.0 | 1.0 | 1.1 | 1.1 | 0.9 | 0.9 | 0.9 | 0.9 |
| 80 per cent pass along | 1.0 | 1.0 | 1.0 | 1.0 | 0.9 | 0.9 | 0.9 | 0.9 |
| 50 per cent pass along | 0.8 | 0.9 | 0.9 | 0.9 | 0.7 | 0.7 | 0.8 | 0.8 |
| Excise tax cut 2 (large) | | | | | | | | |
| 100 per cent pass along | 1.0 | 1.2 | 1.5 | 1.7 | 0.9 | 1.1 | 1.3 | 1.5 |
| 80 per cent pass along | 0.8 | 1.2 | 1.5 | 1.7 | 0.7 | 1.0 | 1.3 | 1.4 |
| 50 per cent pass along | 0.8 | 1.2 | 1.5 | 1.7 | 0.7 | 1.0 | 1.3 | 1.5 |

a) Stimulus introduced beginning 1960:3.

different lags and response patterns, the final absolute gaps between multipliers for the simulations may not be the same as those shown.

Nevertheless, some tentative conclusions can be drawn. On a real input basis, judged at the end of ten quarters, real nonemployment government expenditures seemingly are the most powerful stimulant to real *GNP*. An income tax cut without an accommodating monetary policy does not appear to be very effective. For the cut with such a monetary policy, the ten-quarter multiplier is 1.8 when no account is taken of the implied monetary input and 1.7 when an equivalent input basis is used. In other words, the two policies seem to be highly complementary.

The reserve requirements and open market policies have relatively moderate real input multipliers for real *GNP*. As pointed out in chapter 2, although these monetary policy shifts produce substantial absolute increases in real output, the magnitude of the policy changes themselves are large. Consequently, moderate multipliers are to be expected.

The economies of scale of larger cuts noted earlier are shown by the excise tax real input multipliers. After ten quarters the cut with an initial real input of \$2.5 billion has a multiplier nearly twice that of the \$1.5 billion tax reduction. The result (not cited in chapter 4) is that this conclusion is almost completely independent of the percentage of the reduction passed along. For the smaller cut the real input multipliers under the 50 per cent pass-along assumption are slightly lower than for the 80 and 100 per cent. For the larger cut there is virtually no difference between the three assumptions, indicating the importance of adjusting inputs for leakages and for the prices of their components.

The behavior of real input multipliers for real consumption is much the same as for real *GNP*. However, as might be expected, those policies which have a greater direct impact on consumer disposable incomes have relatively larger multipliers for real consumption than for real *GNP*. This pattern is particularly striking for the income and excise tax cuts in which most of the stimulus of the policies is in the consumption area.

The levels of fiscal multipliers for real *GNP* and real consumption are lower than the corresponding real input multipliers because prices in 1960–62 are higher than in the price base year, 1954. The results also reflect the movement of relative prices between the base year and the simulation period. The prices of government nondurables purchases rose least (mainly due to the stability of farm prices), and those for government employment rose most (measured by an index of compensation per employee) over the interval. This difference in price levels causes the ranking of policies to shift, giving nondurables expenditures the greatest real effect per dollar of current expenditure. The fiscal multiplier superiority of this policy over the durable outlay option is clear.

In case of employment, the apparent superiority might be questioned. It is a convention of the national income and product accounts that no adjustment is made for the increasing productivity of government employees in estimating real output, that is, output is measured on an input basis. This practice biases both the real input and the fiscal multipliers of the employment policy downward. Assuming a productivity increase of from 2 to $2\frac{1}{2}$ per cent per year, the fiscal multiplier for employment is probably about on a par with that for nondurables purchases by 1962:4.

A similar problem occurs with the output measurement of the construction policy which is also on an input basis. However, for these expenditures the bias is probably smaller than for employment.

### *5.5.3. Discounted multipliers*

So far, the multiplier results of the various simulations have been examined quarter by quarter. The need for integrating these results over the entire time path has already been mentioned. One method which accounts for time preference (that is, the desirability of achieving higher outputs earlier in the period) is to determine the average quarterly present "value" of the multiplier stream. The multipliers can be discounted (at the social rate of time preference) as follows:

$$pv_n = \frac{1}{n}\sum_{t=1}^{n} \frac{MULT_t}{(1+r)^t} \tag{5.7}$$

where $MULT_t$ equals the multiplier in quarter $t$; $r$ equals the social rate of time preference; $t$ equals the number of quarters from the start of the simulation; and $n$ equals the number of quarters for which the present value is being determined. These results are given, for a time preference rate of six per cent ($r = 0.06$), in table 5.3. Taking the durables simulation as an example, the entries in the table show that per discounted dollar of inputs over ten quarters, 2.2 discounted dollars of real *GNP* are generated per quarter.

Perhaps the simplest way of contrasting these discounted multiplier results with those computed on a dynamic basis is to review the rank order of policies after a period of ten quarters. These results are shown in table 5.4.

TABLE 5.3

*Average quarterly discounted multipliers for gross national product and real consumption.*

| | Real input multipliers | | | | Fiscal multipliers | | | |
|---|---|---|---|---|---|---|---|---|
| Number of quarters | 1 | 4 | 7 | 10 | 1 | 4 | 7 | 10 |
| Final quarter | 1960:3 | 1961:2 | 1962:1 | 1962:4 | 1960:3 | 1961:2 | 1962:1 | 1962:4 |
| | Average quarterly discounted multipliers for gross national product [a] | | | | | | | |
| Government | | | | | | | | |
| Durables expenditures | 1.6 | 2.0 | 2.0 | 2.2 | 1.3 | 1.6 | 1.7 | 1.8 |
| Nondurables expenditures | 1.4 | 2.0 | 2.1 | 2.2 | 1.5 | 1.9 | 2.1 | 2.2 |
| Employment | 1.6 | 1.9 | 1.8 | 1.8 | 1.4 | 1.5 | 1.5 | 1.4 |
| Construction | 1.6 | 2.1 | 2.3 | 2.3 | 1.4 | 1.8 | 2.2 | 2.0 |
| Income tax cut | 0.8 | 1.0 | 1.0 | 1.0 | 0.7 | 0.9 | 0.9 | 0.9 |
| Income tax cut plus monetary policy with tax cut input | 0.7 | 1.0 | 1.2 | 1.3 | 0.7 | 0.9 | 1.1 | 1.1 |
| Income tax cut plus monetary policy with equivalent input | 0.7 | 1.0 | 1.2 | 1.2 | 0.7 | 0.9 | 1.0 | 1.1 |
| Reserve requirements reduction | 1.2 | 1.6 | 1.4 | 1.4 | 1.0 | 1.3 | 1.2 | 1.1 |
| Open market operations | 1.3 | 1.7 | 1.5 | 1.4 | 1.1 | 1.4 | 1.2 | 1.1 |
| Excise tax cut 1 (small) | | | | | | | | |
| 100 per cent pass along | 1.1 | 1.2 | 1.3 | 1.3 | 1.0 | 1.1 | 1.1 | 1.1 |
| 80 per cent pass along | 1.0 | 1.2 | 1.2 | 1.2 | 0.9 | 1.0 | 1.1 | 1.1 |
| 50 per cent pass along | 0.9 | 1.0 | 1.1 | 1.0 | 0.8 | 0.9 | 0.9 | 0.9 |
| Excise tax cut 2 (large) | | | | | | | | |
| 100 per cent pass along | 1.0 | 1.3 | 1.5 | 1.6 | 0.9 | 1.1 | 1.3 | 1.4 |
| 80 per cent pass along | 0.9 | 1.1 | 1.4 | 1.5 | 0.8 | 1.0 | 1.2 | 1.3 |
| 50 per cent pass along | 0.9 | 1.1 | 1.4 | 1.6 | 0.8 | 1.0 | 1.2 | 1.3 |
| | Average quarterly discounted multipliers for real consumption [a] | | | | | | | |
| Government | | | | | | | | |
| Durables expenditures | 0.5 | 0.6 | 0.7 | 0.8 | 0.4 | 0.5 | 0.6 | 0.6 |
| Nondurables expenditures | 0.4 | 0.6 | 0.7 | 0.8 | 0.4 | 0.6 | 0.7 | 0.8 |
| Employment | 0.6 | 0.7 | 0.8 | 0.8 | 0.5 | 0.6 | 0.6 | 0.6 |
| Construction | 0.4 | 0.7 | 0.8 | 0.8 | 0.3 | 0.6 | 0.6 | 0.7 |
| Income tax cut | 0.7 | 0.8 | 0.9 | 0.9 | 0.7 | 0.7 | 0.8 | 0.8 |
| Income tax cut plus monetary policy with tax cut input | 0.7 | 0.9 | 1.0 | 1.0 | 0.6 | 0.8 | 0.9 | 0.9 |
| Income tax cut plus monetary policy with equivalent input | 0.7 | 0.8 | 0.9 | 1.0 | 0.6 | 0.8 | 0.8 | 0.9 |
| Reserve requirements reduction | 0.4 | 0.6 | 0.6 | 0.6 | 0.3 | 0.5 | 0.5 | 0.5 |
| Open market operations | 0.4 | 0.6 | 0.6 | 0.6 | 0.3 | 0.5 | 0.5 | 0.5 |
| Excise tax cut 1 (small) | | | | | | | | |
| 100 per cent pass along | 1.0 | 1.0 | 1.0 | 1.0 | 0.9 | 0.9 | 0.9 | 0.9 |
| 80 per cent pass along | 1.0 | 1.0 | 1.0 | 1.0 | 0.9 | 0.9 | 0.8 | 0.8 |
| 50 per cent pass along | 0.8 | 0.8 | 0.8 | 0.8 | 0.7 | 0.7 | 0.7 | 0.7 |
| Excise tax cut 2 (large) | | | | | | | | |
| 100 per cent pass along | 1.0 | 1.1 | 1.2 | 1.3 | 0.9 | 1.0 | 1.0 | 1.1 |
| 80 per cent pass along | 0.8 | 1.0 | 1.1 | 1.2 | 0.7 | 0.9 | 1.0 | 1.0 |
| 50 per cent pass along | 0.8 | 1.0 | 1.1 | 1.2 | 0.7 | 0.9 | 1.0 | 1.0 |

[a]) Average per quarter of sum of multipliers discounted quarterly (at an annual rate of 6 per cent) to the beginning of the simulation period, 1960:2.

TABLE 5.4
*Rank order of policy multipliers for real gross national product and real consumption.*

| | Real input multiplier | | Fiscal multiplier | |
|---|---|---|---|---|
| | Dynamic 1962:4 | Discounted [a] Ten quarters | Dynamic 1962:4 | Discounted [a] Ten quarters |
| | Rank order of policy multipliers for real gross national product | | | |
| Government | | | | |
| Durables expenditures | 3 | 3 | 3 | 3 |
| Nondurables expenditures | 2 | 2 | 1 | 1 |
| Employment | 7 | 4 | 8 | 4 |
| Construction | 1 | 1 | 2 | 2 |
| Income tax cut | 14 | 15 | 14 | 14 |
| Income tax cut plus monetary policy with tax cut input | 8 | 10 | 7 | 9 |
| Income tax cut plus monetary policy with equivalent input | 9 | 12 | 9 | 12 |
| Reserve requirements reduction | 10 | 9 | 10 | 10 |
| Open market operations | 11 | 8 | 11 | 8 |
| Excise tax cut 1 (small) | | | | |
| 100 per cent pass along | 12 | 11 | 12 | 11 |
| 80 per cent pass along | 13 | 12 | 13 | 13 |
| 50 per cent pass along | 15 | 14 | 15 | 15 |
| Excise tax cut 2 (large) | | | | |
| 100 per cent pass along | 4 | 5 | 4 | 5 |
| 80 per cent pass along | 6 | 7 | 6 | 7 |
| 50 per cent pass along | 5 | 6 | 5 | 6 |
| | Rank order of policy multipliers for real consumption | | | |
| Government | | | | |
| Durables expenditures | 10 | 13 | 10 | 12 |
| Nondurables expenditures | 8 | 11 | 8 | 9 |
| Employment | 13 | 12 | 13 | 13 |
| Construction | 7 | 9 | 7 | 11 |
| Income tax cut | 6 | 8 | 6 | 8 |
| Income tax cut plus monetary policy with tax cut input | 4 | 4 | 4 | 4 |
| Income tax cut plus monetary policy with equivalent input | 5 | 5 | 5 | 5 |
| Reserve requirements reduction | 15 | 15 | 15 | 15 |
| Open market operations | 14 | 14 | 14 | 14 |
| Excise tax cut 1 (small) | | | | |
| 100 per cent pass along | 9 | 6 | 9 | 6 |
| 80 per cent pass along | 11 | 7 | 11 | 7 |
| 50 per cent pass along | 12 | 10 | 12 | 10 |
| Excise tax cut 2 (large) | | | | |
| 100 per cent pass along | 2 | 1 | 2 | 1 |
| 80 per cent pass along | 3 | 3 | 3 | 3 |
| 50 per cent pass along | 1 | 2 | 1 | 2 |

[a]) At a time preference rate of 6 per cent.

For the most part, the preference order of policies (derived from the rounded figures of table 5.3) is invariant to their ranking either by dynamic or discounted multipliers. Nevertheless, there are some significant exceptions. For real *GNP*, real input and fiscal multiplier rankings tend to fall for the income tax policies and improve for the monetary policies. Also, the rankings for the multipliers for real consumption tend to shift, making the position of the smaller excise tax more favorable and that of the non-employment government expenditure policies less favorable.

## *5.6. Other policy ranking criteria*

However, as noted, increases in real *GNP* and real consumption are not the only criteria relevant to proper policy choice. Price stability is another criterion which has recently received nearly as much attention. It is important because, in the short run, price changes alter the distribution of real and current dollar income and affect the balance of payments. Moreover, price increases may increase the difficulty of attaining full employment when the economy is operating at less than its output potential.

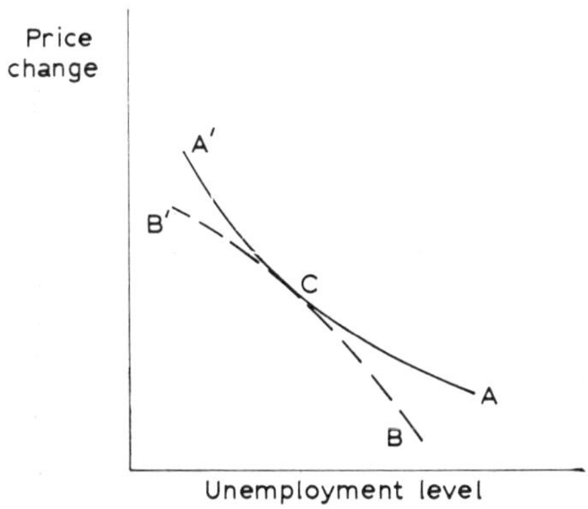


*Figure 5.3. Static Phillips price curve.*

The relationship between the rate of change in prices and the level of unemployment may be shown by using a Phillips price curve. (Given a production function, the rate of unemployment, and some additional information, it is possible to derive real *GNP*. Alternatively, a modified Phillips curve could be drawn to relate price changes to real *GNP* instead of unemployment, and the latter could be derived using a production function.) The usual

Phillips curve, shown as $AA'$ in figure 5.3, summarizes the combination of minimum price changes and unemployment which are obtainable as a given policy is applied in varying amounts [7]). Lower unemployment is accompanied by increased prices (and acceleration of price changes) because of higher wage rates, diminishing returns to scale, and imperfect competition in product markets. $BB'$, one of a set of indifference curves, shows mixtures of price changes and unemployment, no one of which society at large would prefer to any other. The $BB'$ curve is drawn so that as unemployment becomes lower, it must fall even faster to compensate for a fixed increase in prices. Combining $AA'$ and $BB'$, the tangency point $C$ is the price-unemployment position where welfare is maximized for the given policy.

Every policy can be used to generate a Phillips curve. Assuming these curves to be independent, not only can they be represented as in figure 5.4, but they can also form an envelope of Phillips curves such as $D'FE'$. Again, $BB'$ could be superimposed to find the best policy and its size. While this approach seems simple and correct, it suffers from two deficiencies.

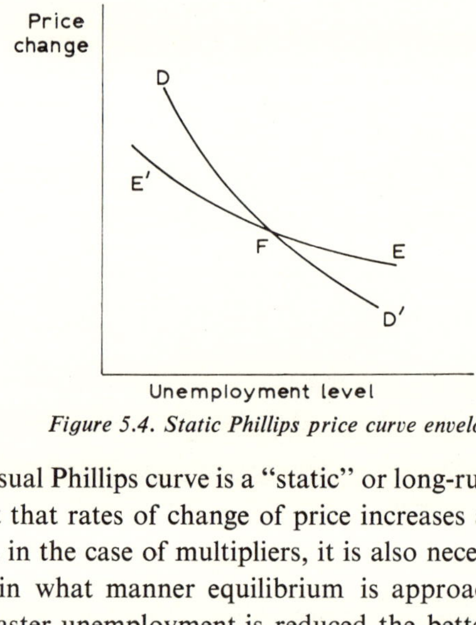


*Figure 5.4. Static Phillips price curve envelopes.*

First, the usual Phillips curve is a "static" or long-run equilibrium concept in the respect that rates of change of price increases are not taken into account. But as in the case of multipliers, it is also necessary to consider how quickly and in what manner equilibrium is approached, because, *ceteris paribus*, the faster unemployment is reduced the better. Moreover, as long as prices are of concern because of income distribution and balance of payments considerations, price changes over time should also be discounted.

---

7) Cf. R. Lipsey, "Structural and Deficient-Demand Unemployment Reconsidered" in A. M. Ross (ed.), *Employment Policy and the Labor Market*, (University of California, 1965) pp. 210–56.

That is, if inflation produces undesirable redistributive effects, then the more distant these are in the future, the less impact they have on current welfare. From a political standpoint such a time lag is not unimportant. Furthermore, the price rises are brought about by lower unemployment, which also acts to redistribute income. Phillips curves, therefore, should be put on a dynamic, discounted basis; figures 5.3 and 5.4 can be redrawn to obtain the relevant dynamic envelope curve.

The second difficulty with the usual Phillips curve concept (even after adjusting it to a dynamic basis) is that it assumes that application of a policy to an increased extent has no adverse effects other than price movements. But, for example, points on *DD'* in figure 5.4 may require smaller amounts of fiscal action and involve a smaller increase in government debt than would be required for points on *EE'*. However, achieving *DD'* may necessitate greater government intervention into the market system than would be necessary to achieve *EE'*. Consequently, even within the framework of the Phillips curve, to make a valid choice between policies, criteria other than prices and unemployment should be considered. Here the focus is on debt because it is possible to show the results diagrammatically.

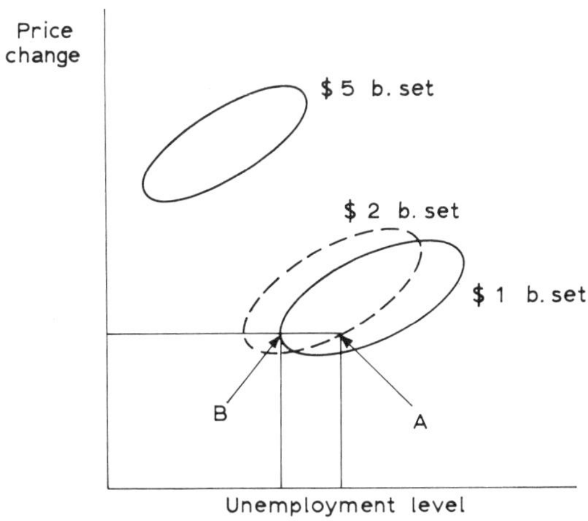


*Figure 5.5. Phillips price curve sets and fiscal action.*

Figure 5.5 shows some representative sets of combinations of prices, unemployment and debt which result from different amounts of fiscal action. The limits of each set are established by examining dynamic discounted Phillips curves for *all* potential policies for given increments in government debt. When the debt is increased, for example, from \$1 billion to \$2 billion, unemployment is lowered and prices are raised along every Phillips curve; thus, all points in the \$2 billion set must lie above and to the left of the *corresponding* points in the \$1 billion set. Of course, the sets can intersect and the distance between corresponding points in the two sets can vary for different policies.

In each set, some points are not relevant because others are more efficient. That is, for any given amount of unemployment the lowest attainable price change is the desired effect, and vice versa. Thus, the most efficient points lie in the southwest quadrant of the set on its boundary. This condition is necessary but insufficient to prove desirability of any boundary point. Efficient points of higher cost sets also must not lie within, or on, lower cost sets. For instance, a point such as *A* on the boundary of the \$2 billion set is not truly efficient because the same amount of unemployment may be obtained with a lower price rise and only \$1 billion of debt.

The converse obviously does not hold; points on lower cost sets are not necessarily dominated by points on higher cost sets when the latter yield lower prices at the same rate of unemployment. For example, point *B* lies on the boundary of the \$1 billion set within the \$2 billion set. To reach the "better" points of the \$2 billion set, extra debt is required.

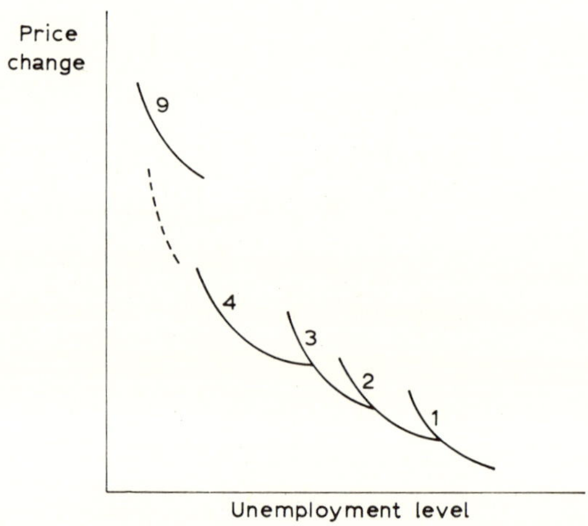


*Figure 5.6. Fiscal action Phillips curve envelope.*

All feasible points from each set can be plotted as in figure 5.6 where 1 indicates the relevant points from the \$1 billion set, 2 those from the \$2 billion set, etc. The discontinuities previously described are shown. The envelope of Phillips curves is not a continuous scallop as in figure 5.4, but is a scallop with interior tails.

To determine the optimum policy graphically, given such an overlapping three-dimensional envelope (in prices, unemployment, and outlays or debt), requires a certain amount of artifice. Assuming that the *utility* of the policy outcomes can be separated into two components, a price-unemployment component and a debt component, a point can be located where the highest price-unemployment partial indifference curve is tangent (or intersects at an extremity) the relevant portion of each cost subset. Connecting these points yields a new envelope adjusted for size of outlay.

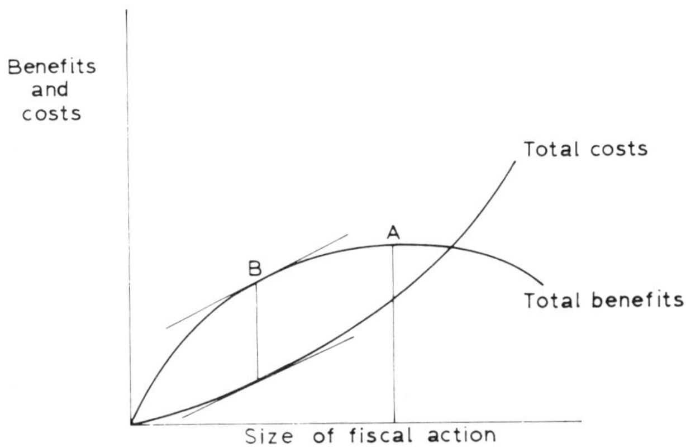


*Figure 5.7. Choice of optimum size fiscal action.*

In effect, each point along this new curve shows the maximum price-unemployment benefits that can be received from a given dollar amount of fiscal policy. To find the best policy, it is necessary to compare these benefits with the disutility costs of increasing fiscal action. This is shown in figure 5.7. The benefits (or total utility) along any envelope do not increase indefinitely. For example, in figure 5.3, *C* is the "best" or highest utility point; thus the benefit curve has a maximum.

If the costs (disutility) of increased size of fiscal action are zero, then the cost function is horizontal and the maximum point (*A*) is chosen as the optimum policy. If, as is more likely, the cost curve rises continuously, the best size and policy choice is where the slopes of the total cost and benefit functions are equal. (The slope of the cost curve becomes steeper as the size of outlays grows, because if the funds are raised by additional taxation the marginal utility of income foregone rises. If the funds are raised by borrowing, the arguments presented earlier apply.)

This consideration of Phillips curve effects is static. Furthermore, it has presumed knowledge of an indifference tradeoff between at least two elements (prices and unemployment or prices and real output), if not three (the third being debt or the size of policy expenditure). An implicit, if not explicit, utility function has entered the analysis. If it can be used to provide answers to three-dimensional tradeoffs, then certainly other criteria relevant to policy choices might also be included. And perhaps it might be possible also to include dynamic response considerations in the utility function measurements.

## 5.7. *Utility evaluation of alternative policies*

### 5.7.1. *Utility functions*

A utility function represents subjective tradeoffs between different criteria. In two-dimensional diagrammatic form it is a curve which show the amounts of two elements that leave the chooser equally well off, in subjective terms. As previously discussed, when more criteria are added this technique becomes cumbersome; hence, it is desirable to convert the analysis to the equivalent mathematical form.

The basic format for any utility function is:

$$u = u(x_1, x_2, \ldots, x_n) \tag{5.8}$$

where $u$ is the utility function which depends on the arguments $x_1, x_2, \ldots x_n$. These arguments would be such variables as consumption, investment, unemployment, and prices. For the purpose of measuring or ranking the desirability of policy alternatives, it is necessary to be more specific about the form of the functional dependency.

One of the simplest forms is the linear:

$$u = \sum_i \beta_i x_i = \beta_1 x_1 + \beta_2 x_2 + \ldots + \beta_n x_n. \tag{5.9}$$

In terms of changes, in this function the willingness to trade an amount of $x_i$ for a unit of any other argument $x_j$ (denoted the marginal rate of substitution), is $-\beta_j/\beta_i$. In other words, this form has the property that the increase in any $x_i$ always adds an equal amount to $u$ regardless of the *level* of all other $x$'s. This seems unrealistic for most situations since the level of unemployment, for example, affects the tolerance for price movements [8]). However, except under extraordinary circumstances or unusual preferences, the linear form is a limiting case; therefore, it will be one of the functions used in the subsequent illustrative utility computations.

Once interdependence between variables is introduced, an infinite number of forms of the utility function is available. A Cobb-Douglas and a constant elasticity of substitution type have been selected for the analysis because they have the desired properties (with appropriate parameters) of diminishing marginal utilities and rates of substitution and are also well known and well explored.

The Cobb-Douglas function is:

$$u = \prod x_i^{\beta_i} = x_1^{\beta_1} x_2^{\beta_2} \ldots x_n^{\beta_n}, \tag{5.10}$$

which has a marginal rate of substitution between any two arguments (the $x$'s) of:

$$-\frac{\beta_j}{\beta_i}\frac{x_i}{x_j}. \tag{5.11}$$

A constant elasticity of substitution (CES) function is:

$$u = [\sum_i \beta_i x_i^\delta]^{1/\delta} = [\beta_1 x_1^\delta + \beta_2 x_2^\delta + \ldots + \beta_n x_n^\delta]^{1/\delta}. \tag{5.12}$$

Its marginal rates of substitution (MRS) are:

$$-\frac{\beta_j}{\beta_i}\left[\frac{x_i}{x_j}\right]^{1-\delta}. \tag{5.13}$$

Furthermore, the elasticity of substitution (which is the quotient of the rates of proportional change of the ratio of the arguments and the marginal rate of substitution), $\sigma$, equals $1/(1-\delta)$. By substitution for $\delta$ in the last MRS expression, it can be seen that the linear and Cobb-Douglas functions are special cases of the CES. For the former, $\delta = 1$ and $\sigma = \infty$; for the latter, $\delta = 0$ and $\sigma = 1$. Also, if the arguments in the function are demanded in fixed proportions, this is given by the special case of $\delta = -\infty$, $\sigma = 0$.

These characteristics may be shown for two arguments as in figure 5.8. Each curve represents a utility isoquant for exchanges of $x_1$ and $x_2$. [The functions are scaled arbitrarily to coincide at the point (1,1).]

---

[8]) In the Phillips curve diagram, the indifference set becomes a series of straight lines with constant slope equaling the marginal rate of substitution.

The case in which $\delta$ is larger than unity implies that the greater the amount of an argument obtained (moving along the curve), the more it is preferred to the other argument. Obviously, this case is only applicable in very unusual circumstances and normally can be neglected.

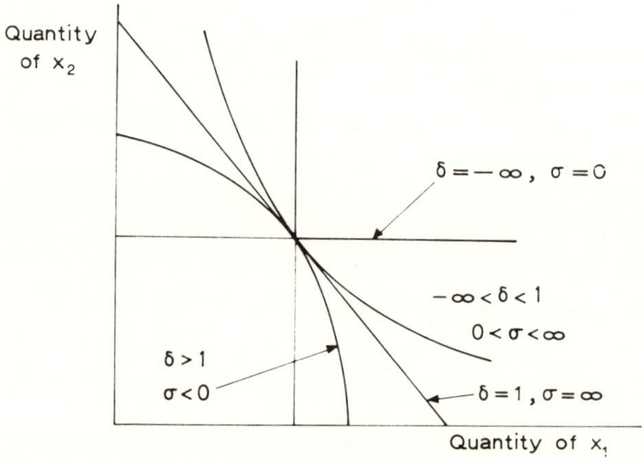


*Figure 5.8. Utility functions.*

### 5.7.2. *Ambiguity of quadratic utility functions*

An additional type of utility function is the quadratic. In its simplest form this is simply the square of a linear function, for example:

$$u = (\sum_i \beta_i x_i)^2. \tag{5.14}$$

It can be shown that the marginal rates of substitution for this function are identical to the linear, that is, $(\beta_i/\beta_j)$. The quadratic can also be transformed into disutility terms. Rather than having the objective to maximize a function with the arguments expressed as deviations from zero, the objective is to minimize the deviations from desired targets [9]). Call these $x_i^*$. Then a linear disutility function would read:

$$d = \sum_i \beta_i(x_i - x_i^*), \tag{5.15}$$

and a quadratic,

$$d = [\sum_i \beta_i(x_i - x_i^*)]^2. \tag{5.16}$$

[9]) Cf. H. Theil, *Economic Forecasts and Policy* (North-Holland, 1958).

(Except in perverse instances, all $\beta_i$ are greater than or equal to zero.) Again, the marginal rates of substitution in these two forms are identical.

However, this is not true with more general forms of the quadratic, as in the two-variable case which might be written:

$$d = \beta_1'(x_1-x_1^*)^2+\beta_2'(x_2-x_2^*)^2+\beta_3'(x_1-x_1^*)(x_2-x_2^*). \qquad (5.17)$$

If $\beta_1' = \beta_1^2$, $\beta_2' = \beta_2^2$ and $\beta_3' = 2\beta_1\beta_2$, then this is simply the square of the linear function $d = \beta_1(x_1-x_1^*)+\beta_2(x_2-x_2^*)$. If the parameters are not so constrained, then the marginal rates of substitution are ratios of linear combinations of the deviation arguments.

The temptation is strong to drop the last interaction term (that is, to let $\beta_3' = 0$) to simplify subsequent analyses. This has the unfortunate consequence of invalidating the entire approach, as is shown in figure 5.9.

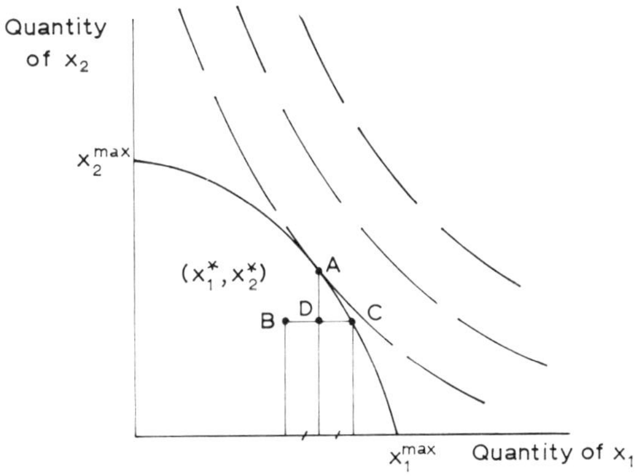


*Figure 5.9. Quadratic utility function ambiguity.*

In this figure, the solid line is the production possibilities frontier; it shows the limit of all combinations of $x_1$ and $x_2$ that are technically achievable. The dashed lines are utility isoquants before being put in deviation from target form. If $A$ is the optimum point which defines the desired quantities $x_1^*$ and $x_2^*$, and the interaction term is dropped, then the disutility function does not discriminate between points $B$ and $C$ [10]). That is, because $BD = DC$, it yields identical values for the two points and does not indicate that $C$ is preferred.

---

[10]) $A$ is the optimum point on both the utility and disutility functions. But even if $A$ were not optimal, for instance, if it were located at the point where the perpendicular intersects the $x_1$ axis, the disutility function would not discriminate between $B$ and $C$.

It might seem that this problem could be avoided by arbitrarily selecting low values for $x_1^*$ and $x_2^*$ so that deviations from them are always positive; however, this forces the solution to interior points in the production possibility set even though higher utilities are attainable. The alternative of making all deviations negative by choosing a point outside of the set greater than $(x_1^{max}, x_2^{max})$ also yields incorrect answers if the utility function is nonlinear.

By now it should be clear that quadratic disutility functions (or, in general, nonlinear functions) expressed in terms of deviations from desired positions must include interaction terms. In addition, the desired positions cannot be chosen arbitrarily (as some writers have erroneously assumed) and must be on the production possibility frontier [11]). Also, the desired points about which the disutility of deviations are calculated depend on the utility function, and must be such that when all deviations are zero, no higher utility positions are achievable.

Taken together, these conditions require that the evaluation of disutilities of given policies be undertaken in a two-step procedure. In the initial step, with a specified model of the economy and a disutility function, disutility is minimized subject to a potential real *GNP* constraint; this yields the desired target values. In the second step, these targets and the disutility function are used to determine the desirability of the outcomes of different policies. The procedure produces a measure of the deviations from optimum positions, but has little else to recommend it.

Policies may be ranked more easily simply by applying a utility function to the values of the arguments resulting from each policy directly (which requires no knowledge of the technical frontier), rather than employing the indirect disutility approach. Moreover, the latter's requirement for the complete determination of the technical possibilities frontier cannot always be met, and even if satisfied, often involves many additional assumptions and approximations. For these reasons only the direct approach is used here.

### *5.7.3. Adjustments for dynamic response*

Some adjustments to the standard method of utility evaluation are required, however, because of the dynamic response of the economy to fiscal and

---

[11]) For example, John H. Wood, "Linear Decision Rules for Economic Stabilization and Growth: Comment," *Quarterly Journal of Economics*, May 1965, pp. 310–316. Theil, *op. cit.*, does not make this error.

monetary policy changes. These lag responses are different for each policy and vary over (simulation) time. Therefore, one cannot select the "best" policy for period 1 and then the "best" for period 2 because the solution for the latter period depends on that for the former (exclusive of any additional policy measures undertaken in the second period). Thus, it becomes necessary to determine the utility value of the entire path for each policy.

This problem has received attention from other writers, the most impressive treatment being that of Koopmans [12]). A less technical discussion is given by J. R. Hicks [13]). The Koopmans-Hicks analysis begins with a statement of certain assumptions. The first is that the utility function is homogenous with marginal rates of substitution independent of the absolute (but not the relative) level of the arguments. For the formulation of optimal growth programs this may be an important condition. For the evaluation of stabilization policies it is not of great significance since the differences in levels between policies are likely to be small.

The second assumption is that the utility function is stationary, that is, that the inter-temporal want system remains fixed in time, and choices are independent of when they are made. Therefore, the marginal rate of substitution between periods $t$ and $t+m$ is constant and does not depend on whether the choice is made at present, or in the future, or whether $t$ is today or several years from now. This assumption is valid only when tastes do not change. Again, as for the first condition, the requirement that the utility function be stationary is far more important for growth than cyclical analyses. In the short run, tastes can be assumed to be constant, so stationarity is assured.

Finally, the third condition is that the utilities of different periods are separate and independent. This means that they may be added to determine the total utility of the outcome path of a policy.

Combining these three conditions results in the requirement that the economy be on a constant growth path, that is, be on a ray solution with equiproportional growth in each period. Assuming that there is a positive rate of time preference, $r$, then aggregate utility is the discounted sum of all future period utilities, or:

$$u_0(x) = \sum_{t=1}^{\infty} \frac{u_t(x)}{(1+r)^t}. \tag{5.18}$$

The discount rate, $r$, need not be constant.

---

[12]) Tjalling C. Koopmans, "Stationary Ordinal Utility and Impatience," *Econometrica*, Vol. 28, No. 2, April 1960.

[13]) John R. Hicks, *Capital and Growth* (New York, Oxford University Press, 1965).

This approach cannot, however, be applied directly to the determination of the utility of a cyclical path which is not characterized by equiproportional growth. The principal adjustment to be made is to remove the restriction of the independence assumption. This adjustment has two aspects. First, there is the distribution of total output over time. For example, a policy which provided for subsistence income in initial periods while creating a larger amount in the more distant future would probably not be considered acceptable by most observers. Second, there is the own rate of change of the arguments in the utility function and their relationship to the rates of change of the other arguments. For example, the consumer would probably prefer an equal interperiod rate of change in the supply of bread to one that fluctuated wildly. Moreover, he would probably want the availability of butter to have nearly the same pattern. While these are complementary goods, the same probably holds true for substitutes; at the margin (as well as on the average) there is some utility to freedom of choice.

Taking these two aspects into account leads to the conclusion that utilities must be calculated for each period on the basis of the arguments of that period, then discounted, and then summed over all periods. For example, with two arguments and two periods ($x_{ij}$—$i$ is the argument number, and $j$ the period) and a Cobb-Douglas function:

$$u_1 = x_{11}^{\beta_1} x_{21}^{\beta_2}; \qquad u_2 = x_{12}^{\beta_1} x_{22}^{\beta_2}; \tag{5.19}$$

and

$$u_0 = \frac{u_1}{1+r} + \frac{u_2}{(1+r)^2}. \tag{5.19}$$

(For most nonlinear utility functions, using discounted utilities is preferable to taking the utility of the discounted arguments because the marginal rate of substitution between $x_{11}$ and $x_{12}$ depends on the values of $x_{21}$ and $x_{22}$ under the former, but not under the latter discounting alternative.)

Furthermore, a variance-covariance matrix of the arguments should be included in the multiperiod function to reflect the disutility of increased variability of the arguments [14]). To simplify the analysis, in many instances

---

[14]) For example, in the Cobb-Douglas and CES cases, the utility functions might be written as (ignoring discounting and scaling factors):

$$u_o = \Pi\, (\sum_j x_{ij})^{\beta_i}, \quad \text{and} \tag{5.20}$$

$$u_o = (\sum_i \beta_i (\sum_j x_{ij})^{\delta}]^{1/\delta}, \tag{5.21}$$

respectively.

merely accounting for the disutility of the variances might suffice. This could be done by using as elements in the utility function the reciprocal of the variances of the $x_i$ arguments ($1/v_i$), i.e., utility increases as the variances decrease. In the Cobb-Douglas case, for example:

$$u_v = \prod \left(\frac{1}{v_i}\right)^{\beta_i} = \left(\frac{1}{v_1}\right)^{\beta_1} \left(\frac{1}{v_2}\right)^{\beta_2} \cdots \left(\frac{1}{v_n}\right)^{\beta_n}. \tag{5.22}$$

The $\beta_i$'s here need not necessarily be the same values (implying relative weights) as those on the corresponding $x_i$'s. However, for the sake of simplicity and in the absence of any other information or a priori estimates, this seems to be a reasonable assumption.

Presumably, just as in behavioral models of individuals' expected value-risk aversion decisions, there are tradeoffs between the levels of a set of outcomes and their variances [15]). Moreover, these tradeoffs tend to take the form of the usual convex indifference surface with an elasticity of substitution ranging between zero and infinity. Thus, given $u_v$, there are many alternatives for defining the total utility of a cyclical path as a combination of $u_0$ and $u_v$. All the same functional forms as were used in the determination of utility within a period could be applied. Since the calculations are for illustration, only those for the linear form are presented. Total utility is defined as the sum of the outcome and variance utilities, or:

$$u_T = \gamma_1 u_0 + \gamma_2 u_v \tag{5.23}$$

where the $\gamma$'s are relative weights.

### *5.7.4. Scaling*

Interest centers on the impact of policy action in changing the path of movement of the economy. All policies start from the same base—the original solution. Therefore, the arguments might be scaled by calculating them as differences between the simulation and original solutions. This approach has two drawbacks. The deviations are in absolute terms (for example, the constant dollar difference in consumption or investment), making the selection of appropriate weights more difficult. Furthermore, a zero deviation of *any* argument in a quarter, irrespective of the values of other arguments,

---

[15]) Much has been written on investment decisions under uncertainty. The classic article on the subject is Harry Markowitz, "Portfolio Selection," *Journal of Finance*, VII, March 1952, pp. 77–91.

involves a zero utility for that quarter because two of the utility functions are multiplicative. For both reasons, the arguments are defined as the ratios of the simulation to the control solution results, that is, a zero change equals a ratio of unity. The weights that must be selected then apply to percentage changes in the arguments.

Similarly, scaling is necessary to prevent a zero variance of any argument in a multiplicative function from indicating infinite utility. Also, for the purpose of specifying weights, the variances should be put in standardized rather than absolute units. One way of doing this is to use a modified coefficient of variation. If the standard deviation of an argument $x_i$ about its mean is $s_i$ ($s_i^2 = v_i$), and the mean of $x_i$ is $\bar{x}_i$, then the coefficient of variation is:

$$c_{x_i} = \frac{s_i}{\bar{x}_i}. \tag{5.24}$$

If the numerator is redefined so that it includes the mean, or

$$c'_{x_i} = \frac{s_i + \bar{x}_i}{\bar{x}_i}, \tag{5.25}$$

then when $s_i = 0$, $c'_{x_i} = 1$. The bounds of $c'_{x_i}$ are 1 and $\infty$. Other things being equal, utility increases as $c'_{x_i}$ approaches unity. Therefore, the arguments in the variance utility function are the reciprocals of the $c'_{x_i}$. For example, the Cobb-Douglas function reads:

$$u_v = \prod \left(\frac{1}{c'_{x_i}}\right)^{\beta_i} = \left(\frac{1}{c'_{x_1}}\right)^{\beta_1} \left(\frac{1}{c'_{x_2}}\right)^{\beta_2} \left(\frac{1}{c'_{x_n}}\right)^{\beta_n} \cdots \tag{5.26}$$

*5.7.5. Summary of utility evaluation procedure*

Before presenting the numerical results, it may be helpful to summarize the preceding discussion.

1. Three different utility functions are to be applied in the evaluation of the various policies:

a. Linear $u_t = \sum_i \beta_i x_i$

b. Cobb-Douglas $u_t = \prod x_i^{\beta_i}$

c. CES $u_t = (\sum_i \beta_i x_i^{\delta})^{1/\delta}$

where $u_t$ is the utility in period $t$ of the ratios of simulation to original solution values ($x_i$). For the CES, $\delta$ is set at 0.5, $-0.5$, $-1.0$, and 2.0.

2. The following sets of weights are used:
a. Equal weights, $\beta_i = 1$ for all $i$;
b. Proportional weights, $\beta_i$ = average share in real *GNP* for expenditure items (with one exception) and 0.5 for all other items.

3. Six arguments ($x_i$) are employed ($\beta$'s are the proportional weights):
a. Real personal consumption expenditures ($\beta = 0.67$);
b. Real gross private domestic investment other than inventory investment ($\beta = 0.13$);
c. Real government expenditures ($\beta = 0.19$);
d. The reciprocal of the rate of unemployment ($\beta = 0.5$);
e. Current dollar government surplus ($\beta = 0.10$);
f. The reciprocal of the implicit price deflator for *GNP*.

4. The utility of outcomes is to be aggregated over time by:

$$u_0 = \sum_{t=1}^{m} \frac{u_t}{(1+r)^t},$$

where $r$ equals a time preference rate (in ratio form—4, 6, 8 and 10 per cent are used) and $m$ is some time horizon limit.

5. The utility of the variance of outcomes is calculated with the modified coefficients of variation, $c'_{x_i}$, as arguments in the same respective form of function as for the utility of the outcomes, that is, linear, Cobb-Douglas, and CES. The identical $\beta$ and $\delta$ weights are used. Total utility is taken as the sum of the outcome and variance utilities (with equal weights):

$$u_T = u_0 + u_v.$$

### 5.7.6. *Illustrative results*

The foregoing summary outlines a large number of utility computations; only a sample of the results can readily be presented. Table 5.5 shows indexes of utility in selected quarters (that is, indexes of $u_t$ for four functions: linear, Cobb-Douglas, CES ($\delta$ = —0.5), and CES ($\delta = -1$), with the arguments weighted on a proportional basis. The index base is the utility of the income tax cut plus monetary policy in 1960:3. This policy has the lowest utility of any of the alternative policies in that quarter using any of the four functions. Despite a substantially higher real *GNP*, its utility is lower than that of the pure monetary policies because of its much lower government surplus. It is also lower than the pure income tax cut because its slightly lower interest rates in the first quarter, through their effect on interest income, cause somewhat lower real consumption.

The results should be examined separately for each utility function. No comparisons of index values should be made across functions. Deliberately, adjustments have not been introduced to make the absolute scales of the functions comparable. The choice to be made is not between functions (which is the province of the political process) but between policies, given the functions. Therefore, for a function one might look at the percentage differences in the utility indexes (the latter, of course, is a cardinal type measure). But, for reasons of statistical significance, accuracy of data inputs, and uncertainty about the validity of equation specifications in the model, this should only be done in an orders of magnitude sense. Consequently, an ordinal ranking (with some awareness of absolute differences) is probably a preferred method of comparison.

On this basis it appears, judging from within quarter utilities (table 5.5) in the initial quarter, that the government employment, monetary policies, and small excise cut are the superior alternatives; the construction and durable expenditure increases and large excise cut are about comparable and somewhat less preferred; and the nondurables expenditures and income tax cuts are quite inferior. In the tenth quarter some of these rankings have changed. The monetary policies still rank at the top, but they are joined by all the expenditure increases. The small excise tax cut has fallen to the bottom to join the pure income tax cut, while the income tax cut plus monetary policy has moved up to join the large excise tax cut in the middle range.

These shifts in within-quarter rankings indicate the importance of calculating discounted utilities (see table 5.6). Here, except for the linear function, the smaller excise cut maintains its superiority over the larger excise cut in all ten quarters. Also, the degree of this superiority depends on the elasticity of substitution—the higher the elasticity the lower is the superiority [16]). Some of the other rankings also shift; the income tax cut plus monetary policy is again nearer to the bottom; and the employment policy has fallen to the middle range.

---

[16]) This conclusion is not affected by the choice of alternative discount rates in the range from 4 to 10 per cent. Similarly, none of the other rankings change if different time preference rates in this range are used to calculate discounted utility.

TABLE 5.5

*Indexes of utility in selected quarters* [a)]

*(arguments weighted on a proportional basis).*

| | Number of quarters and final quarter | | | | | | | |
|---|---|---|---|---|---|---|---|---|
| | 1 | 4 | 7 | 10 | 1 | 4 | 7 | 10 |
| | 1960:3 | 1961:2 | 1962:1 | 1962:4 | 1960:3 | 1961:2 | 1962:1 | 1962:4 |
| | Utility function Linear ($\delta = 1, \sigma = \infty$) | | | | Utility function Cobb-Douglas ($\delta = 0, \sigma = 1$) | | | |
| Government | | | | | | | | |
| Durables expenditures | 102.1 | 104.9 | 106.2 | 107.7 | 108.7 | 116.4 | 120.0 | 123.4 |
| Nondurables expenditures | 100.4 | 104.3 | 106.0 | 107.1 | 101.3 | 114.7 | 119.7 | 122.1 |
| Employment | 102.7 | 107.2 | 106.1 | 106.4 | 110.5 | 122.1 | 119.6 | 120.5 |
| Construction | 101.8 | 105.5 | 107.0 | 107.9 | 107.4 | 118.1 | 121.8 | 123.9 |
| Income tax cut | 100.1 | 101.3 | 103.4 | 104.4 | 100.3 | 104.7 | 113.2 | 115.7 |
| Income tax cut plus monetary policy | 100.0 | 101.8 | 104.6 | 105.5 | 100.0 | 106.6 | 116.0 | 118.5 |
| Reserve requirements reduction | 102.4 | 106.7 | 108.7 | 108.6 | 111.3 | 120.5 | 125.4 | 125.3 |
| Open market operations | 102.3 | 106.8 | 108.7 | 108.6 | 111.2 | 120.7 | 125.4 | 125.2 |
| Excise tax cut 1 (small) | | | | | | | | |
| 100 per cent pass along | 102.4 | 102.8 | 103.7 | 103.8 | 111.0 | 111.8 | 114.4 | 114.6 |
| 80 per cent pass along | 102.4 | 102.7 | 103.6 | 103.7 | 111.0 | 111.7 | 114.1 | 114.2 |
| 50 per cent pass along | 102.3 | 102.5 | 103.2 | 103.3 | 110.9 | 111.3 | 113.3 | 113.4 |
| Excise tax cut 2 (large) | | | | | | | | |
| 100 per cent pass along | 101.5 | 102.2 | 104.8 | 105.6 | 107.5 | 108.3 | 116.7 | 118.7 |
| 80 per cent pass along | 101.5 | 102.0 | 104.3 | 105.1 | 107.7 | 108.1 | 115.5 | 117.5 |
| 50 per cent pass along | 101.3 | 101.7 | 103.9 | 104.6 | 107.4 | 107.5 | 114.6 | 116.4 |
| | Utility function CES ($\delta = -0.5, \sigma = 0.67$) | | | | Utility function CES ($\delta = -1, \sigma = 0.5$) | | | |
| Government | | | | | | | | |
| Durables expenditures | 106.1 | 110.0 | 111.9 | 113.3 | 109.3 | 113.8 | 116.0 | 117.5 |
| Nondurables expenditures | 100.9 | 109.2 | 111.7 | 112.8 | 101.3 | 113.0 | 115.8 | 116.9 |
| Employment | 107.0 | 112.7 | 111.7 | 112.0 | 110.4 | 116.8 | 115.7 | 116.1 |
| Construction | 105.2 | 110.9 | 112.6 | 113.5 | 108.0 | 114.9 | 116.8 | 117.6 |
| Income tax cut | 100.2 | 103.3 | 108.7 | 109.8 | 100.3 | 105.0 | 112.6 | 113.8 |
| Income tax cut plus monetary policy | 100.0 | 104.5 | 110.0 | 111.1 | 100.0 | 106.8 | 114.0 | 115.2 |
| Reserve requirements reduction | 107.9 | 111.9 | 114.1 | 114.1 | 111.9 | 116.0 | 118.2 | 118.1 |
| Open market operations | 107.9 | 112.0 | 114.1 | 114.0 | 111.9 | 116.0 | 118.2 | 118.1 |
| Excise tax cut 1 (small) | | | | | | | | |
| 100 per cent pass along | 107.7 | 108.0 | 109.3 | 109.4 | 111.6 | 111.9 | 113.4 | 113.5 |
| 80 per cent pass along | 107.7 | 108.0 | 109.2 | 109.2 | 111.6 | 111.9 | 113.2 | 113.3 |
| 50 per cent pass along | 107.7 | 107.9 | 108.8 | 108.9 | 111.6 | 111.8 | 112.8 | 112.9 |
| Excise tax cut 2 (large) | | | | | | | | |
| 100 per cent pass along | 105.6 | 105.7 | 110.3 | 111.3 | 108.8 | 108.5 | 114.4 | 115.4 |
| 80 per cent pass along | 105.7 | 105.7 | 109.8 | 110.7 | 109.1 | 108.7 | 113.8 | 114.8 |
| 50 per cent pass along | 105.6 | 105.4 | 109.4 | 110.2 | 108.9 | 108.4 | 113.4 | 114.3 |

[a)] Table values are $u_t$ in the quarter of the column headings placed on an index basis. For each type of function the index base equals the utility of the income tax cut plus monetary policy in 1960:3.

TABLE 5.6

*Quarterly averages of indexes of discounted utility* [a]
*(arguments weighted on a proportional basis).*

| | Number of quarters and final quarter | | | | | | | |
|---|---|---|---|---|---|---|---|---|
| | 1<br>1960:3 | 4<br>1961:2 | 7<br>1962:1 | 10<br>1962:4 | 1<br>1960:3 | 4<br>1961:2 | 7<br>1962:1 | 10<br>1962:4 |
| | Utility function Linear ($\delta = 1, \sigma = \infty$) | | | | Utility function Cobb-Douglas ($\delta = 0, \sigma = 1$) | | | |
| Government | | | | | | | | |
| Durables expenditures | 100.6 | 100.0 | 98.8 | 97.4 | 107.2 | 109.2 | 109.4 | 108.8 |
| Nondurables expenditures | 99.0 | 98.7 | 98.0 | 96.7 | 99.9 | 104.0 | 106.3 | 106.4 |
| Employment | 101.3 | 101.2 | 99.7 | 97.7 | 108.9 | 111.9 | 111.3 | 109.5 |
| Construction | 100.3 | 100.2 | 99.1 | 97.7 | 105.8 | 109.6 | 110.1 | 109.5 |
| Income tax cut | 98.6 | 96.9 | 96.0 | 94.7 | 98.8 | 74.8 | 87.1 | 91.5 |
| Income tax cut plus monetary policy | 98.6 | 97.0 | 96.3 | 95.1 | 98.6 | 75.3 | 88.0 | 92.7 |
| Reserve requirements reduction | 100.9 | 101.2 | 100.2 | 98.8 | 109.7 | 112.6 | 112.9 | 112.0 |
| Open market operations | 100.9 | 101.3 | 100.4 | 98.8 | 109.6 | 112.8 | 113.2 | 112.2 |
| Excise tax cut 1 (small) | | | | | | | | |
| 100 per cent pass along | 100.9 | 98.9 | 97.2 | 95.4 | 109.4 | 107.2 | 106.0 | 104.4 |
| 80 per cent pass along | 100.9 | 98.8 | 97.1 | 95.3 | 109.4 | 107.1 | 105.8 | 104.2 |
| 50 per cent pass along | 100.8 | 98.7 | 96.9 | 95.0 | 109.3 | 106.8 | 105.4 | 103.7 |
| Excise tax cut 2 (large) | | | | | | | | |
| 100 per cent pass along | 100.0 | 97.9 | 96.9 | 95.6 | 105.9 | 101.6 | 103.3 | 103.4 |
| 80 per cent pass along | 100.0 | 97.8 | 96.6 | 95.3 | 106.1 | 101.5 | 102.9 | 102.9 |
| 50 per cent pass along | 100.0 | 97.5 | 96.4 | 95.0 | 105.8 | 100.6 | 102.0 | 102.0 |
| | Utility function CES ($\delta = -0.5, \sigma = 0.67$) | | | | Utility function CES ($\delta = -1, \sigma = 0.5$) | | | |
| Government | | | | | | | | |
| Durables expenditures | 104.6 | 104.6 | 103.6 | 102.3 | 107.7 | 108.1 | 107.3 | 105.9 |
| Nondurables expenditures | 99.4 | 101.3 | 101.7 | 100.8 | 99.8 | 103.3 | 104.5 | 103.8 |
| Employment | 105.5 | 105.8 | 104.5 | 102.5 | 108.8 | 109.3 | 108.1 | 106.2 |
| Construction | 103.7 | 104.8 | 103.9 | 102.6 | 106.4 | 108.3 | 107.6 | 106.2 |
| Income tax cut | 98.8 | 100.6 | 100.1 | 99.0 | 98.9 | 102.5 | 102.7 | 101.9 |
| Income tax cut plus monetary policy | 98.6 | 100.9 | 100.6 | 99.6 | 98.6 | 102.9 | 103.3 | 102.6 |
| Reserve requirements reduction | 106.3 | 106.4 | 105.3 | 103.7 | 110.3 | 110.3 | 109.1 | 107.5 |
| Open market operations | 106.3 | 106.4 | 105.4 | 103.8 | 110.2 | 110.3 | 109.2 | 107.6 |
| Excise tax cut 1 (small) | | | | | | | | |
| 100 per cent pass along | 106.1 | 103.9 | 102.2 | 100.4 | 109.9 | 107.6 | 105.9 | 104.0 |
| 80 per cent pass along | 106.1 | 103.8 | 102.1 | 100.3 | 110.0 | 107.6 | 105.9 | 103.9 |
| 50 per cent pass along | 106.1 | 103.7 | 102.0 | 100.0 | 110.0 | 107.5 | 105.7 | 103.7 |
| Excise tax cut 2 (large) | | | | | | | | |
| 100 per cent pass along | 104.0 | 99.5 | 99.9 | 99.2 | 107.2 | 100.3 | 101.9 | 101.7 |
| 80 per cent pass along | 104.2 | 99.7 | 99.8 | 99.0 | 107.5 | 100.8 | 102.0 | 101.6 |
| 50 per cent pass along | 104.1 | 98.9 | 99.2 | 98.4 | 107.3 | 99.4 | 101.1 | 100.8 |

[a]) Average per quarter of sum of utility indexes discounted quarterly (at an annual rate of 6 per cent to the beginning of the simulation period, 1960:2. That is, table values are $u_0/m$ where $m$ is the number o quarters over which $u_0$ is calculated; $u_0$'s are derived from the indexes of table 5.5, using the formul previously given.

TABLE 5.7

*Rank order of utility indexes—proportional weights (ranked after ten quarters in 1962:4).*

| | $u_t$ | $u_o$ | $u_v$ | $u_T$ | $u_t$ | $u_o$ | $u_v$ | $u_T$ |
|---|---|---|---|---|---|---|---|---|
| | Utility function Linear ($\delta = 1, \sigma = \infty$) | | | | Utility function Cobb-Douglas ($\delta = 0, \sigma = 1$) | | | |
| Government | | | | | | | | |
| Durables expenditures | 4 | 6 | 3 | 4 | 4 | 5 | 6 | 4 |
| Nondurables expenditures | 5 | 5 | 10 | 7 | 5 | 6 | 9 | 9 |
| Employment | 6 | 3 | 8 | 5 | 6 | 4 | 8 | 5 |
| Construction | 3 | 4 | 7 | 3 | 3 | 3 | 7 | 3 |
| Income tax cut | 11 | 14 | 14 | 14 | 11 | 14 | 14 | 14 |
| Income tax cut plus monetary policy | 8 | 11 | 9 | 12 | 8 | 13 | 9 | 13 |
| Reserve requirements reduction | 1 | 2 | 4 | 2 | 1 | 2 | 4 | 2 |
| Open market operations | 2 | 1 | 5 | 1 | 2 | 1 | 5 | 1 |
| Excise tax cut 1 (small) | | | | | | | | |
| 100 per cent pass along | 12 | 8 | 3 | 6 | 12 | 7 | 3 | 6 |
| 80 per cent pass along | 13 | 10 | 2 | 8 | 13 | 8 | 2 | 7 |
| 50 per cent pass along | 14 | 12 | 1 | 9 | 14 | 9 | 1 | 8 |
| Excise tax cut 2 (large) | | | | | | | | |
| 100 per cent pass along | 7 | 7 | 12 | 10 | 7 | 10 | 12 | 10 |
| 80 per cent pass along | 9 | 9 | 10 | 11 | 9 | 11 | 11 | 11 |
| 50 per cent pass along | 10 | 13 | 13 | 13 | 10 | 12 | 13 | 12 |
| | Utility function CES ($\delta = -0.5, \sigma = 0.67$) | | | | Utility function CES ($\delta = -1, \sigma = 0.5$) | | | |
| Government | | | | | | | | |
| Durables expenditures | 4 | 5 | 6 | 4 | 4 | 5 | 6 | 4 |
| Nondurables expenditures | 5 | 6 | 9 | 9 | 5 | 8 | 9 | 9 |
| Employment | 6 | 4 | 8 | 5 | 6 | 4 | 8 | 5 |
| Construction | 3 | 3 | 7 | 3 | 3 | 3 | 7 | 3 |
| Income tax cut | 11 | 12 | 13 | 13 | 11 | 11 | 13 | 13 |
| Income tax cut plus monetary policy | 8 | 10 | 10 | 10 | 8 | 10 | 10 | 10 |
| Reserve requirement reduction | 1 | 2 | 4 | 1 | 1 | 2 | 4 | 1 |
| Open market operations | 2 | 1 | 5 | 1 | 2 | 1 | 5 | 2 |
| Excise tax cut 1 (small) | | | | | | | | |
| 100 per cent pass along | 12 | 7 | 3 | 6 | 12 | 6 | 3 | 6 |
| 80 per cent pass along | 13 | 8 | 2 | 7 | 13 | 7 | 2 | 7 |
| 50 per cent pass along | 14 | 9 | 1 | 8 | 14 | 9 | 1 | 8 |
| Excise tax cut 2 (large) | | | | | | | | |
| 100 per cent pass along | 7 | 11 | 12 | 11 | 7 | 12 | 12 | 12 |
| 80 per cent pass along | 9 | 13 | 11 | 12 | 9 | 13 | 11 | 11 |
| 50 per cent pass along | 10 | 14 | 14 | 14 | 10 | 14 | 14 | 14 |

*Note* $u_t$ = within period outcome utility; $u_o$ = discounted outcome utility; $u_v$ = variance utility; and $u_T$ = total utility.

TABLE 5.8

*Rank order of utility indexes—equal weights (ranked after ten quarters in 1962:4).*

| | $u_t$ | $u_o$ | $u_v$ | $u_T$ | $u_t$ | $u_o$ | $u_v$ | $u_T$ |
|---|---|---|---|---|---|---|---|---|
| | Utility function Linear ($\delta = 1, \sigma = \infty$) | | | | Utility function Cobb-Douglas ($\delta$=0, $\sigma$=1) | | | |
| Government | | | | | | | | |
| Durables expenditures | 4 | 4 | 6 | 4 | 4 | 4 | 6 | 4 |
| Nondurables expenditures | 5 | 6 | 9 | 9 | 5 | 6 | 9 | 9 |
| Employment | 6 | 5 | 8 | 8 | 6 | 5 | 8 | 8 |
| Construction | 3 | 3 | 7 | 3 | 3 | 3 | 7 | 3 |
| Income tax cut | 14 | 14 | 12 | 14 | 14 | 14 | 11 | 14 |
| Income tax cut plus monetary policy | 8 | 13 | 10 | 12 | 8 | 13 | 10 | 12 |
| Reserve requirements reduction | 1 | 2 | 4 | 2 | 1 | 2 | 4 | 2 |
| Open market operations | 2 | 1 | 5 | 1 | 2 | 1 | 5 | 1 |
| Excise tax cut 1 (small) | | | | | | | | |
| 100 per cent pass along | 10 | 7 | 3 | 5 | 10 | 7 | 3 | 5 |
| 80 per cent pass along | 12 | 8 | 2 | 6 | 12 | 8 | 2 | 6 |
| 50 per cent pass along | 13 | 9 | 1 | 7 | 13 | 9 | 1 | 7 |
| Excise tax cut 2 (large) | | | | | | | | |
| 100 per cent pass along | 7 | 10 | 13 | 10 | 7 | 10 | 13 | 10 |
| 80 per cent pass along | 9 | 11 | 11 | 11 | 9 | 11 | 12 | 11 |
| 50 per cent pass along | 11 | 12 | 14 | 13 | 11 | 12 | 14 | 13 |
| | Utility function CES ($\delta = -0.5, \sigma = 0.67$) | | | | Utility function CES ($\delta = -1, \sigma = 0.5$) | | | |
| Government | | | | | | | | |
| Durables expenditures | 4 | 4 | 6 | 4 | 4 | 5 | 6 | 6 |
| Nondurables expenditures | 5 | 9 | 9 | 9 | 5 | 9 | 9 | 9 |
| Employment | 6 | 5 | 8 | 8 | 6 | 4 | 8 | 8 |
| Construction | 3 | 3 | 7 | 7 | 3 | 3 | 7 | 7 |
| Income tax cut | 14 | 14 | 11 | 12 | 14 | 13 | 11 | 11 |
| Income tax cut plus monetary policy | 8 | 13 | 10 | 10 | 8 | 10 | 10 | 10 |
| Reserve requirements reduction | 1 | 2 | 4 | 1 | 1 | 2 | 4 | 1 |
| Open market operations | 2 | 1 | 5 | 2 | 2 | 1 | 5 | 2 |
| Excise tax cut 1 (small) | | | | | | | | |
| 100 per cent pass along | 10 | 6 | 3 | 3 | 10 | 6 | 3 | 5 |
| 80 per cent pass along | 12 | 7 | 2 | 5 | 12 | 7 | 2 | 3 |
| 50 per cent pass along | 13 | 8 | 1 | 6 | 13 | 8 | 1 | 4 |
| Excise tax cut 2 (large) | | | | | | | | |
| 100 per cent pass along | 7 | 10 | 13 | 13 | 7 | 12 | 13 | 13 |
| 80 per cent pass along | 9 | 11 | 12 | 11 | 9 | 11 | 12 | 12 |
| 50 per cent pass along | 11 | 12 | 14 | 14 | 11 | 14 | 14 | 14 |

The effect of discounting utilities may be seen more clearly in tables 5.7 and 5.8, which show the rank order of utility indexes in 1962:4. Generally, the high ranked monetary and expenditure policies have nearly the same positions on a current or discounted basis, while there is some switching in the lower and middle ranked policies. The rank order of variance utilities is also shown. At high elasticities of substitution there seems to be no consistent relationship between the variance and outcome utilities. As the elasticity decreases, however, the two rank orderings begin to have nearly the same pattern. Contrasting total utilities (the sum of the outcome and variance utilities) using proportional versus equal weights, it appears that the rank orders are not greatly different. But, again, this conclusion depends on the elasticity of substitution: the lower the elasticity, the greater the divergence.

Another interesting comparison is the rank order of policies using discounted real input and fiscal multipliers versus that using discounted total utilities (see table 5.9). Except with the lowest elasticity of substitution, the "best" policies, ranked in terms of utilities, are the shifts in monetary variables. After that, ranking by utilities, come the government expenditure policies (other than for nondurables) and the excise tax cuts. In terms of multipliers, some of these positions are reversed; the expenditure increases are in first position, followed by the monetary policies. In fact, the larger excise cut ranks ahead of the monetary policies when the judgment is made solely on the basis of multipliers. The difference between the two rankings stems mainly from government surplus. The monetary policies have a higher rank on a utility basis because they increase government surplus while the other policies decrease it. For this same reason, the larger excise tax cut is less highly regarded on a utility basis than the smaller excise cut. Finally, under either set of rankings, the income tax cuts (pure or otherwise) rank far down the scale.

While the monetary policies are high on the preference scale, their rank as indicated by the utility functions may be overstated. No costs (disutility) comparable to the government surplus costs which are associated with fiscal policy are attached to the manipulation of monetary instruments. An argument could be made that discretionary monetary policy causes volatility in money markets and large swings in interest rates, which impose (unmeasured) costs on the economy. Furthermore, greater uncertainty probably attaches to the impact and lags of monetary than fiscal policy, tending to make the use of monetary instruments less desirable than fiscal action,

TABLE 5.9

*Comparison of multiplier vs. utility rank ordering (ranked after ten quarters ending 1962:4).*

| | (1) [a] | (2) [a] | (3) | (4) | (5) | (6) |
|---|---|---|---|---|---|---|
| | Rank of discounted multipliers for $GNP^{54}$ | | Rank of discounted total utility with utility functions [b] | | | |
| | Real input | Fiscal | Linear | Cobb-Douglas | CES ($\delta = -0.5$) | CES ($\delta = -1$) |
| Government | | | | | | |
| Durables expenditures | 3 | 3 | 4 | 4 | 4 | 4 |
| Nondurables expenditures | 2 | 1 | 7 | 9 | 9 | 9 |
| Employment | 4 | 4 | 5 | 5 | 5 | 5 |
| Construction | 1 | 2 | 3 | 3 | 3 | 3 |
| Income tax cut | 14 | 13 | 14 | 14 | 13 | 13 |
| Income tax cut plus monetary policy | 11 | 11 | 12 | 13 | 10 | 10 |
| Reserve requirements reduction | 9 | 9 | 2 | 2 | 1 | 1 |
| Open market operations | 8 | 8 | 1 | 1 | 1 | 2 |
| Excise tax cut 1 (small) | | | | | | |
| 100 per cent pass along | 10 | 10 | 6 | 6 | 6 | 6 |
| 80 per cent pass along | 11 | 12 | 8 | 7 | 7 | 7 |
| 50 per cent pass along | 13 | 14 | 9 | 8 | 8 | 8 |
| Excise tax cut 2 (large) | | | | | | |
| 100 per cent pass along | 5 | 5 | 10 | 10 | 11 | 12 |
| 80 per cent pass along | 7 | 7 | 11 | 11 | 12 | 11 |
| 50 per cent pass along | 6 | 6 | 13 | 12 | 14 | 14 |

| | Difference in rankings | | | | | | | |
|---|---|---|---|---|---|---|---|---|
| | Column 1 less indicated column | | | | Column 2 less indicated column | | | |
| | (3) | (4) | (5) | (6) | (3) | (4) | (5) | (6) |
| Government | | | | | | | | |
| Durables expenditures | −1 | −1 | −1 | −1 | −1 | −1 | −1 | −1 |
| Nondurables expenditures | −5 | −7 | −7 | −7 | −6 | −8 | −8 | −8 |
| Employment | −1 | −1 | −1 | −1 | −1 | −1 | −1 | −1 |
| Construction | −2 | −2 | −2 | −2 | −1 | −1 | −1 | −1 |
| Income tax cut | 0 | 0 | 1 | 1 | −1 | −1 | 0 | 0 |
| Income tax cut plus monetary policy | −1 | −2 | 1 | 1 | −1 | −2 | 1 | 1 |
| Reserve requirements reduction | 7 | 7 | 8 | 8 | 7 | 7 | 8 | 8 |
| Open market operations | 7 | 7 | 7 | 6 | 7 | 7 | 7 | 6 |
| Excise tax cut 1 (small) | | | | | | | | |
| 100 per cent pass along | 4 | 4 | 4 | 4 | 4 | 4 | 4 | 4 |
| 80 per cent pass along | 3 | 4 | 4 | 4 | 4 | 5 | 5 | 5 |
| 50 per cent pass along | 4 | 5 | 5 | 5 | 5 | 6 | 6 | 6 |
| Excise tax cut 2 (large) | | | | | | | | |
| 100 per cent pass along | −5 | −5 | −6 | −7 | −5 | −5 | −6 | −7 |
| 80 per cent pass along | −4 | −4 | −5 | −4 | −4 | −4 | −5 | −4 |
| 50 per cent pass along | −7 | −6 | −8 | −8 | −7 | −6 | −8 | −8 |

a) Ranked using equivalent inputs for the income tax cut plus monetary policy.

b) Calculated using proportional weights.

especially if the latter can be directed to specific areas of the economy [17]). Nevertheless, it would appear that monetary policy is powerful (in both an impact and utility sense) and has a role to play in cyclical stabilization.

## *5.8. Conclusion*

This chapter has attempted to provide some perspective and some new methodology on the analysis of alternative government fiscal and monetary policy instruments. It has been shown that larger scale models of the economy than have previously been employed for such analyses can produce meaningful, reasonable results. No claims are advanced for the particular model used here. As indicated in chapter 1, this model is tentative and in need of improvement. Much remains to be done. Not only should individual sector specifications be given further scrutiny, but the entire system should be subjected to stability (via stochastic shocks) and forecasting tests [18]). Moreover, while the three types of utility functions used to evaluate policies are ones commonly employed, their choice is still quite arbitrary. Unfortunately, there is no evidence available regarding how the forms, arguments, or weights of these functions correspond to the preferences of the Administration, the Congress, or any segment of the public. Thus, only future research will provide a check on the present conclusions.

These orderings of policies are not to be regarded as a prescription for government decisionmakers. Aside from any questions of the validity and accuracy of the model, neither the multipliers nor the utility functions (even if augmented with additional arguments endogenous to the model) reflect the many other considerations which impinge on a policy choice. Such issues as the degree of government intervention, intergroup and interregional inequities, implications for long-run resource allocation, and other social costs and benefits which are difficult to quantify must be taken into account.

In addition, even within the model framework, the desirability of a *type* of policy is not independent of the initial conditions under which a choice is made, nor is it independent of the degree to which the policy is to be under-

---

[17]) Cf. William C. Brainard, "Uncertainty and the Effectiveness of Policy," *American Economic Review*, Vol. LVII, May 1967, no. 2, pp. 411–425.

[18]) Some preliminary stability tests results appear in A. L. Nagar, "Stochastic Simulation of the Brookings Econometric Model," paper presented at the San Francisco Meetings of the Econometric Society, December 1966.

taken. (Both these dependencies stem from the nonlinear nature of the behavioral relationships which characterize the economy.) For example, adopting an easy monetary policy when credit is already plentiful will not provide as much stimulus as when credit is highly rationed. Thus, at any given point in time, policy alternatives should be evaluated in the context of the situation to which they are to be applied. If the illustrative utility functions are accepted, the rankings described provide a tentative indication of how policies might fare in general [19]); however, they need not hold in any particular instance.

[19]) In the foregoing utility comparisons no account is taken of the differing scale of the various policies. Yet, the percentage changes in inputs for the monetary policy shifts are among the smallest of those introduced. They are about 5 to 6 per cent, while for government expenditures they range from 7 per cent for employment to nearly 50 per cent for nondurables. It is possible to include the scale factors as arguments in the utility computations, assuming (if no further adjustments are made) that equal percentage changes of different policies involve the same disutility consequences—an extremely dubious assumption.

# APPENDIX A. BROOKINGS ECONOMETRIC MODEL CONDENSED SYSTEM OF EQUATIONS AND LIST OF VARIABLES AND DEFINITIONS

The system of equations used in the simulation experiments appears below. Equations are arranged by concepts which generally correspond to the national income and product accounts. For example, the first group of equations explain personal consumption expenditures.

Following each group of equations, variables are defined generally in their order of appearance. For the last group, a list of identities, the variables are listed alphabetically.

Monetary variables are in billions of dollars, seasonally adjusted. Monetary stock variables are, unless otherwise indicated, end-of-period; and monetary flow variables, including changes in stocks between ends of periods, are at annual rates. In the definitions, the variables are generally defined as if they are in current dollars. In the equations, the distinction is made between current and constant 1954 dollars. Variables in the latter units are superscripted 54. Other modifiers of the variables are:

1. Sector subscripts. These refer only to producing sectors and government; those that appear in the system of equations presented here are as follows:

| | |
|---|---|
| *A* | = agriculture, forestry and fisheries |
| *AF* | = farming |
| *C* | = contract construction |
| *EAF* | = nonfarm business |
| *F* | = federal government (used only as a subscript for government expenditure variables) |
| *G* | = government and government enterprises |
| *GF* | = federal government |
| *GSL* | = state and local government |

$M$ = manufacturing

$MD$ = durable manufacturing

$MN$ = nondurable manufacturing

$O$ = residual industries: mining; finance, insurance, and real estate; and services

$O{*}2$ = mining, wholesale and retail, services, finance, and contract construction

$O{*}4$ = all industries except manufacturing, wholesale and retail trade, and farming

$O{*}6$ = wholesale and retail trade and contract construction plus residual industries (mining; finance, insurance, and real estate; and services)

$R$ = regulated industries: railroad and nonrail transportation, communications, and public utilities

$T$ = wholesale and retail trade

2. Other subscripts are defined with the variables to which they apply. An example is modification of the symbol for employment, $E$. $E_p$ stands for employment of production workers; $E_o$, employment of overhead workers. Many of these modified variables will also have sector subscripts.

*Consumer demand*

$$C^{54}_{\mathrm{DEA}} = 1.9795+0.2094Y^{54}_{\mathrm{D}}-14.7464\frac{P_{\mathrm{CDEA}}}{P_{\mathrm{C}}}-0.0809[K^{54}_{\mathrm{CDEA}}]_{-1} \tag{A.1}$$

$$C^{54}_{\mathrm{DA}} = 16.4097+0.0558Y^{54}_{\mathrm{D}}-14.4938\frac{P_{\mathrm{CDA}}}{P_{\mathrm{C}}}+3.4405DMY55-92.0635RU \tag{A.2}$$

$$C^{54}_{\mathrm{NFB}} = 65.5208+0.0922Y^{54}_{\mathrm{D}}-39.9710\frac{P_{\mathrm{CNFB}}}{P_{\mathrm{C}}}+0.2587[\tfrac{1}{4}\sum_{i=-4}^{-1}[C^{54}_{\mathrm{NFB}}]_i] \tag{A.3}$$

$$C^{54}_{\mathrm{NEFB}} = 36.6546+0.1272Y^{54}_{\mathrm{D}}-30.4330\frac{P_{\mathrm{CNEFB}}}{P_{\mathrm{C}}}+0.2856[\tfrac{1}{4}\sum_{i=-4}^{-1}[C^{54}_{\mathrm{NEFB}}]_i] \tag{A.4}$$

$$C_S^{54} = -6.2186 + 0.0278\,Y_D^{54} - 10.9454\,\frac{P_{CS}}{P_C} + 0.9256[\tfrac{1}{4}\sum_{i=-4}^{-1}[C_S^{54}]_i] + 0.1049\left[\frac{ALQD}{P_C}\right]_{-1} \quad \text{(A.5)}$$

The variables in order of appearance are:

$C_{DEA}$ = personal consumption expenditures for durable goods other than new and net used automobiles, billions of dollars

$Y_D$ = disposable personal income, billions of dollars

$P_{CDEA}$ = implicit price deflator for personal consumption expenditures on durable goods other than new and net used automobiles, 1954 = 1.00

$P_C$ = implicit price deflator for personal consumption expenditures, 1954 = 1.00

$K_{CDEA}$ = stock of consumer durable goods excluding automobiles, billions of dollars

$C_{DA}$ = personal consumption expenditures for new and net used automobiles, billions of dollars

$DMY55$ = 1, in 1955 (to reflect a major easing of credit terms)
= 0, in all other years

$RU$ = rate of unemployment, fraction

$P_{CDA}$ = implicit price deflator for personal consumption expenditures on new and used automobiles, 1954 = 1.00

$C_{NFB}$ = personal consumption expenditures on food and beverages, billions of dollars

$P_{CNFB}$ = implicit price deflator for personal consumption expenditures on food and beverages, 1954 = 1.00

$C_{NEFB}$ = personal consumption expenditures on nondurables goods other than food and beverages, billions of dollars

$C_S$ = personal consumption expenditures on services including imputations, billions of dollars

$P_{CS}$ = implicit price deflator for personal consumption expenditures on services, 1954 = 1.00

$ALQD$ = currency liabilities of the Treasury and Federal Reserve less commercial banks' currency holdings; plus private demand deposit liabilities of commercial banks less interbank deposits, cash items in process of collection, and Federal Reserve float; plus private time deposit liabilities of commercial banks less time deposit holdings of commercial banks, all average during quarter, billions of dollars

*Residential construction*

$$HU_{STS} = 0.3140-0.1272[\tfrac{1}{4}\sum_{i=1}^{3}[RM_{GBS3}]_{t-i}]+0.3966[HU_{STS}]_{-1}$$

$$-0.2470[HU_{VAC*}]_{-1}+0.6908\left[\frac{CPI_{SR}}{P_{ICNFR}}\right]_{-1}+0.0131TIME \qquad (A.6)$$

$$\frac{PM_{ICRD}}{P_{ICNFR}} = 3.6667+1.2587\left\{\frac{1}{3}\sum_{i=-2}^{-4}\left[\frac{Y_D}{P_C[HH]_{-1}}\right]_i\right\}$$

$$-0.0714\{\tfrac{1}{3}\sum_{i=-2}^{-4}[RM_{GBS3}]_i\} \qquad (A.7)$$

$$I^{54}_{CNFRH} = 0.41\left\{\left[\frac{PM_{ICRD}}{P_{ICNFR}}\right]\cdot[HU_{STS}]\right\}+0.49\left\{\left[\frac{PM_{ICRD}}{P_{ICNFR}}\right]\cdot[HU_{STS}]\right\}_{-1}$$

$$+0.10\left\{\left[\frac{PM_{ICRD}}{P_{ICNFR}}\right]\cdot[HU_{STS}]\right\}_{-2} \qquad (A.8)$$

$$I^{54}_{CNFREH} = -6.1643+0.1871[HU_{AVL}]_{-1}+0.3189[P_{ICNFR}/P_C]_{-2} \qquad (A.9)$$

$$I^{54}_{CNFR*} = I^{54}_{CNFRH}+I^{54}_{CNFREH} \qquad (A.10)$$

$$I^{54}_{CNFR} = DMY15[I^{54}_{CNFR*}] \qquad (A.11)$$

$$I^{54}_{CO} = -6.3028+1.5203\left\{\frac{1}{8}\sum_{i=-1}^{-8}\left[\frac{Y_D}{P_C[HH]_{-1}}\right]_i\right\} \qquad (A.12)$$

$$\Delta HU_{AVL} = 0.0172-0.0033[HU_{AVL}]_{-1}$$

$$+0.3058[0.25HU_{STS_{-1}}+0.50HU_{STS_{-2}}+0.25HU_{STS_{-3}}] \qquad (A.13)$$

$$HU_{VAC} = [HU_{VAC}]_{-1} + \Delta HU_{AVL} - \Delta HH \tag{A.14}$$

$$[HU_{VAC*}]_{-1} = [HU_{VAC}]_{-1} - 0.0476 + 0.0012TIME \tag{A.15}$$

$$CPI_{SR} = 0.9392 - 0.0302\left[\frac{Y_D}{P_C[HH]_{-1}}\right] + 0.0253[HU_{VAC*}]_{-1} + 0.0057TIME \tag{A.16}$$

New variables in order of appearance are:

$HU_{STS}$ = number of private housing units started, millions

$RM_{GBS3}$ = average market yield on three-month U. S. Treasury bills, per cent

$HU_{VAC*}$ = adjusted vacant available housing units, millions

$CPI_{SR}$ = rent component of consumer price index, 1954 = 1.00

$P_{ICNFR}$ = implicit price deflator for residential, nonfarm new private construction, 1954 = 1.00

$TIME$ = time trend, 1947:1 = 1.00

$PM_{ICRD}$ = average cost per unit of private housing starts, thousands of dollars

$HH$ = number of households, millions

$I_{CNFRH}$ = value of new private nonfarm housing units put in place, billions of dollars

$I_{CNFREH}$ = value of new additions and alterations to private nonfarm residential buildings plus value of new private nonfarm nonhousekeeping residential buildings put in place, billions of dollars

$HU_{AVL}$ = total available housing units, millions

$I_{CNFR*}$ = value of new private nonfarm residential buildings put in place, billions of dollars

$I_{CNFR}$ = private residential nonfarm new construction, billions of dollars

$DMY15$ = dummy variable to convert from Bureau of the Census value of new private nonfarm residential buildings put in place to *GNP* expenditures on private residential nonfarm new construction, both billions of 1954 dollars

$I_{CO}$ = value of new private nonfarm, nonresidential, nonbusiness construction put in place, billions of dollars

$\Delta$ = first difference operator

$HU_{VAC}$ = vacant available housing units, millions

*Inventory investment*

$$\Delta INV_{MD}^{54} = -17.2596+0.2221[GNP_{\mathrm{D}}^{54}-\Delta INV_{\mathrm{D}}^{54}+GNP_{\mathrm{IC}}^{54}]$$
$$-0.4517[INV_{MD}^{54}]_{-1}+0.0977[\Delta(O_{\mathrm{U}_{MD}}^{54})_{-1}]+0.0660[O_{\mathrm{U}_{MD}}^{54}]_{-1} \quad \text{(A.17)}$$

$$\Delta INV_{MN}^{54} = -2.7816+0.2037[GNP_{\mathrm{N}}^{54}-\Delta INV_{\mathrm{N}}^{54}]-1.1537[INV_{MN}^{54}]_{-1}$$
$$-0.1841[\Delta(GNP_{\mathrm{N}}^{54}-\Delta INV_{\mathrm{N}}^{54})]+0.5692[O_{\mathrm{U}_{MN}}^{54}]_{-1}$$
$$+0.3937[\Delta INV_{MN}^{54}]_{-1} \quad \text{(A.18)}$$

$$\Delta INV_{T}^{54} = 0.2784+0.8784\Delta RM_{\mathrm{GBS3}}$$
$$+0.0472\left[GNP^{54}-\Delta INV^{54}-C_{\mathrm{S}}^{54}-\frac{WS_G}{P_G}\right]$$
$$+80.3392\left[\frac{\Delta WPI_{EAF}}{WPI_{EAF_{-1}}}\right]-0.3484[INV_{T}^{54}]_{-1} \quad \text{(A.19)}$$

$$\Delta INV_{O*4}^{54} = -0.0300-0.1280\Delta RM_{\mathrm{GBS3}}$$
$$+6.1992\left[\frac{\Delta WPI_{EAF}}{WPI_{EAF_{-1}}}\right]-0.1452[INV_{O*4}^{54}]_{-1}$$
$$+0.0032\left[GNP^{54}-\Delta INV^{54}-\frac{WS_G}{P_G}\right] \quad \text{(A.20)}$$

$$INV_j^{54} = \tfrac{1}{4}\Delta INV_j^{54}+INV_{j-1}^{54} \quad \text{(A.21)}$$

$$\Delta O_{\mathrm{U}j}^{54} = 4\{O_{\mathrm{U}j}^{54}-[O_{\mathrm{U}j}^{54}]_{-1}\} \quad \text{(A.22)}$$

The variables in order of appearance are:

$INV$ = business inventory stock, billions of dollars

$GNP_{\mathrm{D}}$ = durable goods component of gross national product, billions of dollars

$INV_{\mathrm{D}}$ = inventory stock of durable goods, billions of dollars

$GNP_{\mathrm{IC}}$ = construction component of gross national product, billions of dollars

$O_{\mathrm{U}}$ = manufacturers' unfilled orders, billions of dollars

$GNP_{\mathrm{N}}$ = nondurable goods component of gross national product, billions of dollars

$INV_{\mathrm{N}}$ = inventory stock of nondurable goods, billions of dollars

$RM_{\mathrm{GBS3}}$ = average market yield on three-month U. S. Treasury bills, per cent

$GNP$ = gross national product, billions of dollars

$WS_G$ = government wage and salary disbursements, billions of dollars

$P_G$ = implicit price deflator for government purchases of goods and services, 1954 = 1.00

$WPI_{EAF}$ = wholesale price index of all commodities except farm products, 1954 = 1.00

*Orders*

$$O_{MD}^{54} = -691.3272+2.2812[GNP_D^{54}-\Delta INV_D^{54}+GNP_{\mathrm{IC}}^{54}] - 1.008[GNP_{\mathrm{D}}^{54}-\Delta INV_{\mathrm{D}}^{54}+GNP_{\mathrm{IC}}^{54}]_{-2}+682.2264\left[\frac{WPI_{MD}}{[WPI_{MD}]_{-1}}\right] + 4.37044\Delta\left[\frac{G_{\mathrm{ML}_F}}{P_{\mathrm{GF}}}\right] \tag{A.23}$$

$$O_{MN}^{54} = -192.0888+1.4844[GNP_{\mathrm{N}}^{54}-\Delta INV_{\mathrm{N}}^{54}]+146.5728\left[\frac{WPI_{MN}}{[WPI_{MN}]_{-1}}\right] + 3.636DMY1 \tag{A.24}$$

$$O_{\mathrm{U}_{MD}}^{54} = \left\{\frac{[WPI_{MD}]_{-1}}{WPI_{MD}}\right\}[O_{\mathrm{U}_{MD}}^{54}]_{-1}+0.25[O_{MD}^{54}]-[0.25][2.4310]X_{MD}^{54} + 0.25\Delta INV_{MD}^{54} \tag{A.25}$$

$$O_{\mathrm{U}_{MN}}^{54} = \left\{\frac{[WPI_{MN}]_{-1}}{WPI_{MN}}\right\}[O_{\mathrm{U}_{MN}}^{54}]_{-1}+0.25[O_{MN}^{54}]-[0.25][3.2344]X_{MN}^{54} + 0.25\Delta INV_{MN}^{54} \tag{A.26}$$

New variables in order of appearance are:

$O$ = manufacturers' net new orders, billions of dollars

$P_{GF}$ = implicit price deflator for federal government purchases of goods and services, 1954 = 1.00

$DMY1$ = 1, 1950: 3 through 1951: 2
= 0, all other quarters

$X$ = gross product originating, billions of dollars

$WPI$ = wholesale price index, 1954 = 1.00

$G_{\mathrm{ML}_F}$ = federal government purchases of goods and services for national defense, billions of dollars

*Investment in nonfarm business plant and equipment*

$$I^{54}_{\mathrm{BUS}_{MD}} = -0.8987 - 0.1374[K^{54}_{MD}]_{-1} + 0.0600[X^{54}_{MD}]_{-1} + 0.0902[X^{54}_{MD}]_{-5} + 0.9642[RM_{\mathrm{GBL}}]_{-2} - 1.0523[RM_{\mathrm{GBL}}]_{-5} + 0.0380[X^{54}_{MD}]_{-2} \quad \text{(A.27)}$$

$$I^{54}_{\mathrm{BUS}_{MN}} = 0.5958 - 0.1577[K^{54}_{MN}]_{-1} + 0.1110[X^{54}_{MN}]_{-1} + 0.3672[X^{54}_{MN}]_{-5} - 0.7156[RM_{\mathrm{GBL}}]_{-1} - 2.5870[RM_{\mathrm{GBL}}]_{-5} \quad \text{(A.28)}$$

$$I^{54}_{\mathrm{BUS}_{R}} = 8.2383 - 0.0867[K^{54}_{R}]_{-1} + 0.1061[X^{54}_{R}]_{-1} + 0.1357[X^{54}_{R}]_{-5} + 0.6933[RM_{\mathrm{GBL}}]_{-1} - 1.6955[RM_{\mathrm{GBL}}]_{-5} + 0.1551[X^{54}_{R}]_{-6} \quad \text{(A.29)}$$

$$I^{54}_{\mathrm{BUS}_{O*2}} = 0.6340 - 0.1577[K^{54}_{O*2}]_{-1} + 0.1202[X^{54}_{C} + X^{54}_{T} + X^{54}_{O}]_{-1} - 1.7933[RM_{\mathrm{GBL}}]_{-1} \quad \text{(A.30)}$$

New variables in order of appearance are:

$I_{\mathrm{BUS}}$ = business gross investment in plant and equipment, billions of dollars

$K$ = stock of business capital, billions of dollars

$RM_{\mathrm{GBL}}$ = average yield during quarter on U. S. securities maturing or callable in ten years or more, per cent

*Foreign trade*

$$M_{\text{FIN}}^{54} = 0.4833 + 0.0294 Y_{\text{D}}^{54} - 4.3917 \frac{PM_{\text{MFIN}}}{P_{\text{GOOD}}} + 0.6269[M_{\text{FIN}}^{54}]_{-1} \quad \text{(A.31)}$$

$$M_{\text{EFIN}}^{54} = 3.1483 + 0.0282 \Delta INV_{EAF}^{54} + 0.0337 X_{M}^{54} - 2.1324 \frac{PM_{\text{MEFIN}}}{P_{\text{GOOD}}} + 0.3680[M_{\text{EFIN}}^{54}]_{-1} \quad \text{(A.32)}$$

$$EX^{54} = 9.9873 - 10.9873 \frac{P_{\text{EX}}}{PM_{\text{EXW}}} + 0.6275[EX^{54}]_{-1} + 0.1012 EX_{\text{W}}^{54} \quad \text{(A.33)}$$

New variables in order of appearance are:

$M_{\text{FIN}}$ = imports of finished goods and services, billions of dollars

$PM_{\text{MFIN}}$ = unit value index of imports of finished goods and services, 1954 = 1.00

$P_{\text{GOOD}}$ = implicit price deflator for *GNP* goods, 1954 = 1.00

$M_{\text{EFIN}}$ = imports of crude materials, crude foodstuffs, and semimanufactures, billions of dollars

$PM_{\text{MEFIN}}$ = unit value index of imports of crude materials, crude foodstuffs, and semimanufactures, 1954 = 1.00

$EX$ = U.S. exports of goods and services, billions of dollars

$PM_{\text{EXW}}$ = unit value index of world exports exluding U.S. components, 1954 = 1.00

$EX_{\text{W}}$ = world exports excluding U.S. exports, billions of dollars

$P_{\text{EX}}$ = implicit price deflator for exports of goods and services, 1954 = 1.00

*Government taxes and transfer payments*

$$TP = -21.2849 + 0.1784 Y_{\text{P}} \quad \text{(A.34)}$$

$$TX = -19.1451 + 0.1299 GNP \quad \text{(A.35)}$$

$$TC = -0.3543 + 0.4976 Z_{\text{BU}} \quad \text{(A.36)}$$

$$TW = -17.9061 + 0.1306 WSS \quad \text{(A.37)}$$

$$V_{\text{US}_{GF}} = -0.5261 + 0.6482 U + 0.0226[GNP_{\text{K}}^{54} - GNP^{54}]P_{\text{GNP}} \quad \text{(A.38)}$$

$$V_{\text{OA}_{GF}} + V_{\text{VET}} = -0.1047 + 1.0314[V_{\text{OA}_{GF}} + V_{\text{VET}}]_{-1} \quad \text{(A.39)}$$

$$V_{\text{O}_G} = 0.2470 + 0.9657[V_{\text{O}_G}]_{-1} + 0.0080[GNP_{\text{K}}^{54} - GNP^{54}]P_{\text{GNP}} \quad \text{(A.40)}$$

$$V_{\text{G}} = V_{\text{US}_{GF}} + V_{\text{OA}_{GF}} + V_{\text{VET}} + V_{\text{O}_G} \quad \text{(A.41)}$$

New variables in order of appearance are:

$TP$ = personal tax and nontax receipts (or payments), billions of dollars

$Y_P$ = personal income, billlions of dollars

$TX$ = indirect business tax and nontax accruals, billions of dollars

$TC$ = corporate profits tax accruals to government, billions of dollars

$TW$ = contributions for social insurance, billions of dollars

$Z_{BU}$ = corporate profits before taxes and before inventory valuation adjustment, billions of dollars

$WSS$ = compensation of employees, billions of dollars

$V_{US_{GF}}$ = state unemployment insurance benefits paid by the federal government, billions of dollars

$GNP_K^{54}$ = capacity gross national product, billions of 1954 dollars [$GNP^{54}$ in 1955 (392.7 billion dollars) is extrapolated quarterly at a 3.5 per cent annual rate of growth]

$V_{OA_{GF}}$ = old-age and survivors' insurance benefits, billions of dollars

$V_{VET}$ = veterans' benefits, billions of dollars

$P_{GNP}$ = implicit price deflator for $GNP$, 1954 = 1.00

$V_{O_G}$ = government transfer payments to persons other than OASI benefits, state unemployment insurance benefits, and veterans' benefits, billions of dollars

*Production functions*

$$E_{P_{MD}} = 0.7788+0.0671X_{MD}^{54}-0.0431[X_{MD}^{54}]_{-1}-0.0253[K_{MD}^{54}]_{-1} +0.0720[\Delta H_{P_{MD}}]_{-1}+0.8149[E_{P_{MD}}]_{-1} \tag{A.42}$$

$$E_{P_{MN}} = 0.3215+0.0423X_{MN}^{54}-0.0344[X_{MN}^{54}]_{-1}-0.0115[K_{MN}^{54}]_{-1} +0.1033[\Delta H_{P_{MN}}]_{-1}+0.9686[E_{P_{MN}}]_{-1} \tag{A.43}$$

$$E_{P_T} = 0.0158+0.0246X_T^{54}-0.0053[X_T^{54}]_{-1}-0.0056TIME +0.8625[E_{P_T}]_{-1} \tag{A.44}$$

$$E_{P_C} = 0.0742+0.0657X_C^{54}+0.0004[X_C^{54}]_{-1}-0.0025TIME +0.5089[E_{P_C}]_{-1} \tag{A.45}$$

$$E_{O_{MD}} = -0.1121+0.0044X_{MD}^{54}+0.0025[K_{MD}^{54}]_{-1}+0.8845[E_{O_{MD}}]_{-1} \quad \text{(A.46)}$$

$$E_{O_{MN}} = 0.0524+0.0021X_{MN}^{54}-0.0029[K_{MN}^{54}]_{-1}+0.9949[E_{O_{MN}}]_{-1} \quad \text{(A.47)}$$

$$E_{O_T} = 0.4062+0.0020X_T^{54}+0.0042\,TIME+0.6990[E_{O_T}]_{-1} \quad \text{(A.48)}$$

$$E_{O_C} = 0.0530+0.0053X_C^{54}+0.0017\,TIME+0.4187[E_{O_C}]_{-1} \quad \text{(A.49)}$$

$$MH_O = 2.4473+0.0473X_O^{54}+0.0065\,TIME+0.6478[MH_O]_{-1} \quad \text{(A.50)}$$

$$H_{P_{MD}} = 5.7081+7.1241\left[\frac{\Delta X_{MD}^{54}}{[X_{MD}^{54}]_{-1}}\right]+0.8577[H_{P_{MD}}]_{-1} \quad \text{(A.51)}$$

$$H_{P_{MN}} = 8.6754+12.5242\left[\frac{\Delta X_{MN}^{54}}{[X_{MN}^{54}]_{-1}}\right]+0.7769[H_{P_{MN}}]_{-1} \quad \text{(A.52)}$$

$$H_{P_T} = 0.2980+0.3568\left[\frac{\Delta X_T^{54}}{[X_T^{54}]_{-1}}\right]+0.9915[H_{P_T}]_{-1} \quad \text{(A.53)}$$

$$H_{P_C} = 7.6701+1.0497\left[\frac{\Delta X_C^{54}}{[X_C^{54}]_{-1}}\right]+0.7937[H_{P_C}]_{-1} \quad \text{(A.54)}$$

$$E_R = 0.9941+0.0392X_R^{54}-0.0190[X_R^{54}]_{-1}-0.0112[K_R^{54}]_{-1} +0.9010[E_R]_{-1} \quad \text{(A.55)}$$

$$H_R = 11.5676+4.3575\left[\frac{\Delta X_R^{54}}{[X_R^{54}]_{-1}}\right]+0.7160[H_R]_{-1} \quad \text{(A.56)}$$

New variables in order of appearance are:

$E_P$ = employment of production workers, millions of persons

$H_P$ = average workweek of production workers, hours

$TIME$ = time trend, 1947:1 = 1.00

$MH$ = manhours, billions per year

$E_0$ = employment of nonproduction workers, millions of persons

$X$ = gross product originating, billions of dollars

$K$ = stock of business capital, billions of dollars

*Prices and wage rates (compensation per manhour)*

$$PV_{MD} = 0.2109+1.1068ULC^{N}_{MD}+0.8155[ULC_{MD}-ULC^{N}_{MD}]$$
$$-0.2427\left\{\frac{INV^{54}_{MD}}{X^{54}_{MD}}-\frac{1}{12}\sum_{i=-11}^{0}\left[\frac{INV^{54}_{MD}}{X^{54}_{MD}}\right]_{i}\right\}_{-1} \tag{A.57}$$

$$PV_{MN} = 0.0881+1.3109ULC^{N}_{MN}+0.1033P_{S*AF}$$
$$-0.2945\left\{\frac{INV^{54}_{MN}}{X^{54}_{MN}}-\frac{1}{12}\sum_{i=-11}^{0}\left[\frac{INV^{54}_{MN}}{X^{54}_{MN}}\right]_{i}\right\}_{-1}$$
$$+0.9321[ULC_{MN}-ULC^{N}_{MN}] \tag{A.58}$$

$$PV_{T} = 0.3511+1.1916ULC^{N}_{T}+0.8643[ULC_{T}-ULC^{N}_{T}]$$
$$+0.0719\left\{\frac{INV^{54}_{T}}{X^{54}_{T}}-\frac{1}{12}\sum_{i=-11}^{0}\left[\frac{INV^{54}_{T}}{X^{54}_{T}}\right]_{i}\right\}_{-1} \tag{A.59}$$

$$PV_{C} = 0.0745+1.3527ULC^{N}_{C}+1.4689[ULC_{C}-ULC^{N}_{C}] \tag{A.60}$$

$$PV_{O} = 0.1112+2.4464ULC^{N}_{O}+3.1369[ULC_{O}-ULC^{N}_{O}] \tag{A.61}$$

$$PV_{R} = 0.2563+1.0747[ULC^{N}_{R}+UCCA^{N}_{R}]$$
$$+1.2326[ULC_{R}+UCCA_{R}-(ULC^{N}_{R}+UCCA^{N}_{R})] \tag{A.62}$$

$$WPI_{MD} = 0.0272+0.9783PV_{MD} \tag{A.63}$$

$$WPI_{MN} = 0.5833+0.4234PV_{MN} \tag{A.64}$$

$$WPI_{EAF} = 0.0286+0.4572WPI_{MD}+0.5169WPI_{MN} \tag{A.65}$$

$$P_{GOOD} = 0.1775+0.8405WPI_{EAF}-0.0175P_{S*AF} \tag{A.66}$$

$$\Delta CPI = -0.0003+1.1250\Delta P_{C} \tag{A.67}$$

$$P_{C} = \left[\frac{\sum P_{k}C^{54}_{k}}{\sum C^{54}_{k}}\right] \tag{A.68}$$

$$P_{GNP} = \left[\frac{\sum P_{k}GNP^{54}_{k}}{\sum GNP^{54}_{k}}\right] \tag{A.69}$$

$$\left[\frac{RWSS_{MD}-RWSS_{MD_{-4}}}{RWSS_{MD_{-4}}}\right] = -0.0007+0.8196\left\{\frac{1}{4}\sum_{i=-3}^{0}\left[\frac{CPI-CPI_{-4}}{CPI_{-4}}\right]_i\right\}$$

$$+0.1717\left\{\frac{1}{4}\sum_{i=-4}^{-1}\left[\frac{Z_{B_{MD}}}{X_{MD}^{54}}\right]_i\right\}+0.0012\left[\frac{1}{RU*}\right]$$

$$-0.2768\left[\frac{RWSS_{MD_{-4}}-RWSS_{MD_{-8}}}{RWSS_{MD_{-8}}}\right] \qquad \text{(A.70)}$$

$$\left[\frac{RWSS_{MN}-RWSS_{MN_{-4}}}{RWSS_{MN_{-4}}}\right] = +0.0444+0.6894\left\{\frac{1}{4}\sum_{i=-3}^{0}\left[\frac{CPI-CPI_{-4}}{CPI_{-4}}\right]_i\right\}$$

$$-0.0741\left\{\frac{1}{4}\sum_{i=-4}^{-1}\left[\frac{Z_{B_{MN}}}{X_{MN}^{54}}\right]_i\right\}+0.0012\left[\frac{1}{RU*}\right]$$

$$-0.5304\left[\frac{RWSS_{MN_{-4}}-RWSS_{MN_{-8}}}{RWSS_{MN_{-8}}}\right] \qquad \text{(A.71)}$$

$$\left[\frac{RWSS_{T}-RWSS_{T_{-4}}}{RWSS_{T_{-4}}}\right] = 0.2090+0.7738\left\{\frac{1}{4}\sum_{i=-3}^{0}\left[\frac{CPI-CPI_{-4}}{CPI_{-4}}\right]_i\right\}$$

$$-0.6471\left\{\frac{1}{4}\sum_{i=-4}^{-1}\left[\frac{(Z_{B_T}+Y_{ENT_T})}{X_T^{54}}\right]_i\right\}$$

$$+0.0012\left[\frac{1}{RU*}\right]$$

$$-0.8411\left[\frac{RWSS_{T_{-4}}-RWSS_{T_{-8}}}{RWSS_{T_{-8}}}\right] \qquad \text{(A.72)}$$

$$\left[\frac{RWSS_{R}-RWSS_{R_{-4}}}{RWSS_{R_{-4}}}\right] = 0.0292+0.7062\left\{\frac{1}{4}\sum_{i=-3}^{0}\left[\frac{CPI-CPI_{-4}}{CPI_{-4}}\right]_i\right\}$$

$$+0.2378\left\{\frac{1}{4}\sum_{i=-4}^{-1}\left[\frac{Z_{B_R}}{X_R^{54}}\right]_i\right\}$$

$$-0.0703\times10^{-4}\left[\frac{1}{RU*}\right]$$

$$-0.5120\left[\frac{RWSS_{R_{-4}}-RWSS_{R_{-8}}}{RWSS_{R_{-8}}}\right] \qquad \text{(A.73)}$$

$$\left[\frac{RWSS_C - RWSS_{C_{-4}}}{RWSS_{C_{-4}}}\right] = -0.0146 + 0.8528 \left\{\frac{1}{4}\sum_{i=-3}^{0}\left[\frac{CPI - CPI_{-4}}{CPI_{-4}}\right]_i\right\}$$
$$+0.1346 \left\{\frac{1}{4}\sum_{i=-4}^{-1}\left[\frac{(Z_{BC} + Y_{ENTC})}{X_C^{54}}\right]_i\right\} + 0.0013 \frac{1}{RU*}$$
$$-0.3119 \left[\frac{RWSS_{C_{-4}} - RWSS_{C_{-8}}}{RWSS_{C_{-8}}}\right] \qquad (A.74)$$

$$\left[\frac{RWSS_O - RWSS_{O_{-4}}}{RWSS_{O_{-4}}}\right] = -0.0522 + 0.6382 \left\{\frac{1}{4}\sum_{i=-3}^{0}\left[\frac{CPI - CPI_{-4}}{CPI_{-4}}\right]_i\right\}$$
$$+0.4871 \left\{\frac{1}{4}\sum_{i=-4}^{-1}\left[\frac{(Z_{BO} + Y_{ENTO})}{X_O^{54}}\right]_i\right\} + 0.0004 \frac{1}{RU*}$$
$$-0.5473 \left[\frac{RWSS_{O_{-4}} - RWSS_{O_{-8}}}{RWSS_{O_{-8}}}\right] \qquad (A.75)$$

New variables in order of appearance are:

$PV$ = implicit price deflator for gross product originating, 1954 = 1.00

$ULC^N$ = normal unit labor costs, dollars per dollar

$$= \frac{WSS}{MH} \Big/ \frac{1}{12}\left\{\sum_{i=-11}^{0}\left[\frac{X^{54}}{MH}\right]_i\right\}$$

$ULC$ = unit labor cost (compensation of employees per unit of gross product originating), dollars per dollar of real gross product

$UCCA^N$ = normal unit capital consumption allowances, dollars per dollar

$$= \frac{1}{12}\left\{\sum_{i=-11}^{0}\left[\frac{CCA}{X^{54}}\right]_i\right\}$$

$CCA$ = capital consumption allowances, billions of dollars

$UCCA$ = unit capital consumption allowances (capital consumption allowance per unit of real gross product originating), dollars per dollar of real product

$WPI$ = wholesale price index, 1954 = 1.00

$CPI$ = consumer price index, 1954 = 1.00

$RWSS$ = compensation of employees per manhour, dollars per hour

$Z_B$ = corporate profits before taxes including inventory valuation adjustment, billions of dollars

$RU*$ = five-quarter average of $RU$ centered on ($t$-2), fraction

$= 1/8RU_{-4}+1/4RU_{-3}+1/4RU_{-2}+1/4RU_{-1}+1/8RU$

$P_{S*_{AF}}$ = implicit price deflator for value of cash receipts from farm marketings and CCC loans plus value of farm products consumed directly in farm households, 1954 = 1.00

$Y_{ENT}$ = proprietors' income, billions of dollars

*Final demand and price conversion*

$$\hat{F}^{54}_{MD} = 0.555C^{54}_{DA}+0.664C^{54}_{DEA}+0.8377[I^{54}_{PDE}+G^{54}_{CD}]+\Delta INV^{54}_{MD} +0.3170[EX^{54}+\Delta INV^{54}_{T}]+5.288DMY12 \quad (A.76)$$

$$\hat{F}^{54}_{MN} = 0.664[C^{54}_{NEFB}-C^{54}_{INEFB}]+0.838G^{54}_{CN}+\Delta INV^{54}_{MN} +0.379[C^{54}_{NFB}-C^{54}_{INFB}+\Delta INV^{54}_{T}+EX^{54}-M^{54}] +0.163[DMY13][TIME] \quad (A.77)$$

$$\hat{F}^{54}_{T} = 0.250[C^{54}-C^{54}_{DA}]+0.359C^{54}_{DA} +0.0761[GNP^{54}-C^{54}-EX^{54}-\Delta INV^{54}_{AF}-\Delta INV^{54}_{M}] \quad (A.78)$$

$$\hat{F}^{54}_{R} = 0.0640[GNP^{54}-\Delta INV^{54}_{AF}-\Delta INV^{54}_{M}] \quad (A.79)$$

$$\hat{F}^{54}_{C} = 9.68+0.8377[I^{54}_{CNFR}+I^{54}_{CO}+(I^{54}_{CPL_{EAF}}+I^{54}_{C_{AF}})+G^{54}_{IC}] \quad (A.80)$$

$$\hat{F}^{54}_{O} = C^{54}_{SR}+0.686[C^{54}_{S}-C^{54}_{IS}]+0.0222[GNP^{54}-C^{54}_{SR}-(C^{54}_{S}-C^{54}_{IS})] \quad (A.81)$$

(A.82) through (A.88) – continued on p. 140.

$$\begin{bmatrix} 0.7304 & -0.0025 & -0.1758 & -0.0134 & -0.0005 & -0.0032 & -0.0015 \\ -0.0112 & 0.6318 & -0.0281 & -0.0341 & -0.0361 & -0.3276 & -0.0310 \\ -0.0908 & -0.0684 & 0.6786 & -0.0912 & -0.0558 & -0.0529 & -0.0670 \\ -0.0399 & -0.0200 & -0.0171 & 0.9597 & -0.0216 & -0.0995 & -0.0205 \\ -0.0260 & -0.0376 & -0.0348 & -0.0324 & 0.9239 & -0.0467 & -0.0559 \\ -0.0059 & -0.0031 & -0.0002 & -0.0046 & -0.0550 & 0.9998 & -0.0554 \\ -0.0709 & -0.0377 & -0.0364 & -0.1164 & -0.0575 & -0.0498 & 0.9075 \end{bmatrix}$$

$$\cdot\begin{bmatrix}\hat{X}_{AF}(1.8716)(1.225)\\ \hat{X}_{MD}(2.4310)(0.752)\\ \hat{X}_{MN}(3.3244)(0.859)\\ \hat{X}_{T}\ (1.2684)(0.866)\\ \hat{X}_{R}\ (1.4564)(0.821)\\ \hat{X}_{C}\ (3.1893)(0.738)\\ \hat{X}_{O}\ (1.4391)(0.734)\end{bmatrix}=\begin{bmatrix}\hat{F}_{AF}(1.225)\\ \hat{F}_{MD}(0.752)\\ \hat{F}_{MN}(0.859)\\ \hat{F}_{T}\ (0.866)\\ \hat{F}_{R}\ (0.821)\\ \hat{F}_{C}\ (0.738)\\ \hat{F}_{O}\ (0.734)\end{bmatrix}$$

Note: $\hat{X}$'s and $\hat{F}$'s are in billions of 1954 dollars.

*Autoregressive output corrections*

$$\hat{\hat{X}}_{MD}^{54} = 2.8755+0.9516\hat{X}_{MD}^{54}+0.4700(X_{MD}^{54}-\hat{X}_{MD}^{54})_{-1} \tag{A.89}$$

$$\hat{\hat{X}}_{MN}^{54} = 5.3576+0.8893\hat{X}_{MN}^{54}+0.4683(X_{MN}^{54}-\hat{X}_{MN}^{54})_{-1} \tag{A.90}$$

$$\hat{\hat{X}}_{T}^{54} = 4.6300+0.9136\hat{X}_{T}^{54}+0.5336(X_{T}^{54}-\hat{X}_{T}^{54})_{-1} \tag{A.91}$$

$$\hat{\hat{X}}_{R}^{54} = -2.2370+1.0668\hat{X}_{R}^{54}+0.8592(X_{R}^{54}-\hat{X}_{R}^{54})_{-1} \tag{A.92}$$

$$\hat{\hat{X}}_{C}^{54} = 0.9938+0.9442\hat{X}_{C}^{54}+0.8907(X_{C}^{54}-\hat{X}_{C}^{54})_{-1} \tag{A.93}$$

$$\hat{\hat{X}}_{O}^{54} = -1.6565+1.0177\hat{X}_{O}^{54}+0.8845(X_{O}^{54}-\hat{X}_{O}^{54})_{-1} \tag{A.94}$$

*Reconciliation of real GNP and industry gross product originating*

$$\varepsilon_{\hat{\hat{X}}54} = GNP^{54}-\sum_{j}\hat{\hat{X}}_{j}^{54}-X_{A}^{54}-X_{W}^{54}-X_{G}^{54}-\varepsilon_{X54} \tag{A.95}$$

$$X_{j}^{54} = \left[\frac{\hat{\hat{X}}_{j}^{54}}{\sum\hat{\hat{X}}_{j}^{54}}\right]_{-1}\varepsilon_{\hat{\hat{X}}54}+\hat{\hat{X}}_{j}^{54} \tag{A.96–A.101}$$

$j \quad = MD, MN, T, R, C, O.$

*Price conversions*

$$\hat{P}_{\text{CDEA}} = 0.6643PV_{MD}+0.2495PV_{T}+0.0640PV_{R}+0.0222PV_{O} \tag{A.102}$$

$$\hat{P}_{\text{CDA}} = 0.5550PV_{MD}+0.3588PV_{T}+0.0640PV_{R}+0.0222PV_{O} \tag{A.103}$$

$$\hat{P}_{\text{CNEFB}} = 0.6643PV_{MN}+0.2495PV_T+0.0640PV_R+0.0222PV_O \quad \text{(A.104)}$$

$$\hat{P}_{\text{CNFB}} = 0.2856PV_A+0.3787PV_{MN}+0.2495PV_T+0.0640PV_R+0.0222PV_O \quad \text{(A.105)}$$

$$\hat{P}_{\text{CS}} = 0.2495PV_T+0.0640PV_R+0.6865PV_O \quad \text{(A.106)}$$

$$\hat{P}_{\text{IBUS}} = 0.4964PV_{MD}+0.0761PV_T+0.0640PV_R+0.3413PV_C+0.0222PV_O \quad \text{(A.107)}$$

$$\hat{P}_{\text{ICNFR}} = 0.0761PV_T+0.0640PV_R+0.8377PV_C+0.0222PV_O \quad \text{(A.108)}$$

$$\hat{P}_{\text{EX}} = 0.2181PV_{\text{A}}+0.3170PV_{MD}+0.3787PV_{MN}+0.0640PV_R+0.0222PV_O \quad \text{(A.109)}$$

$$\hat{P}_{\text{G}} = 0.0420PV_A+0.1886PV_{MD}+0.0703PV_{MN}+0.0728PV_T +0.0612PV_R+0.1247PV_C+0.0213PV_O+0.4188J_{\text{WSG/EG}} \quad \text{(A.110)}$$

*Autoregressive price corrections*

$$P_{\text{CDEA}} = 0.2102+0.7811\hat{P}_{\text{CDEA}}+0.7520[P_{\text{CDEA}}-\hat{P}_{\text{CDEA}}]_{-1} \quad \text{(A.111)}$$

$$P_{\text{CDA}} = 0.0935+0.9415\hat{P}_{\text{CDA}}+0.1546[P_{\text{CDA}}-\hat{P}_{\text{CDA}}]_{-1} \quad \text{(A.112)}$$

$$P_{\text{CNEFB}} = 0.1861+0.8222\hat{P}_{\text{CNEFB}}+0.1514[P_{\text{CNEFB}}-\hat{P}_{\text{CNEFB}}]_{-1} \quad \text{(A.113)}$$

$$P_{\text{CNFB}} = 0.0338+0.9637\hat{P}_{\text{CNFB}}+0.7925[P_{\text{CNFB}}-\hat{P}_{\text{CNFB}}]_{-1} \quad \text{(A.114)}$$

$$P_{\text{CS}} = -0.0163+1.0157\hat{P}_{\text{CS}}+0.6759[P_{\text{CS}}-\hat{P}_{\text{CS}}]_{-1} \quad \text{(A.115)}$$

$$P_{\text{IBUS}} = -0.0163+1.0225\hat{P}_{\text{IBUS}}+0.5942[P_{\text{IBUS}}-\hat{P}_{\text{IBUS}}]_{-1} \quad \text{(A.116)}$$

$$P_{\text{ICNFR}} = 0.1733+0.8328\hat{P}_{\text{ICNFR}}+0.4974[P_{\text{ICNFR}}-\hat{P}_{\text{ICNFR}}]_{-1} \quad \text{(A.117)}$$

$$P_{\text{EX}} = 0.0843+0.9153\hat{P}_{\text{EX}}+0.5785[P_{\text{EX}}-\hat{P}_{\text{EX}}]_{-1} \quad \text{(A.118)}$$

$$P_G = -0.0169+1.0203\hat{P}_G+0.9369[P_G-\hat{P}_G]_{-1} \quad \text{(A.119)}$$

New variables in order of appearance are:

$F$ = estimated final demand, billions of dollars

$I_{\text{PDE}}$ = investment in producers' durable equipment, billions of dollars

$G_{\text{CD}}$ = government purchases of durable goods, billions of dollars

$EX$ = exports, billions of dollars

$DMY12$ = 1, 1953 through 1955
0, other years

$C_{\text{INEFB}}$ = personal consumption expenditures for nondurable goods except food and beverages, imputed or in kind, billions of dollars

$M$ = imports, billions of dollars

$DMY13$ = 0, 1947 through 1957
1, in other years

$C$ = personal consumption expenditures, billions of dollars

$I_{\text{CNFR}}$ = private residential nonfarm new construction, billions of dollars

$I_{\text{CO}}$ = value of new private nonfarm, nonresidential, nonbusiness construction put in place, billions of dollars

$I_{\text{CPL}_{EAF}}$ = new nonfarm business construction, billions of dollars

$I_{\text{C}_{AF}}$ = new farm residential and nonresidential construction, billions of dollars

$G_{\text{IC}}$ = new public construction activity, billions of dollars

$C_{\text{SR}}$ = personal consumption expenditures for rent (space-rental value of owner-occupied nonfarm dwellings, space rent of tenant-occupied nonfarm dwellings, and rental value of farm houses), billions of dollars

$C_{\text{IS}}$ = imputed personal consumption expenditures on services, billions of dollars

$X$ = gross product originating, billions of dollars

$\varepsilon_{\hat{\hat{\text{X}}}54}$ = complete system solution endogenous epsilon: difference between real *GNP* and the sum of autoregressive corrected industry gross product originating

$\varepsilon_{\text{X}54}$ = real industry gross product originating epsilon: difference between real *GNP* in the gross national product expenditure accounts and the sum of real industry gross product originating from Brookings quarterly interpolations of annual data prepared by Martin L. Marimont of the Office of Business Economics

$PV$ = implicit price deflator for gross product originating, 1954 = 1.00

$P_{\text{CDEA}}$ = implicit price deflator for personal consumption expenditures on durable goods other than new and net used automobiles, 1954 = 1.00

$P_{CDA}$ = implicit price deflator for personal consumption expenditures on new and net used automobiles, 1954 = 1.00

$P_{CNEFB}$ = implicit price deflator for personal consumption expenditures on nondurable goods other than food and beverages, 1954 = 1.00

$P_{CNFB}$ = implicit price deflator for personal consumption expenditures on food and beverages, 1954 = 1.00

$P_{CS}$ = implicit price deflator for personal consumption expenditures on services, 1954 = 1.00

$P_{IBUS}$ = implicit price deflator for business gross investment in plant and equipment, 1954 = 1.00

$P_{ICNFR}$ = implicit price deflator for residential nonfarm new private construction, 1954 = 1.00

$P_{EX}$ = implicit price deflator for exports of goods and services, 1954 = 1.00

$P_G$ = implicit price deflator for government purchases of goods and services, 1954 = 1.00

$J_{WSG/EG}$ = index of wages and salaries per employee in government, 1954 = 1.00

*Financial sector*

$$RES_F = RES_{NB} - RES_R \tag{A.120.1}$$

$$RES_R = 0.84[RRR_{DD}][DD + DD_{GF}] + 0.82[RRR_{DT}][DT] \tag{A.120.2}$$

$$\frac{\Delta DD}{WLTH} = -0.00281 - 0.108\left[\frac{[DD]_{-1}}{WLTH}\right] - 0.00491 RM_{GBL} - 0.00236 RM_{BDT} + 0.067\frac{Y_D}{WLTH} + 0.031\left[\frac{[Y_D]_{-1}}{[WLTH]_{-1}}\right] - 0.196\left[\frac{I_{BUS} + I_{CO}}{[WLTH]_{-1}}\right] \tag{A.121}$$

$$\frac{\Delta DT}{WLTH} = -0.00205 - 0.123\left[\frac{[DT]_{-1}}{WLTH}\right] + 0.00627 RM_{BDT} - 0.00266 RM_{GBS3} + 0.021\left[\frac{[Y_D]_{-1}}{[WLTH]_{-1}}\right] \tag{A.122}$$

$$\frac{\Delta RES_{F}}{[DD+DT]_{-1}} = -0.00156-0.387\left[\frac{[RES_{F}]_{-1}}{[DD+DT]_{-1}}\right]-0.00216RM_{GBS3}$$
$$+0.00235RM_{FRB}$$
$$+0.053\left[\frac{\Delta[(DD+DD_{GF})(1-0.84RRR_{DD})+DT(1-0.82RRR_{DT})]}{[DD+DT]_{-1}}\right] \qquad (A.123)$$

$$\Delta RM_{BDT} = -1.255-0.388[RM_{BDT}]_{-1}+0.331RM_{BDTM}$$
$$+0.142RM_{GBL}+1.02\left[\frac{ALNPS_{B}}{[DD+DT]}\right]_{-2} \qquad (A.124)$$

$$RM_{GBL}-RM_{GBS3} = 1.315-1.115\{\sum_{i=0}^{10}[w_{1-i}][\Delta RM_{GBL-i}]\} \qquad (A.125)$$

$$-1.413\{\sum_{i=0}^{10}[w_{2-i}][\Delta RM_{GBL-i}]\}-0.366\{\sum_{i=0}^{10}[w_{3-i}][\Delta RM_{GBL-i}]\}$$
$$-5.1\Delta\left[\frac{BF_{1}}{BF_{PUB}}\right]-5.2\Delta\left[\frac{BF_{1-5}}{BF_{PUB}}\right] \qquad (A.126)$$

$$WLTH = 0.114\sum_{i=1}^{20}(0.9)^{i-1}(GNP)_{-i} \qquad (A.127)$$

New variables in order of appearance are:

$RES_{F}$ = free reserves of Federal Reserve member banks, average during quarter, billions of dollars

$RES_{NB}$ = unborrowed reserves of Federal Reserve member banks, average during quarter, billions of dollars

$RES_{R}$ = required reserves of Federal Reserve member banks, average during quarter, billions of dollars

$RRR_{DD}$ = weighted average of required reserve ratios against demand deposits, proportion

$DD$ = private demand deposit liabilities of commercial banks less interbank deposits, cash items in process of collection, and Federal Reserve float, average during quarter, billions of dollars

$DD_{GF}$ = federal government demand deposits at commercial banks, average during quarter, billions of dollars

$RRR_{DT}$ = average reserve ratio required against time deposits, proportion

$WLTH$ = weighted average of recent values of *GNP*, billions of dollars

$RM_{GBL}$ = average yield during quarter on U.S. securities maturing or callable in ten years or more, per cent

$RM_{BDT}$ = yield on commercial bank time deposits, per cent

$RM_{GBS3}$ = average market yield on three-month U.S. Treasury bills, per cent

$RM_{FRB}$ = Federal Reserve Bank of New York discount rate, daily average during quarter, per cent

$ALNPS_{B}$ = commercial bank holdings of loans and other private securities, billions of current dollars

$BF_{1}$ = U. S. marketable debt maturing within 1 year, average during quarter, billions of dollars

$BF_{PUB}$ = marketable federal debt of all maturities outside Federal Reserve and U. S. government agencies and trust funds, average during quarter, billions of dollars

$BF_{1-5}$ = U. S. marketable debt of 1 to 5 year maturity, average during quarter, billions of dollars

$w_n$ = fourth degree polynomial weights

$I_{BUS} = \sum_j [I_{BUS_j}] + [P_{IBUS}][\varepsilon_{IBUS54}] + \varepsilon_{IBUS}$

*Non-wage income*

$$\Delta INT_G = 0.0669 + 0.0043[RM_{GBS3}][\Delta BF_{PUB}] + 0.0007[BF_{PUB}][\Delta RM_{GBS3}] \quad \text{(A.128)}$$

$$\Delta DIV = -0.0036 + 0.0957[Z_A + CCAC] - 0.3149[DIV]_{-1} \quad \text{(A.129)}$$

$$\Delta Y_{ENT_{EAF}} = 0.0955 + 0.0450[\Delta WSS - \Delta WSS_A - \Delta WSS_W - \Delta WSS_G - \Delta \varepsilon_{WSS}] + 0.0882\Delta[Z_B - Z_{B_A} - Z_{B_W} - \varepsilon_{ZB} + Y_{ENT_{EAF}} - \varepsilon_{YENT_{EAF}}] + \Delta\varepsilon_{YENT_{EAF}} \quad \text{(A.130)}$$

$$\Delta INT_{BUS_O} = 0.0554 + 0.0006\{[RM_{GBL}(C_D + I_{CNFR})] + [RM_{GBL}(C_D + I_{CNFR})]_{-1}\} \quad \text{(A.131)}$$

$$\begin{aligned} IVA = {} & 0.0980 - 3.3595[INV^{54}_{MD_{-1}} \Delta WPI_{MD}] - 1.6056[INV^{54}_{T_{-1}} \Delta WPI_{MD}] \\ & - 3.6843[INV^{54}_{O*4_{-1}} \Delta WPI_{MD}] - 3.3796[INV^{54}_{MN_{-1}} \Delta WPI_{MN}] \\ & - 1.1777[INV^{54}_{T_{-1}} \Delta WPI_{MN}] - 0.1662[INV^{54}_{T_{-1}} \Delta P_{\mathrm{S}*_{AF}}] \end{aligned} \tag{A.132}$$

*Note* Exogenous in present model solutions.

New variables in order of appearance are:

$INT_{\mathrm{G}}$ = personal interest income paid by government, billions of dollars

$DIV$ = dividends, billions of dollars

$Z_{\mathrm{A}}$ = corporate profits after taxes and after inventory valuation adjustment, billions of dollars

$CCAC$ = corporate capital consumption allowances, billions of dollars

$Y_{\mathrm{ENT}_{EAF}}$ = business and professional proprietors' income, billions of dollars

$\varepsilon_{\mathrm{WSS}}$ = compensation of employees epsilon: the difference between compensation of employees from the national income accounts and the sum of unpublished data by industry for the same concept (supplements to wages and salaries by industry are quarterly interpolations of annual data). Both sets of data are from the Office of Business Economics. In the late years, the epsilon also stems from use of revised aggregate and unrevised WSS data by industry.

$Z_{\mathrm{B}}$ = corporate profits before tax, billions of dollars

$\varepsilon_{\mathrm{ZB}}$ = corporate profits epsilon: the difference between corporate profits before tax including inventory valuation adjustment in the national income accounts (on a company basis) and the sum of the same concept by industry from quarterly interpolations of annual data (on an establishment basis) – basic source for both sets of data is the Office of Business Economics.

$\varepsilon_{\mathrm{YENT}_{EAF}}$ = business and professional proprietors' income epsilon: the difference between nonfarm proprietors' income from the national income accounts (late years revised) and the sum of unpublished data by industry for the same concept (late years unrevised). All data are from the Office of Business Economics.

$INT_{\mathrm{BUS}}$ = personal interest income paid by business, billions of dollars

$C_{\mathrm{D}}$ = personal consumption expenditures on durable goods, billions of dollars

$IVA$ = inventory valuation adjustment, billions of dollars

*Capital consumption allowances*

$$CCA_{MD} = [CCA_{MD}]_{-1} + 0.0202 + 0.0248\{\tfrac{1}{2}I_{BUS_{MD}} + \tfrac{1}{2}[I_{BUS_{MD}}]_{-1} - [CCA_{MD}]_{-1}\} + 0.0432DMY19 + 0.242DMY23 \quad (A.133)$$

$$CCA_{MN} = [CCA_{MN}]_{-1} + 0.0189\{\tfrac{1}{2}I_{BUS_{MN}} + \tfrac{1}{2}[I_{BUS_{MN}}]_{-1} - [CCA_{MN}]_{-1}\} + 0.0446DMY20 + 0.216DMY23 \quad (A.134)$$

$$CCA_{R} = [CCA_{R}]_{-1} + 0.0162\{\tfrac{1}{2}I_{BUS_{R}} + \tfrac{1}{2}[I_{BUS_{R}}]_{-1} - [CCA_{R}]_{-1}\} + 0.0506DMY21 + 0.101DMY23 \quad (A.135)$$

$$CCA_{O*6} = [CCA_{O*6}]_{-1} + 0.0204\{I_{BUS_{O*2}} + \tfrac{1}{2}[I_{BUS_{O*2}}]_{-1} - [CCA_{O*6}]_{-1}\} + 0.0539\{\tfrac{1}{2}I_{BUS_{O*2}} + \tfrac{1}{2}[I_{BUS_{O*2}}]_{-1}\} + 1.7485\left[\frac{\tfrac{1}{2}I_{BUS_{O*2}} + \tfrac{1}{2}[I_{BUS_{O*2}}]_{-1}}{\tfrac{1}{2}[I_{BUS_{O*2}}]_{-1} + \tfrac{1}{2}[I_{BUS_{O*2}}]_{-2}}\right] - 1.7485 + 0.0021DMY22 + 0.184DMY23 \quad (A.136)$$

Variables in order of appearance are:

$CCA$ = capital consumption allowances, billions of dollars

$I_{BUS}$ = business gross investment in plant and equipment, billions of dollars

$DMY19$ = 1, 1954:1 through 1955:4
0, all other quarters

$DMY23$ = 1, in 1962
0, in all other years

$DMY20$ = 1, 1954:1 through 1955:4
0, all other quarters

$DMY21$ = 1, 1955:1 through 1955:4
0, all other quarters

$DMY22$ = 1, 1954:1 through 1957:4
0, all other quarters

*Proprietors' income*

$$\Delta Y_{\mathrm{ENT}_{MD}} = -0.0069+0.0072\Delta WSS_{MD}+0.0152\Delta[PV_{MD}X_{MD}^{54}-WSS_{MD} - Y_{\mathrm{RENT}_{MD}}-INT_{\mathrm{BUS}_{MD}}-CCA_{MD}-(TX_{MD}+V_{\mathrm{BUS}_{MD}})] \quad \text{(A.137)}$$

$$\Delta Y_{\mathrm{ENT}_{MN}} = -0.0051+0.0159\Delta WSS_{MN}+0.0042\Delta[PV_{MN}X_{MN}^{54}-WSS_{MN} - Y_{\mathrm{RENT}_{MN}}-INT_{\mathrm{BUS}_{MN}}-CCA_{MN}-(TX_{MN}+V_{\mathrm{BUS}_{MN}})] \quad \text{(A.138)}$$

$$\Delta Y_{\mathrm{ENT}_{T}} = -0.0144+0.0737\Delta WSS_{T}+0.0972\Delta[PV_{T}X_{T}^{54}-WSS_{T} - Y_{\mathrm{RENT}_{T}}-INT_{\mathrm{BUS}_{T}}-CCA_{T}-(TX_{T}+V_{\mathrm{BUS}_{T}})] \quad \text{(A.139)}$$

$$\Delta Y_{\mathrm{ENT}_{R}} = 0.0049+0.0019\Delta WSS_{R}+0.0056\Delta[PV_{R}X_{R}^{54}-WSS_{R}- Y_{\mathrm{RENT}_{R}}-INT_{\mathrm{BUS}_{R}}-CCA_{R}-(TX_{R}+V_{\mathrm{BUS}_{R}})] \quad \text{(A.140)}$$

$$\Delta Y_{\mathrm{ENT}_{C}} = -0.0046+0.0681\Delta WSS_{C}+0.7580\Delta[PV_{C}X_{C}^{54}-WSS_{C} - Y_{\mathrm{RENT}_{C}}-INT_{\mathrm{BUS}_{C}}-CCA_{C}-(TX_{C}+V_{\mathrm{BUS}_{C}})] \quad \text{(A.141)}$$

$$\Delta Y_{\mathrm{ENT}_{O}} = 0.0739+0.0676\Delta WSS_{O}+0.2394\Delta[PV_{O}X_{O}^{54}-WSS_{O}- Y_{\mathrm{RENT}_{O}}-INT_{\mathrm{BUS}_{O}}-CCA_{O}-(TX_{O}+V_{\mathrm{BUS}_{O}})] \quad \text{(A.142)}$$

The variables in order of appearance are:

$Y_{\mathrm{ENT}}$ = proprietors' income, billions of dollars

$WSS$ = compensation of employees, billions of dollars

$PV$ = implicit price deflator for gross product originating, 1954 = 1.00

$X$ = gross product originating, billions of dollars

$Y_{\mathrm{RENT}}$ = rental income of persons, billions of dollars

$INT_{\mathrm{BUS}}$ = net interest paid by business, billions of dollars

$CCA$ = capital consumption allowances, billions of dollars

$TX$ = indirect business tax and nontax accruals, billions of dollars

$V_{\mathrm{BUS}}$ = business transfer payments, billions of dollars

*Indirect business taxes and business transfer payments*

$$\Delta\left[\frac{TX_R+V_{\text{BUS}_R}}{TX+V_{\text{BUS}}}\right] = -0.0004+0.6793\Delta\left[\frac{PV_R X_R^{54}}{\sum_j (PV_j X_j^{54})}\right] \tag{A.143}$$

$$\Delta\left[\frac{TX_C+V_{\text{BUS}_C}}{TX+V_{\text{BUS}}}\right] = 0.0001+0.0603\Delta\left[\frac{PV_C X_C^{54}}{\sum_j (PV_j X_j^{54})}\right] +0.1592\Delta\left[\frac{CCA_C}{\sum_j CCA_j}\right] \tag{A.144}$$

$$\Delta\left[\frac{TX_O+V_{\text{BUS}_O}}{TX+V_{\text{BUS}}}\right] = -0.0001+0.8427\Delta\left[\frac{PV_O X_O^{54}}{\sum_j (PV_j X_j^{54})}\right] \tag{A.145}$$

$$\Delta\left[\frac{TX_{MD}+V_{\text{BUS}_{MD}}}{TX+V_{\text{BUS}}}\right] = 0.4916\Delta\left[\frac{PV_{MD} X_{MD}^{54}}{\sum_j PV_j X_j^{54}}\right] \tag{A.146}$$

$$\Delta\left[\frac{TX_{MN}+V_{\text{BUS}_{MN}}}{TX+V_{\text{BUS}}}\right] = -0.0010+0.4493\Delta\left[\frac{PV_{MN} X_{MN}^{54}}{\sum_j PV_j X_j^{54}}\right] \tag{A.147}$$

$$\Delta\left[\frac{TX_T+V_{\text{BUS}_T}}{TX+V_{\text{BUS}}}\right] = 0.0007+0.6130\Delta\left[\frac{PV_T X_T^{54}}{\sum_j PV_j X_j^{54}}\right] +0.1471\Delta\left[\frac{CCA_T}{\sum_j CCA_j}\right] \tag{A.148}$$

The variables are:

$TX$ = indirect business tax and nontax accruals, billions of dollars

$V_{\text{BUS}}$ = business transfer payments, billions of dollars

$PV$ = implicit price deflator for gross product originating, 1954 = 1.00

$X$ = gross product originating, billions of dollars

$CCA$ = capital consumption allowances, billions of dollars

*Labor force*

$$L = 11.992+0.7987E+0.4860U_{-1}+0.6566\Delta U_{-1}+0.0637TIME \tag{A.149}$$

The variables are:

$L$ = civilian labor force, millions of persons

$E$ = employment, millions of persons

$U$ = unemployment, millions of persons

*Identities and fixed proportions*

Gross national product or expenditures

$$GNP^{54} = C^{54}+I^{54}_{\mathrm{CNFR}}+I^{54}_{\mathrm{CO}}+\Delta INV^{54}+I^{54}_{\mathrm{BUS}}+EX^{54}-M^{54}+G^{54} \quad \text{(A.150)}$$

$$C^{54} = C^{44}_{\mathrm{DA}}+C^{54}_{\mathrm{DEA}}+C^{54}_{\mathrm{NFB}}+C^{54}_{\mathrm{NEFB}}+C^{44}_{\mathrm{S}} \quad \text{(A.151)}$$

$$P_{\mathrm{C}} = [\sum P_{\mathrm{C}_k}C^{54}_k]/[\sum C^{54}_k] \quad \text{(A.152)}$$

$$\Delta INV^{54} = \Delta INV^{54}_{AF}+\Delta INV^{54}_{MD}+\Delta INV^{54}_{MN}+\Delta INV^{54}_{T}+\Delta INV^{54}_{O*4} \quad \text{(A.153)}$$

$$M^{54} = M^{54}_{\mathrm{FIN}}+M^{54}_{\mathrm{EFIN}} \quad \text{(A.154)}$$

$$\varepsilon_{\mathrm{IBUS54}} = [I^{54}_{\mathrm{CPL}_{EAF}}+I^{54}_{\mathrm{C}_{AF}}]+I^{54}_{\mathrm{PDE}}-I^{54}_{\mathrm{BUS}_{AF}}-I^{54}_{\mathrm{BUS}_{MD}}-I^{54}_{\mathrm{BUS}_{MN}} -I^{54}_{\mathrm{BUS}_{R}}-I^{54}_{\mathrm{BUS}_{O*2}} \quad \text{(A.155)}$$

$$I^{54}_{\mathrm{BUS}} = I^{54}_{\mathrm{BUS}_{AF}}+I^{54}_{\mathrm{BUS}_{MD}}+I^{54}_{\mathrm{BUS}_{MN}}+I^{54}_{\mathrm{BUS}_{R}}+I^{54}_{\mathrm{BUS}_{O*2}}+\varepsilon_{\mathrm{IBUS54}} \quad \text{(A.156)}$$

$$[I^{54}_{\mathrm{CPL}_{EAF}}+I^{54}_{\mathrm{C}_{AF}}] = 0.3830I^{54}_{\mathrm{BUS}} \quad \text{(A.157)}$$

$$I^{54}_{\mathrm{C}} = I^{54}_{\mathrm{CNFR}}+I^{54}_{\mathrm{CO}}+[I^{54}_{\mathrm{CPL}_{EAF}}+I^{54}_{\mathrm{C}_{AF}}] \quad \text{(A.158)}$$

$$GNP^{54}_{\mathrm{IC}} = I^{54}_{\mathrm{C}}+G^{54}_{\mathrm{IC}} \quad \text{(A.159)}$$

$$C^{54}_{\mathrm{D}} = C^{54}_{\mathrm{DA}}+C^{54}_{\mathrm{DEA}} \quad \text{(A.160)}$$

$$C_{\mathrm{D}} = [P_{\mathrm{CDA}}][C^{54}_{\mathrm{DA}}]+[P_{\mathrm{CDEA}}][C^{54}_{\mathrm{DEA}}] \quad \text{(A.161)}$$

$$I^{54}_{\mathrm{PDE}} = 0.6170I^{54}_{\mathrm{BUS}} \quad \text{(A162)}$$

$$EX^{54}_{\mathrm{D}} = 0.3711EX^{54} \quad \text{(A.163)}$$

$$M^{54}_{\mathrm{D}} = 0.2658M^{54} \quad \text{(A.164)}$$

$$[GNP^{54}_{\mathrm{D}}-\Delta INV^{54}_{\mathrm{D}}] = C^{54}_{\mathrm{D}}+I^{54}_{\mathrm{PDE}}+G^{54}_{\mathrm{CD}}+EX^{54}_{\mathrm{D}}-M^{54}_{\mathrm{D}} \quad \text{(A.165)}$$

$$EX_{\mathrm{N}}^{54} = 0.3320EX^{54} \tag{A.166}$$

$$M_{\mathrm{N}}^{54} = 0.3739M^{54} \tag{A.167}$$

$$[GNP_{\mathrm{N}}^{54} - \Delta INV_{\mathrm{N}}^{54}] = C_{\mathrm{NFB}}^{54} + C_{\mathrm{NEFB}}^{54} + G_{\mathrm{CN}}^{54} + EX_{\mathrm{N}}^{54} - M_{\mathrm{N}}^{54} \tag{A.168}$$

$$I_{\mathrm{BUS}_j} = [P_{\mathrm{IBUS}}][I_{\mathrm{BUS}_j}^{54}], \text{ where } j = MD, MN, R, O{*}2, \text{ and } AF \tag{A.169}$$

$$I_{\mathrm{BUS}} = \sum_j [I_{\mathrm{BUS}_j}] + [P_{\mathrm{IBUS}}][\varepsilon_{\mathrm{IBUS54}}] + \varepsilon_{\mathrm{IBUS}} \tag{A.170}$$

$$\begin{aligned} \Delta INV = {} & [P_{\mathrm{S}*_{AF}}][\Delta INV_{AF}^{54}] + [WPI_{MD}][\Delta INV_{MD}^{54}] \\ & + [WPI_{MN}][\Delta INV_{MN}^{54}] \\ & + [0.5462WPI_{MD} + 0.3722WPI_{MN} + 0.0816P_{\mathrm{S}*_{AF}}][\Delta INV_{T}^{54}] \\ & + [WPI_{MD}][\Delta INV_{O*4}^{54}] + \varepsilon_{\Delta\mathrm{INV}} \end{aligned} \tag{A.171}$$

$$I_{\mathrm{CO}} = [P_{\mathrm{ICNFR}}][I_{\mathrm{CO}}^{54}] + \varepsilon_{\mathrm{ICO}} \tag{A.172}$$

$$I_{\mathrm{CNFR}} = [P_{\mathrm{ICNFR}}][I_{\mathrm{CNFR}}^{54}] \tag{A.173}$$

$$\begin{aligned} GNP = {} & [P_{\mathrm{C}}][C^{54}] + I_{\mathrm{CO}} + I_{\mathrm{CNFR}} + \Delta INV + I_{\mathrm{BUS}} + [P_{\mathrm{EX}}][EX^{54}] \\ & - [P_{\mathrm{M}}][M^{54}] + [P_{G}][G^{54}] \end{aligned} \tag{A.174}$$

$$P_{\mathrm{GNP}} = GNP/GNP^{54} \tag{A.175}$$

Relations among gross national product, national income, personal income, and disposable personal income

$$Y_{\mathrm{N}} = GNP - CCA - TX - V_{\mathrm{BUS}} - STAT + SUB \tag{A.176}$$

$$CCA = CCA_{A} + CCA_{MD} + CCA_{MN} + CCA_{R} + CCA_{O*6} + \varepsilon_{\mathrm{CCA}} \tag{A.177}$$

$$CCAC = 0.5982CCA \tag{A.178}$$

$$CCA_{C} = 0.0587CCA_{O*6} \tag{A.179}$$

$$CCA_{T} = 0.2204CCA_{O*6} \tag{A.180}$$

$$CCA_{O} = 0.7209CCA_{O*6} \tag{A.181}$$

$$Z_{\mathrm{B}} = Y_{\mathrm{N}} - WSS - Y_{\mathrm{ENT}_{EAF}} - Y_{\mathrm{ENT}_{AF}} - Y_{\mathrm{RENT}} - INT_{\mathrm{BUS}} + WALD \tag{A.182}$$

$$
\begin{aligned}
WSS &= WSS_A + WSS_G + WSS_W + [RWSS_{MD}][(E_{P_{MD}})(H_{P_{MD}}) \\
&\quad + 40.0E_{O_{MD}}][0.052] \\
&\quad + [RWSS_{MN}][(E_{P_{MN}})(H_{P_{MN}}) + 40.0E_{O_{MN}}][0.052] \\
&\quad + [RWSS_C][(E_{P_C})(H_{P_C}) = 40.0E_{O_C}][0.052] \\
&\quad + [RWSS_T][(E_{P_T})(H_{P_T}) + 40.0E_{O_T}][0.052] \\
&\quad + [RWSS_R][(E_R)(H_R)][0.052] \\
&\quad + [RWSS_O][MH_O] + \varepsilon_{\mathrm{WSS}}
\end{aligned}
\tag{A.183}
$$

$$
\begin{aligned}
INT_{\mathrm{BUS}} &= INT_{\mathrm{BUS}_A} + INT_{\mathrm{BUS}_C} + INT_{\mathrm{BUS}_T} + INT_{\mathrm{BUS}_R} + INT_{\mathrm{BUS}_O} \\
&\quad + INT_{\mathrm{BUS}_{MD}} + INT_{\mathrm{BUS}_{MN}} + INT_{\mathrm{BUS}_W}
\end{aligned}
\tag{A.184}
$$

$$Z_{\mathrm{BU}} = Z_{\mathrm{B}} - IVAC \tag{A.185}$$

$$IVAC = 0.86IVA \text{ (exogenous in present solutions)} \tag{A.186}$$

$$Z_{\mathrm{AU}} = Z_{\mathrm{BU}} - TC \tag{A.187}$$

$$Z_{\mathrm{A}} = Z_{\mathrm{AU}} + IVAC \tag{A.188}$$

$$RE = Z_{\mathrm{AU}} - DIV \tag{A.189}$$

$$Y_{\mathrm{P}} = Y_{\mathrm{N}} - RE - TC - IVAC - TW - WALD + V_G + INT_G + V_{\mathrm{BUS}} \tag{A.190}$$

$$Y_{\mathrm{D}} = Y_{\mathrm{P}} - TP \tag{A.191}$$

$$Y_{\mathrm{D}}^{54} = Y_{\mathrm{D}}/P_{\mathrm{C}} \tag{A.192}$$

$$T = TP + TC + TX + TW \tag{A.193}$$

$$DEF_G = T - G - V_G - V_{\mathrm{FOR}_G} - INT_G - SUB \tag{A.194}$$

Corporate profits by producing sector

$$
\begin{aligned}
Z_{B_{MD}} &= [PV_{MD}][X_{MD}^{54}] - WSS_{MD} - Y_{\mathrm{ENT}_{MD}} - Y_{\mathrm{RENT}_{MD}} - INT_{\mathrm{BUS}_{MD}} \\
&\quad - CCA_{MD} - [TX_{MD} + V_{\mathrm{BUS}_{MD}}]
\end{aligned}
\tag{A.195}
$$

$$
\begin{aligned}
Z_{B_{MN}} &= [PV_{MN}][X_{MN}^{54}] - WSS_{MN} - Y_{\mathrm{ENT}_{MN}} - Y_{\mathrm{RENT}_{MN}} - INT_{\mathrm{BUS}_{MN}} \\
&\quad - CCA_{MN} - [TX_{MN} + V_{\mathrm{BUS}_{MN}}]
\end{aligned}
\tag{A.196}
$$

$$Z_{B_T} = [PV_T][X_T^{54}] - WSS_T - Y_{ENT_T} - Y_{RENT_T} - INT_{BUS_T} - CCA_T - [TX_T + V_{BUS_T}] \quad (A.197)$$

$$Z_{B_R} = [PV_R][X_R^{54}] - WSS_R - Y_{ENT_R} - Y_{RENT_R} - INT_{BUS_R} - CCA_R - [TX_R + V_{BUS_R}] \quad (A.198)$$

$$Z_{B_C} = [PV_C][X_C^{54}] - WSS_C - Y_{ENT_C} - Y_{RENT_C} - INT_{BUS_C} - CCA_C - [TX_C + V_{BUS_C}] \quad (A.199)$$

$$Z_{B_O} = [PV_O][X_O^{54}] - WSS_O - Y_{ENT_O} - Y_{RENT_O} - INT_{BUS_O} - CCA_O - [TX_O + V_{BUS_O}] \quad (A.200)$$

$$Z_B = \varepsilon_{ZB} + Z_{B_A} + Z_{B_C} + Z_{B_T} + Z_{B_R} + Z_{B_O} + Z_{B_{MD}} + Z_{B_{MN}} + Z_{B_W} \quad (A.201)$$

Miscellaneous relationships

$$K_{CDEA}^{54} = \sum_{i=0}^{39} (0.92784)^i C_{DEA_{-i}}^{54} \quad (A.202)$$

$$ALQD = DD + DT + CURR \quad (A.203)$$

$$K_{MD}^{54} = [K_{MD}^{54}]_{-1} + 0.25[I_{BUS_{MD}}^{54} - DPNR_{MD}^{54}] \quad (A.204)$$

$$K_{MN}^{54} = [K_{MN}^{54}]_{-1} + 0.25[I_{BUS_{MN}}^{54} - DPNR_{MN}^{54}] \quad (A.205)$$

$$K_R^{54} = [K_R^{54}]_{-1} + 0.25[I_{BUS_R}^{54} - DPNR_R^{54}] \quad (A.206)$$

$$K_{O*2}^{54} = [K_{O*2}^{54}]_{-1} + 0.25[I_{BUS_{O*2}}^{54} - DPNR_{O*2}^{54}] \quad (A.207)$$

$$DPNR_{MD}^{54} = 0.1116[K_{MD}^{54}]_{-1} \quad (A.208)$$

$$DPNR_{MN}^{54} = 0.1060[K_{MN}^{54}]_{-1} \quad (A.209)$$

$$DPNR_R^{54} = 0.04588[K_R^{54}]_{-1} \quad (A.210)$$

$$DPNR_{O*2}^{54} = 0.09840[K_{O*2}^{54}]_{-1} \quad (A.211)$$

$$RU = U/L \quad (A.212)$$

$$U = L - E_A - E_{P_{MD}} - E_{O_{MD}} - E_{P_{MN}} - E_{O_{MN}} - E_{P_T} - E_{O_T} - E_{P_C} - E_{O_C} - E_R - [MH_O]/[40.0 \times 0.052] - E_G - \varepsilon_E \quad (A.213)$$

$$X_M^{54} = X_{MD}^{54} + X_{MN}^{54} \quad (A.214)$$

$$\Delta INV_M^{54} = \Delta INV_{MD}^{54} + \Delta INV_{MN}^{54} \quad (A.215)$$

$$\Delta INV_{EAF}^{54} = \Delta INV_M^{54} + \Delta INV_T^{54} + \Delta INV_{O*4}^{54} \quad (A.216)$$

An alphabetical list of the variables which appear in the identities and fixed-proportion equations follows. All monetary variables are in billions of dollars, seasonally adjusted. Monetary flow variables are at annual rates; stocks are end of period unless otherwise indicated. All prices are based 1954 = 1.00. The units of other variables are given with the definitions.

$C$ = personal consumption expenditures

$C_D$ = personal consumption expenditures on durable goods

$C_{DA}$ = personal consumption expenditures on new and net used automobiles

$C_{DEA}$ = personal consumption expenditures on durable goods other than new and net used automobiles

$C_{NEFB}$ = personal consumption expenditures on nondurable goods other than food and beverages

$C_{NFB}$ = personal consumption expenditures on food and beverages

$C_S$ = personal consumption expenditures on services

$CCA$ = capital consumption allowances

$CCAC$ = corporate capital consumption allowances

$CURR$ = currency liabilities of the Treasury and Federal Reserve less commercial banks' currency holdings, average during quarter

$\Delta$ = first difference operator

$DD$ = private demand deposit liabilities of commercial banks less interbank deposits, cash items in process of collection, and Federal Reserve float, average during quarter

$DEF_G$ = government surplus or deficit on income and product account

$DIV$ = dividends

$DPNR$ = replacement-cost depreciation

$DT$ = private time deposit liabilities of commercial banks less time deposit holdings of commercial banks, average during quarter

$E$ = employment, millions of persons

$E_O$ = employment of nonproduction workers, millions of persons

$E_P$ = employment of production workers, millions of persons

$EX$ = exports

$EX_D$ = exports of durable goods

$EX_N$ = exports of nondurable goods

$G$ = government purchases of goods and services

$G_{CD}$ = government purchases of durable goods

$G_{CN}$ = government purchases of nondurable goods

$G_{IC}$ = new public construction activity

$GNP$ = gross national product

$GNP_D$ = durable goods component of gross national product

$GNP_{IC}$ = construction component of gross national product

$GNP_N$ = nondurable goods component of gross national product

$H$ = average weekly hours of all workers, hours

$H_P$ = average weekly hours of production or nonsupervisory workers, hours

$I_{BUS}$ = business gross investment in fixed plant and equipment

$I_C$ = new construction component of gross private domestic investment

$I_{C_{AF}}$ = new private farm residential and nonresidential construction

$I_{CNFR}$ = private residential nonfarm new construction

$I_{CO}$ = value of new private nonfarm, nonresidential, nonbusiness construction put in place

$I_{CPL}$ = business construction

$I_{PDE}$ = investment in producers' durable equipment

$INT_{BUS}$ = personal interest income paid by business

$INT_G$ = personal interest income paid by government

$INV$ = business inventory stock

$INV_D$ = inventory stock of durable goods

$INV_N$ = inventory stock of nondurable goods

$IVA$ = corporate and unincorporated enterprises' inventory valuation adjustment

$IVAC$ = corporate inventory valuation adjustment

$K$ = stock of business fixed capital

$K_{CDEA}$ = stock of consumer durable goods other than automobiles

$L$ = civilian labor force, millions of persons

$M$ = imports

$M_D$ = imports of durable goods

$M_{EFIN}$ = imports of crude materials, crude foodstuffs, and semimanufactures

$M_{FIN}$ = imports of finished goods and services

$M_N$ = imports of nondurable goods

$MH$ = manhours, billions per year

$P_C$ = implicit price deflator for personal consumption expenditures

$P_{EX}$ = implicit price deflator for exports

$P_G$ = implicit price deflator for government purchases of goods and services

$P_{GNP}$ = implicit price deflator for gross national product

$P_{IBUS}$ = implicit price deflator for business gross investment in plant and equipment

$P_{ICNFR}$ = implicit price deflator for residential nonfarm new private construction

$P_M$ = implicit price deflator for imports

$P_{S*AF}$ = implicit price deflator for value of cash receipts from farm marketings and CCC loans plus value of farm products consumed directly in farm households

$PV$ = implicit price deflator for gross product originating

$RE$ = undistributed corporate profits

$RU$ = rate of unemployment, fraction

$RWSS$ = compensation of employees per manhour, dollars per hour

$STAT$ = statistical discrepancy

$T$ = government receipts

$SUB$ = subsidies less current surplus of government enterprises

$TC$ = corporate profits tax liability

$TP$ = personal tax and nontax receipts (or payments)

$TW$ = contributions for social insurance

$TX$ = indirect business tax and nontax accruals

$U$ = unemployed civilian labor force, millions of persons

$V_{\mathrm{BUS}}$ = business transfer payments

$V_G$ = government transfer payments to persons

$WALD$ = excess of wage accruals over disbursements

$WPI$ = wholesale price index

$WSS$ = compensation of employees

$X$ = gross product originating

$Y_{\mathrm{D}}$ = disposable personal income

$Y_{\mathrm{ENT}}$ = proprietors' income

$Y_{\mathrm{N}}$ = national income

$Y_{\mathrm{P}}$ = personal income

$Y_{\mathrm{RENT}}$ = rental income of persons

$Z_{\mathrm{A}}$ = corporate profits after tax, including inventory valuation adjustment

$Z_{\mathrm{AU}}$ = corporate profits after tax, excluding inventory valuation adjustment

$Z_{\mathrm{B}}$ = corporate profits before tax, including inventory valuation adjustment

$Z_{\mathrm{BU}}$ = corporate profits before tax, excluding inventory valuation adjustment

$\varepsilon_{\Delta\mathrm{INV}}$ = inventory investment epsilon: the difference between current dollar inventory investment in the gross national product accounts and the sum of real inventory investment by industry inflated as indicated on page 151.

$\varepsilon_E$ = employment epsilon: the difference between employment estimates based on the Bureau of Labor Statistics' household survey, from which unemployment estimates are derived, and the sum of employment by industry from BLS's establishment survey.

$\varepsilon_{IBUS}$ = business investment epsilon in current dollars: the difference between current dollar producers' durable equipment and business construction expenditures in the gross national product accounts and the sum of investment by industry inflated as indicated on page 151.

$\varepsilon_{IBUS54}$ = business investment epsilon in 1954 dollars: the difference between real producers' durable equipment and business construction expenditures in the gross national product accounts and the sum of real investment by industry, estimates of which are derived by deflating data from the Office of Business Economics – Securities and Exchange Commission investment survey.

$\varepsilon_{ICO}$ = the difference between the current dollar value of new private nonfarm, nonresidential, nonbusiness construction put in place and the real value of such construction inflated by the implicit price deflator for nonfarm residential construction.

$\varepsilon_{ZB}$ = corporate profits epsilon: the difference between corporate profits before tax including inventory valuation adjustment in the national income accounts (on a company basis) and the sum of the same concept by industry from quarterly interpolations of annual data (on an establishment basis) – basic source for both sets of data is the Office of Business Economics.

$\varepsilon_{WSS}$ = compensation of employees epsilon: the difference between compensation of employees from the national income accounts and the sum of unpublished data by industry for the same concept (supplements to wages and salaries by industry are quarterly interpolations of annual data). Both sets of data are from the Office of Business Economics. In the late years, the epsilon also stems from use of revised aggregate and unrevised WSS data by industry.

$\varepsilon_{CCA}$ = capital consumption allowances epsilon: the difference between capital consumption allowances in the national income and product accounts and the sum of the same concept by industry from quarterly interpolations of annual data (on an establishment basis).

# APPENDIX B. CODING OF THE BROOKINGS INDUSTRIES

TABLE B.1

*Coding of the thirty-three-sector Brookings industries.*

| Brookings sector number | Industry composition (OBE numbers) | SIC Code |
|---|---|---|
| 1. Agriculture | 1, 2 | 01, 02 |
| 2. Agricultural services, hunting, trapping, forestry and fisheries | 3, 4 | 07, 08, 09 |
| 3. Mining (includes petroleum, gas) | 5, 6, 7, 8, 9, 10 | 10, 11, 12, 1311, 1322, 14 |
| 4. Construction | 11, 12 | 15, 16, 17, 138, pt. 6561 |
| 5. Transportation | 65 | 40, 41, 42, 44, 45, 46, 47 |
| 6. Communication | 66, 67 | 48 |
| 7. Public utilities | 68 | 49 |
| 8. Trade | 69 | 50, 52, 53, 54, 55, 56, 57, 58, 59, pt. 7399 |
| 9. Finance, insurance, real estate | 70, 71 | 60–67 except 6541, pt. 6561 |
| 10. Services | 72, 73, 74, 75, 76, 77 | 70, 72, 75, 76, 78, 79, 80, 81, 82, 84, 86, 89, 6541, and 73 except 7391 and pt. 7399 |
| 11. Ordnance and accessories | 13 | 19 |
| 12. Lumber and wood products except furniture | 20, 21 | 24 |
| 13. Furniture | 22, 23 | 25 |
| 14. Stone, clay, and glass products | 35, 36 | 32 |
| 15. Primary iron and steel | 37 | 331, 332, 3391, 3399 |
| 16. Primary nonferrous metals | 38 | 2819 (alumina only), 333, 334, 335, 336, 3392 |
| 17. Fabricated metal products except ordnance, machinery and transportation equipment | 39, 40, 41, 42 | 34 |

TABLE B.1 (continued)

| Brookings sector number | Industry composition (OBE numbers) | SIC Code |
|---|---|---|
| 18. Machinery | 43, 44, 45, 46, 47, 48, 49, 50, 51, 52 | 35 |
| 19. Electrical machinery, equipment and supplies | 53, 54, 55, 56, 57, 58 | 36 |
| 20. Motor vehicles and equipment | 59 | 371 |
| 21. Other transportation equipment | 60, 61 | 37 except 371 |
| 22. Professional, scientific, and controlling instruments; photographic and optical goods; watches and clocks | 62, 63 | 38 |
| 23. Miscellaneous manufacturing | 64 | 39 except 3992 |
| 24. Food | 14 | 20 |
| 25. Tobacco | 15 | 21 |
| 26. Textile products | 16, 17, 18, 19 | 22, 23, 3992 |
| 27. Paper and allied products | 24, 25 | 26 |
| 28. Printing and publishing | 26 | 27 |
| 29. Chemicals and allied products | 27, 28, 29, 30 | 28 (except alumina pt. 2819) |
| 30. Petroleum refining and related | 31 | 29 |
| 31. Rubber and misc. plastic products | 32 | 30 |
| 32. Leather and leather products | 33, 34 | 31 |
| 33. Government enterprises | 78, 79 | — |

TABLE B.2

*Coding of the eight-sector Brookings industries.*

| Brookings eight-sector number | Composition Brookings thirty-three-sector number |
|---|---|
| 01 Agriculture | 1, 2 |
| 03 Construction | 4 |
| 17 Trade | 8 |
| 18 Regulated | 5, 6, 7 |
| 19 Residual | 3, 9, 10 |
| 51 Durables | 11–23 |
| 56 Nondurables | 24–32 |
| — Government enterprises | 33 |

# APPENDIX C. PRICE BEHAVIOR AFTER EXCISE TAX CHANGES

It would be convenient if it could be proven that all prices were set by markup standards with taxes entering in a particular way. Unfortunately, this cannot be done, because no guarantee can be given that any tax change is fully passed along. However, the information presented is fairly definitive for a few taxes, for example, cigarettes and gasoline.

Except for gasoline, all excises have changed, at the most, one other time since World War II. Time series analysis is not very effective when based on one observation; hence, continuous cross-section data are used to determine the effect of *ad valorem* and specific taxes on prices.

The basic premise of the continuous cross-section analysis is that each price equation can be derived either directly (or as a reduced form) as a function of many variables, including tax rates. For any period, $j$,

$$P_{ij} = (rate_{ij}\, y_{kj}) \qquad j = 1, \ldots M \qquad k = 1, \ldots N \tag{C.1}$$

where $P_{ij}$ = price of the $i^{th}$ good for the $j^{th}$ observation, $rate_{ij}$ is the tax rate on the $i^{th}$ good, $y_k$ is a vector of variables that affect $P_i$, and these $y_k$ can take on different values for each $j$. $y_k$ can include random errors, and for the time period involved $d(y_{kj})/dt$ is a random variable with expected value of zero for all $k$ and $j$. To make this last assumption more acceptable, the length of $dt$ should be minimized. On this assumption, price changes at the time of rate changes can be attributed to the rate changes.

Even employing cross-sections which record prices for different units just before and after tax changes, the problem still remains to distinguish the cross-section units. Two divisions that are theoretically acceptable and practical are geographic location and product differentiation. Data on prices by geographic location can be obtained from the Bureau of Labor Statistics in the form of average prices at a specified date in various cities [1]). (Price *levels* generally vary between locations, but since interest is in price movements in response to tax changes, these variations can be disregarded.) Another source of data is information about prices of different brands of the same product. Furthermore, it is not necessary to restrict the analysis to those products included in the current rate reduction. Instead, data can be used on any product that has had a tax change. However, because behavior patterns are not constant over time, only observations after the Second World War are utilized.

Attention will first be focused on gasoline mainly because that product had three rate changes during the 1950's. The gasoline excise tax is a specific one, that is, the tax is a fixed number of cents per gallon irrespective of dealers' prices. The rate changed from \$ 0.015 per gallon to \$ 0.020 as of November 1, 1951, to \$ 0.030 July 1, 1956, and to \$ 0.040 on October 1, 1959. The Bureau of Labor Statistics has published prices for the latter two dates for 20 cities [2]). Both regular and premium gasoline prices are available, but since most areas have a fixed differential between the two prices, the results obtained were almost identical; hence, here the analysis is restricted to regular gasoline.

Price data were collected from the identical stations on each date for the quarterly changes presented below. The prices are averages based on a small sample in each city. Price increases were computed from the last and first months available before and after the tax changes, for example, in 1956, from April, May or June to July, August or September. The data seemed to be free of seasonal movements; therefore, no adjustment was made.

Table C.1 presents the mean price movement and standard deviation for the 1956 and 1959 periods. Some cities were eliminated because either the initial or terminal price occurred in a price war. (These wars are generally noted in the BLS publications). The year 1956 contains two entries because three cities are borderline cases.

The mean price increase varied from \$ 0.012 to \$ 0.009. Since the tax change was \$ 0.01, one can test whether the mean price change differed

---

[1]) The basic publications describing the sampling procedure and available data are: *Bureau of Labor Statistics Bulletin No.* 1182 (June 1955) and *Bureau of Labor Statistics Bulletin No.* 1197 (June 1956).

[2]) See *Bureau of Labor Statistics Monthly Fuel Index Publication.* Prices are obtained at least quarterly for Atlanta, Baltimore, Boston, Chicago, Cincinnati, Cleveland, Detroit, Houston, Kansas City, Los Angeles, Minneapolis, New York, Philadelphia, Pittsburgh, Portland, St. Louis, San Francisco, Scranton, Pa., Seattle, and Washington, D. C.

from $ 0.01. The last column indicates no significant difference, but this might only be due to the small size of this sample.

TABLE C.1

*Retail price movements in regular gasoline in response to a $0.01 increase in tax: July 1, 1956 and October 1, 1959.*

| Date | Number of cities | Mean price change | Standard deviation [a] $.01-mean price change |
|---|---|---|---|
| 1956 | 14 | 0.0123 | −0.67 |
| 1956 | 17 | 0.0092 | 0.11 |
| 1959 | 15 | 0.0103 | −0.08 |

[a]) Adjusted for sample size.

*Source* Data published by Bureau of Labor Statistics in *Monthly Fuel Index Publication.*

To clarify the situation, the BLS was asked to supply the data from the other twenty six cities sampled in 1956 and 1959, plus any data available for 1951. The BLS was generous enough to furnish the original observations by individual stations. Rather than combine the data into city averages, the individual units were used. The results, given in table C.2, do not include in 1956 or 1959 the observations in table C.1.

The most important aspect of the table is the number of stations which raised their prices by exactly the amount of the tax: 70 per cent in 1959, 40 per cent in 1956, and 80 per cent in 1959. (Since the frequency distributions were not normal, standard deviations were not calculated.) The average price change exceeded the tax change by a small amount in two years, but for most stations it appears that the price change equalled the tax change. This result is of special significance since the gasoline excise tax is imposed on the manufacturer and specific excises are generally thought to be pyramided [3]). Here, however, the retail price movement only equals the tax change, suggesting that the tax is not marked up at any level of production.

Another specific tax for which price data were made available on a store basis is the cigarette tax. The tax changed in 1951 along with the gasoline tax. The results in table C.3 are, if anything, more dramatic than for gasoline

[3]) John F. Due, "The Effect of the 1954 Reduction in the Federal Excise Taxes Upon the List Prices of Electrical Appliances—A Case Study," *National Tax Journal* (September 1954), and Paul Taubman, *op. cit.*

TABLE C.2

*Distribution of changes in retail price of regular gasoline in response to changes in excise taxes, for individual stations.*

A. 1959 Tax change = $0.01

| Price change | −0.040 | −0.010 | 0.000 | 0.005 | 0.010 | 0.020 | 0.030 |
|---|---|---|---|---|---|---|---|
| Stations-72 | 3 | 1 | 9 | 1 | 53 | 2 | 3 |

Simple average price change = $0.0097

B. 1956 Tax change = $0.01

| Price change | −0.050 | −0.020 | −0.010 | −0.003 | 0.000 | 0.006 | 0.009 | 0.010 | 0.014 | 0.015 | 0.016 | 0.017 | 0.019 | 0.020 | 0.021 | 0.029 |
|---|---|---|---|---|---|---|---|---|---|---|---|---|---|---|---|---|
| Stations-75 | 2 | 1 | 1 | 1 | 3 | 1 | 1 | 31 | 5 | 10 | 1 | 1 | 3 | 11 | 2 | 1 |

Simple average price change = $ 0.011

C. 1951 Tax change = $0.005

| Price change | 0.000 | 0.003 | 0.004 | 0.005 | 0.006 | 0.007 | 0.008 | 0.010 | 0.015 | 0.018 | 0.020 | 0.028 | 0.051 | 0.055 | 0.056 |
|---|---|---|---|---|---|---|---|---|---|---|---|---|---|---|---|
| Stations-106 | 3 | 1 | 2 | 87 | 2 | 2 | 1 | 1 | 1 | 1 | 2 | 1 | 2 | 2 | 1 |

Simple average price change = $0.0077[a] or $0.0054[b]

[a] Includes 5 observations from 0.051 to 0.056 which occurred because price wars ended.

[b] Excludes 5 observations from 0.051 to 0.056 which occurred because price wars ended.

*Source* Unpublished data from the Bureau of Labor Statistics.

since 88 per cent of the stores increased their price by the tax. Again, it should be noted that even though this tax is imposed on the manufacturer and even though cigarettes pass through a wholesaling and retailing sector, the net result was that a tax increase of \$ 0.01 led to a price increase of \$ 0.01 [4]). For these specific taxes, the tax is not thought of as a cost which should be marked up, but is always kept separate and merely passed along exactly in price increases.

TABLE C.3

*Distribution of retail price changes for regular size cigarettes in response to a tax change of \$0.01 price from individual stores, various cities.*

| Number of stores | Frequency distribution of price change | | | | | | | Simple average |
|---|---|---|---|---|---|---|---|---|
| | 0.000 | 0.005 | 0.008 | 0.010 | 0.015 | 0.020 | 0.025 | |
| 130 | 3 | 2 | 1 | 114 | 6 | 3 | 1 | 0.0103 |

*Source* Unpublished data from the Bureau of Labor Statistics.

A few *ad valorem* excises, were decreased on April 1, 1954. Some data were gathered at the time on prices of gas and electric appliances, automobiles,face powder, face cream, and light bulbs.

For face powder and face creams, where taxes were reduced from 20 to 10 per cent, the most instructive analysis is cast in terms of the pre-tax cut price, the new price; and what the new price should be if a markup scheme were used (and other factors remain unchanged). If the costs and the markup rate remain the same (the preferred assumption, see pp. 57-58), price should equal [(1 + *tax rate*) (*markup coefficient*) (*costs*)]. Then, multiplying the old price by the ratio of June to March (1 + *tax rate*), that is, 1.10/1.20, should yield the June price if the hypothesized markup scheme were used. Comparing the second and third column of table C.4, it can be observed that if prices are rounded to the nearest cent (the numbers ending in 5 always have a remainder) the columns agree in every instance. The same comparison for columns 5 and 6 reveals that only in Los Angeles does a discrepancy exist.

Both the face powder and face cream taxes are imposed at the retail level. Attention will now be given to *ad valorem* taxes imposed on manufacturers.

---

[4]) In some areas prices are set by the state and the state may only allow tax increases to be just passed on.

TABLE C.4

*Comparison of old and new prices for face powder and face cream, March–June 1954, for tax reduction from 20 to 10 per cent, April 1, 1954.*

| City | Face powder Price/ounce March | June | $\left(\frac{1.10}{1.20}\right)$ March price | Face cream Price/ounce March | June | $\left(\frac{1.10}{1.20}\right)$ March price |
|---|---|---|---|---|---|---|
| Atlanta | 0.65 | 0.60 | 0.595 | 0.18 | 0.17 | 0.165 |
| Baltimore | 0.65 | 0.60 | 0.595 | 0.19 | 0.17 | 0.174 |
| Chicago | 0.65 | 0.60 | 0.595 | 0.20 | 0.18 | 0.183 |
| Cincinnati | 0.65 | 0.60 | 0.595 | 0.20 | 0.18 | 0.183 |
| Detroit | 0.65 | 0.60 | 0.595 | 0.18 | 0.17 | 0.174 |
| Los Angeles | 0.58 | 0.53 | 0.532 | 0.19 | 0.18 | 0.174 |
| New York | 0.67 | 0.61 | 0.614 | 0.19 | 0.17 | 0.174 |
| Philadelphia | 0.65 | 0.58 | 0.577 | 0.19 | 0.17 | 0.174 |
| San Francisco | 0.53 | 0.49 | 0.485 | 0.18 | 0.17 | 0.174 |

*Source Bureau of Labor Statistics Bulletin No.* 1182 *(June* 1955*).*

The most important taxes of this type are on durables, including automobiles. In 1954 the tax on gas and electric appliances was unexpectedly cut from 10 to 5 per cent [5]). John Due originally analyzed the tax reduction effects on manufacturers' suggested retail price [6]). Recently his results were extended by Harry Johnson [7]). Johnson's sample is the larger one; hence, it will form the basis for the present discussion (Johnson's table 1 has been reproduced as table C.5).

The percentage decline in price is calculated as $(1-P_{t+1}/P_t)$. Under the assumption advanced in chapter 3, the decline in price should be $(1-1.05/1.10) = 0.0455$ or 4.55 per cent. An examination of Johnson's table reveals that very few observations are greater than 5 per cent (only 46 out of 676) while many are less than 4 per cent (414 out of 676). If the observations are averaged using the midpoints of the percentage price decline classes (and any value up to 13 for the 8th class), a measure of the average price change

[5]) This cut included refrigerators, gas ranges and toasters, but not radios or television receivers.

[6]) John F. Due, "The Effect of the 1954 Reduction in the Federal Excise Taxes Upon the List Prices of Electrical Appliances—A Case Study," *National Tax Journal* (September 1954).

[7]) H. L. Johnson, "Tax Pyramiding and the Manufacturers' Excise Tax Reduction of 1954," *National Tax Journal* (September 1964), p. 298.

equal to 3.0 per cent is obtained. (This average is a simple average.) However, an examination of Johnson's table 2 reveals that smaller companies usually had smaller price decreases. In fact, Johnson finds that both *between* and *within* industries the larger the companies and the more concentrated the industries, the greater the price decrease [8]). If small companies in table 2 are excluded and a simple average of price declines of the remainder is computed, the result becomes 3.5 per cent. Apparently, even for large companies the tax cut was not fully passed along to consumers, since then the price reduction would have been 4.5 per cent.

TABLE C.5

*Frequency distribution of percentage changes in suggested retail prices, April 1 through August 31, 1954 by appliance group.*

| Appliance group | Number of firms | Number of models observed | Number of models | | | | | | | | |
|---|---|---|---|---|---|---|---|---|---|---|---|
| | | | Percentage decline in price | | | | | | | | |
| | | | 0 | 1 to 2 | 2 to 3 | 3 to 4 | 4 to 5 | 5 to 6 | 6 to 7 | 7 to 8 | 8 and over |
| Major: | | | | | | | | | | | |
| Refrigerators | 22 | 153 | 11 | | 39 | 16 | 76 | 6 | 4 | 1 | |
| Freezers | 16 | 55 | 7 | 3 | 6 | 16 | 17 | 2 | 1 | | 3 |
| Electric ranges | 27 | 176 | 42 | 2 | 22 | 29 | 72 | 5 | 2 | 2 | |
| Gas ranges | 22 | 188 | 77 | 9 | 21 | 25 | 27 | 11 | 5 | 13 | |
| Minor: | | | | | | | | | | | |
| Coffee makers | 14 | 26 | 4 | 7 | 4 | | 11 | | | | |
| Fans | 12 | 42 | 3 | 1 | 34 | 1 | 2 | 1 | | | |
| Irons | 12 | 23 | 2 | 4 | 12 | 4 | 1 | | | | |
| Toasters | 11 | 13 | | 1 | 11 | 1 | | | | | |
| | | 676 | 146 | 27 | 149 | 92 | 206 | 25 | 12 | 16 | 3 |

*Sources* Individual price changes are derived from suggested retail prices recorded in the *Mart*, Buttenheim Publishing Corporation (New York, February–August, 1954), and *Nelda Master System*, Nelda Publications, Inc. (New York, 1954).

[8]) H. L. Johnson, *op. cit.*, p. 298.

But, the foregoing prices are *suggested* retail prices, not the actual amounts paid. In the period involved the suggested prices are supposed to be reasonably good guides to the actual price movements because discounters usually followed a flat 20 per cent off policy, and other sellers adjusted to the fair trade laws [9]). Some BLS data on refrigerator and toaster prices can be employed as a partial check. Refrigerator prices are of special interest because

TABLE C.6

*Refrigerator, standard model retail prices by city; tax decrease from 10 to 5 per cent.*

| City | March | June | (March/June)−1.0 |
|---|---|---|---|
| Atlanta | 275.95 | 262.15 | 0.052 |
| Baltimore | 274.39 | 268.57 | 0.021 |
| Cincinnati | 255.78 | 255.45 | 0.001 |
| Detroit | 287.73 | 275.20 | 0.045 |
| Los Angeles | 281.38 | 268.22 | 0.049 |
| New York | 271.11 | 260.58 | 0.040 |
| Philadelphia | 292.95 | 274.62 | 0.066 |
| St. Louis | 266.62 | 261.00 | 0.021 |
| San Francisco | 266.29 | 256.38 | 0.038 |

*Source* Bureau of Labor Statistics

TABLE C.7

*Ratio of retail prices, March/June 1954—1.00; tax decrease from 10 to 5 per cent for toasters, 15 to 10 per cent for light bulbs.*

| City | Toasters | Light bulbs |
|---|---|---|
| Atlanta | 0.038 | 0 |
| Baltimore | 0.049 | 0 |
| Chicago | 0.039 | −0.059 |
| Cincinnati | 0.039 | 0 |
| Detroit | 0.039 | −0.059 |
| Los Angeles | 0.101 | −0.059 |
| New York | 0.055 | 0 |
| Philadelphia | 0.039 | 0 |
| St. Louis | 0.004 | −0.056 |
| San Francisco | 0.056 | 0.058 |

*Source* Bureau of Labor Statistics

9) John F. Due, *op. cit.*, p. 3.

Johnson's data show a large number of observations in the 4 to 5 per cent range, and most of the lesser declines are for small companies. The average change (see table C.6) is 0.037, which is less than 0.045 but not significantly so; the $t$ value is 0.4. For toasters, the average of change shown in table C.7 is 0.046, which certainly coincides with the expected value of 0.045. For light bulbs, the average change is $-0.175$; that is, prices rose by 17.5 per cent. In fact, only in San Francisco did light bulb prices fall [10]).

The impact of *ad valorem* rate changes certainly is nowhere near as clear as for specific taxes. This lack of clarity is unfortunate since the only specific taxes cut recently are the minor ones such as those on playing cards and matches. (Perhaps price changes in the *ad valorem* case revealed greater disagreement with the constant markup, 100 per cent pass-along, hypotheses than those for the specific excises because of the direction of the tax rate shifts, *ad valorem* rates decreased while specific tax rates increased. That is, perhaps the responses to tax changes are asymmetric.)

---

[10]) Where no change occurred it is possible that rounding is confusing the issue since if the old price were \$0.184, the new price (if the tax cut were passed along) would be \$0.176, which rounds back to the original price.

# APPENDIX D. ADJUSTMENT OF MODEL EQUATIONS FOR EXCISE TAX REDUCTIONS

## *D.1. Prices and profits*

The Brookings model transforms the value-added price indices into *GNP* category implicit price deflators in two steps. First, using a price conversion matrix based on an input-output matrix and final demands, the producing sector prices are aggregated into *GNP* component prices such as $P_{\mathrm{CDA}}$, the implicit price deflator for personal consumption expenditures on new and net used automobiles. These $\hat{P}$ variables would be the correct answers provided the price conversion matrix elements remained constant over time. Second, as these elements do not remain constant, the model uses an adjustment equation of the following type:

$$P_{\mathrm{CDA}} = a + b\hat{P}_{\mathrm{CDA}} + c(\hat{P}_{\mathrm{CDA}} - \hat{P}_{\mathrm{CDA}_{t-1}}). \qquad \text{(D.1)}$$

Equation (D.1) is a distributed lag adjustment process which is also used in the excise analysis.

However, a change must be made in the price conversion technique. Without a modification, the use of the ratios in the last two columns of table 3.1 (or the alternative figures cited in the text) would mean that all value-added prices would remain constant or decrease. This occurs because: (1) the *GNP* component implicit price deflators (before adjustment) are weighted averages of the value-added prices, (2) the weights are nonnegative, and (3) the value-added price of durables has a positive weight in all the weighted averages. Consequently, all the *GNP* implicit price deflators would decrease. While it is conceivable that a drop in telephone tax rates might have an effect on the implicit price deflator for investment goods, a reduction in toaster taxes should not. This is essentially an aggregation problem. Applying an average tax rate index to durables, and then weighting this index in the price conversion matrix on the assumption that all items in an element of the matrix have the same tax index is inappropriate because, for the most part, only consumer items are taxed. The same problem exists for the other industries.

To solve this problem two steps are taken. First, before applying the price conversion matrix, value-added prices are multiplied by the reciprocal of the foregoing rate index ratios. (In the initial quarters, this yields the original pre-tax cut value-added prices. In later quarters the transformed value-added prices are not quite the same as the original prices because of complete system feedbacks of the tax cut.) Second, the price conversion matrix is used to generate *GNP* component implicit price deflators before the tax change. (This assures that the tax change will not affect the investment price deflator.) These answers are then multiplied by a new set of tax markup factors.

The factors apply only to the consumer goods sector, and are defined as $R'_m = [\sum_j C_{mj} + r_j X'_{mj}]/\sum_j C_{mj}$ [1]). For each final demand *GNP* sector, $m$, and each item, $j$, in that sector, $X'_{mj}$ equals gross output originating in current dollars through the stage at which the tax is applied and $C_{mj}$ equals its consumption. Thus, manufacturers' excises are weighted by the relative value of output at the manufacturing level, while the remainder of the value added to the product (distribution and transportation margins) is part of the weight but has an $r_j = 0$.

TABLE D.1

*Ad valorem tax rate markup factors for consumption sectors: 1965–67.*

| (1) Sector | (2) 1-1-65 | (3) 7-1-65 | (4) 1966 | (5) 1967 | (6) (2)/(3) | (7) (2)/(5) |
|---|---|---|---|---|---|---|
| Automobiles | 1.082 | 1.057 | 1.049 | 1.030 | 1.024 | 1.050 |
| Durables other than autos | 1.034 | 1.000 | 1.000 | 1.000 | 1.034 | 1.034 |
| Food | 1.000 | 1.000 | 1.000 | 1.000 | 1.000 | 1.000 |
| Nondurables other than food | 1.003 | 1.000 | 1.000 | 1.000 | 1.003 | 1.003 |
| Services | 1.009 | 1.007 | 1.003 | 1.002 | 1.001 | 1.005 |

Both sets of factors and adjustments are necessary to obtain profits accurately for the six producing sectors (requiring correct sector prices) and *GNP* in current dollars (requiring correct final demand prices). The first set

[1]) The procedure is not correct, if, for example, telephones enter into the cost of investment goods and if the price of investment goods falls because of the tax decrease. This seems unlikely.

of factors are weighted to yield correct sector prices but do not yield correct final demand prices; hence, the second set of factors which are shown in columns six and seven of table D.1 are needed for the conversion.

The reciprocals of the last two columns give approximate measures of the initial cut in prices if the cut is fully passed along. These estimates are not exact because some items included are not sold exclusively to consumers, but their whole value is included in the weight given to the tax rate. The only consumption sectors with large price reductions are automobiles and other durables, but these are also the two sectors where the full tax cut may not be passed along. Assuming, that 80 per cent will be passed along, and using equation (3.2) for automobiles, the 1.024 becomes 1.019 in 1966, while in 1967 the 1.050 changes to 1.040. The corresponding change for other durables for both years is that 1.034 becomes 1.027.

The foregoing procedures will generate "correct" estimates of the implicit price deflators as only consumption prices will feel the initial impact. The model can then generate the implicit price deflator for all consumption, obtain a new value for real disposable income, and use the consumption functions to obtain an initial impact of the multiplier.

Before employing the Brookings model to work out the full implications of the tax cut, there are still a few additional changes to be made. First, wholesale price indexes of manufacturing durables and nondurables are derived from their respective value-added prices. But wholesale price indexes exclude excises; thus, the tax cut should not directly affect wholesale prices. This change can be accomplished by multiplying the new value-added indexes by the reciprocals of the rate adjustments used in the price determination equations.

To obtain profits by industry, $i$, the model splits indirect business taxes and business transfers by using equations of the form:

$$\Delta \left[\frac{(TX+V_{\mathrm{BUS}})_i}{(TX+V_{\mathrm{BUS}})}\right] = b_i \Delta \left[\frac{(value\ added)_i}{value\ added}\right] \tag{D.2}$$

where $(TX+V_{\mathrm{BUS}})$ is total indirect taxes plus business transfers. The underlying assumption made in equation (D.2) is that:

$$(TX+V_{\mathrm{BUS}})_i = R_i(value\ added) \tag{D.3}$$

$$(TX+V_{\mathrm{BUS}}) = R(value\ added) \tag{D.4}$$

where $R$ is a rate index; the change in the ratio of equation (D.3) to equation

(D.4) is equation (D.2.). A change in any excises will affect $R_i$, $R$, and the price used in obtaining value-added. It is assumed that all these shifts will offset each other leaving $b_i$ unchanged. At the date of the tax reduction, however, additive corrections must be used to alter the ratios of industry to total $TX + V_{BUS}$. The corrections are derived by subtracting out of the numerators and denominators the amounts of the excises being cut. A correction factor was calculated for each of the six industries. The largest of these was for manufacturing durables, where the level of the ratio fell from 10.7 to 7.3 per cent. All the changes are given in table D.2.

TABLE D.2

*Expected shifts in levels of* $(TX+V_{BUS})_i/(TX+V_{BUS})$.

| | Tax change in | | |
|---|---|---|---|
| Sector | 1/65–7/65 | 7/65-1/66 | 1/66-1/67 |
| Durable manufacturing | −0.024 | −0.006 | −0.004 |
| Nondurable manufacturing | 0.004 | 0.002 | 0.001 |
| Regulated | 0.004 | −0.011 | −0.002 |
| Trade | 0.003 | 0.006 | 0.002 |
| Construction | 0.001 | 0.000 | 0.000 |
| Other | 0.009 | 0.006 | 0.002 |

## *D.2. Government revenues*

The one remaining set of adjustments is in identities in the revenue sector:

$$Revenue_i = (rate_i)base_i. \qquad \text{(D.5)}$$

Since rates are given, only bases must be determined. These, for *ad valorem* excises are current dollar gross value of output originating at the relevant production level, while for specific excises they are gallons, pounds, or similar measures.

One possible approach is to estimate demand functions for each base. For *ad valorem* rates this would require splitting current dollar gross output into its price and real components. Even for goods taxed at the manufacturing level, no problem exists because demand functions use constant dollar "quantities" as the dependent variable, and changes in retail margins do not alter the constant dollar amounts. This approach would yield price and income elasticities and presumably would be the preferred method to use provided there were no constraints.

Additional constraints do exist. To estimate the demand functions, it would be necessary to make the prices of each taxed commodity endogenous. It would also be necessary to investigate the dynamic specifications of each demand equation. In addition, the inclusion of these functions would increase the size of the model (measured by number of endogenous equations) by twice the number of taxed commodities. This increase in the size of the model affects the speed at which it can be solved. Moreover, the increment in the time required for each additional equation would increase.

These efforts and costs could be borne. But, there is an alternative method which should yield satisfactory results and which would be far easier and cheaper to implement. Suppose that the following equation is valid for the consumption of a taxed commodity which is in the $j^{\text{th}}$ consumption category:

$$C_{ij} = a_{ij} + b_{ij}\frac{P_{ij}}{P} + d_{ij}Y_{\text{D}}, \tag{D.6}$$

$$C_i = \sum a_{ij} + \frac{\sum b_{ij}P_{ij}}{P} + Y_{\text{D}}\sum d_{ij}. \tag{D.7}$$

Solving equation (D.7) for $Y_{\text{D}}$ and substituting back into equation (D.6),

$$C_{ij} = \left\{a_{ij} - d_{ij}\left[\frac{\sum a_{ij}}{\sum d_{ij}}\right]\right\} + \left[b_{ij}\frac{P_{ij}}{P}\right] - \left\{\frac{d_{ij}}{\sum d_{ij}}\left[\frac{\sum b_{ij}P_{ij}}{P}\right]\right\} + \frac{d_{ij}C_i}{\sum d_{ij}}. \tag{D.8}$$

So long as

$$\frac{b_{ij}P_{ij}}{P} = \frac{d_{ij}}{\sum d_{ij}}\,\frac{\sum b_{ij}P_{ij}}{P}$$

in equation (D.8), all relative prices can be ignored. One set of conditions that will satisfy this stipulation is that $b_{ij} = b_i$, $d_{ij} = d_i$ for all $j$, and $P_{ij} = (1/n)\sum P_{ij}$ for each taxed commodity. If only taxed commodities' prices fall, then if these conditions were met before the tax cut, the $P_{ij}$ for all taxed commodities are not equal to the new $(1/n)\sum P_{ij}$. Nevertheless, this difficulty can be assumed to be minor, especially since it refers only to commodities *within* a group, for example, consumption of durables other than automobiles, because the consumption functions for each group use relative prices *between* groups.

Each of the bases with non-zero rates as of July 1, 1965 was regressed on the consumption category to which it belonged. If the tax were a specific one, real consumption was used, but for *ad valorem* taxes, current dollar consumption was employed. The equations were estimated using annual data. Some of the tax bases were available directly, for example, the number of taxable cigarette withdrawals, while others were obtained by dividing revenues by the tax rate. The following equations were estimated from 1954 to 1963. The numbers in parentheses are $t$ statistics.

$$\text{Air passage revenues (billions of dollars)} = \underset{(42.5)}{-0.892 + 0.021\, C_S} \tag{D.9}$$

$$\text{Tire production (millions of tires)} = 28.06 + \underset{(3.99)}{3.579\, C^{54}_{DEA}} \tag{D.10}$$

$$\text{Gasoline production (billions of barrels)} = 0.412 + \underset{(14.3)}{0.017\, C^{54}_{NEFB}} \tag{D.11}$$

$$\text{Lubricants (millions of barrels)} = 28.35 + \underset{(3.32)}{0.463\, C^{54}_{NEFB}} \tag{D.12}$$

$$\text{Cigarettes (billions)} = -66.79 + \underset{(17.89)}{8.06\, C^{54}_{NEFB}} \tag{D.13}$$

$$\text{Cigars (billions)} = 2.57 + \underset{(5.75)}{0.056\, C^{54}_{NEFB}} \tag{D.14}$$

$$\text{Taxable communication sales (millions of dollars)} = 1115.33 + \underset{(119.3)}{75.02\, C_S} \tag{D.15}$$

$$\text{Total taxable alcohol sales (millions of dollars)} = \underset{(5.1)}{3.40\, C^{54}_{NFB}} \tag{D.16}$$

Tires, which are taxed by the pound, have different rates for different types. The number of tires determined are converted to pounds and the tax base by assuming an average weight of 32 pounds per tire and an average rate of about \$ 0.08 per pound, or \$ 2.55 per tire. For automobiles, the tax applies only to the gross output originating at the manufacturing level, but the average rate equals the automobile entry in table D.1 less 1.0. The other excises present no problems. With this information, it is possible to substitute into equation (D.5) and obtain excises in terms of the consumption categories of equations (D.9) through (D.16).

# INDEX


Accommodating monetary policy, 28, 51
Ad valorem tax, 56, 57, 57*n*, 59
Aggregation, 6, 14, 15
Agricultural sector, 12
Analysis of excise tax reduction, 54-61
Ando, Albert, 13*n*, 15
Automobiles: excise tax on, 53, 63; inventories of, 6, 14

Bacharach, Michael, 16, 16*n*
Balance of payments, 9, 29, 89
Belsley, David, 6
Benefit-cost evaluation, 105
Block recursive system, 1, 18, 24
Bond yields, 87, 88
Brainard, William C., 123*n*
Brown, E. Cary, 77

CES, *see* Constant elasticity of substitution function
Cobb-Douglas function, 8, 8*n*, 107, 112, 113, 114, 115
Constant elasticity of substitution function (CES), 107, 114, 115, 121
Consumption: autonomous, 87; of durable goods, 2-3, 49; lag, 77; "portfolio" approach to, 3; real, 95-98
Costs of policy actions, 105, 121; analyses, 91
Credit conditions: demand for durables and, 2, 49; residential construction and, 3

Davidson, P., 75*n*
de Leeuw, Frank, 13*n*
Department of Agriculture, 12
Demand and time deposits, 22, 88
Discount rate, 88, 89
Discounted multiplier, 98-99
Duesenberry, J. S., 2*n*
Durables: consumer demand for, 2; government, 28; potential price reductions, 59
Durbin-Watson statistics: use of, 8
Dynamic multiplier, 25, 49-51, 82, 95-98

Economic history, 27
Economies of scale, 75-77, 97
Eisner, Robert, 7
Elasticity of substitution, *see* Constant elasticity of substitution function
Employment, production functions, 10. *See also* Labor force; Unemployment
Endogenous variables, 2; lagged, 18
Equilibrium multiplier, 81, 82
Evans, Michael, 3*n*, 49
Excise tax: Brookings model, 54 ff; changes in law, 53; effects of reduction in, 53-55, 64, 75, 78-80; impact multiplier for, 65, 75; implicit rates, 58-59; initial equivalent, 55; nonlinear considerations, 60-61; real input multiplier for, 83-84; specific, 56
Exogenous variables, 1, 27, 61; lagged, 18

Factor income payments, 10
Federal debt, 89, 90
Federal National Mortgage Association, 3
Federal Reserve Board, 14
Federal Trade Commission-Securities and Exchange Commission (FTC-SEC), balance sheet data, 13-14
Ferguson, James M., 91*n*
Fiscal multiplier, 91-92
Fisher, F. M., 15, 15*n*
Forecasting, 17, 19-23

Foreign sector, 9
Fox, Karl, 12
Fringe benefits, 11
Fromm, Gary, 2*n*, 12

Galbraith, J. K., 89, 89*n*
GNP, *see* Gross national product
Government sector, 82, 84-85, 89; loss in revenue from excise tax reduction, 79-80; purchase of durables, 28; revenues, 9, 47; state and local, 10
Gross national product (GNP): actual versus predicted, 19-23; expenditure components, 15-16; impact of excise tax reduction on, 64; price deflator, 28, 79; real, 49-51, 91-94, 95-98

Hicks, John R., 88*n*, 111, 111*n*
Holt, Charles C., 25

Impact multiplier, 23-24, 25, 65, 75, 82
Income, disposable, 51, 54-55, 77
Income tax, 55; impact of reduction in, 51; "pure" rise in, 50, 51; real input multiplier for, 82-83
Input: equivalent incremental, 93-95; from excise tax reduction, 63-64
Interest rates, 3, 6, 22, 51
Inventories, 6, 14
Investment: autonomous, 87, 88; effect of excise tax reduction on, 78; intentions, 7–8 lag, 8; real business, 89; realizations, 7

Jorgenson, Dale, 7, 8

Kisselgoff, Avram, 3*n*, 49
Klein, L. R., 2*n*, 15
Koopmans, Tjalling C., 111, 111*n*
Krause, Lawrence, 9
Kresge, David, 16
Kuh, E., 2*n*

Labor force, 12, 29
Lipsey, R., 102*n*

Marginal rate of substitution (MRS), 107, 111
Markowitz, Harry, 113*n*
Markup pricing mechanism, 56, 59
May, S., 25
Mincer, Jacob, 13*n*
Modigliani, Franco, 13*n*
Monetary policy, 47; accommodating, 28, 51; real input multiplier for, 84-88
Monetary sector, 13
MRS, see Marginal rate of substitution
Multiplier: discounted, 98-99; dynamic, 25, 49-51, 82, 95-98; equilibrium, 81, 82; fiscal, 91-92; impact, 23-24, 25, 65, 75, 82; real input, 81-89
Musgrave, R., 55*n*

Nagar, A. L., 123*n*
National Industrial Conference Board, 8
National Planning Association, 7
Nonlinearities, 60–61, 91

Office of Business Economics-Securities and Exchange Commission (OBE-SEC) investment statistics, 8
Orders, 7
Output conversion, 16–17

Parameters, 17, 25
Phillips, A. W., 25
Phillips curve, 25, 101–06
Policy: criteria for choice of, 101–06; response paths, 92–93; utility evaluation of, *see* Utility function
Prices: block structure, 18, 19, 24; changes in, and excise tax reduction, 55, 79; conversion matrix, 15, 16; sector, 11–12; durables, 28; markup mechanism for, 56; potential reduction in, 59; predictions, 11, 22, 29; stability, 101
Productions functions, 8, 10
Profits: effect of excise tax reduction on, 78–79; real input multiplier for, 89
Quality block structure, 18; 19

Real input multiplier, 81–82; excise taxes, 83–84; government expenditures, 82, 84–85, 89; income taxes, 82–83; monetary-policies, 84–88; real debt, 89–90

Reserve requirements, 49
Residential construction: credit conditions and, 3; single versus multi-unit, 6
Rhomberg, Rudolph, 9
Ross, A. M., 102*n*

Samuelson, Paul A., 50*n*
Schultze, C. L., 55*n*
Shinkai, Y., 15
Simon, H. A., 15, 15*n*
Simulation, 24 ff; studies, 24–25, 27; excise tax structure and, 64 ff; experiments, 27–28; results, 28–49
Specific tax, 56
Stabilization policy, 25, 91
Stochastic disturbances, 24, 25
Stone, Richard, 16
Systematic functioning of models, 17–18

Taubman, P., 55*n*, 56*n*
Taxes: passed-along changes in, 56–57, 64; state and local versus federal revenues from, 10. *See also* Excise tax; Income tax
Theil, Henri, 25, 108*n*, 110*n*
Tobin, James, 91*n*
Tryon, J. L., 55*n*
Tustin, A., 25

Unemployment, 12, 13, 47; excise tax reduction and, 80; relations between prices and, 101–04
Utility function, 105, 106–10; maximization, 3; discounting, 121; dynamic response adjustments for, 110–13; ranking by, 121; scaling, 113–14

Wages, 11; effect of excise tax reduction on, 78; government influence on, 11
Weintraub, S., 75*n*, 76*n*
Wharton model, 24
Wood, John H., 110*n*